D0770706

THE "BENEVOLENT" STATE

THE "BENEVOLENT" STATE

The Growth of Welfare in Canada

Allan Moscovitch &
Jim Albert, editors

Garamond Press
Toronto

Garamond Press
67A Portland St.
Toronto, Ontario.
M5V 2M9

Cover design: Peter McArthur
Cover photo: "March on Ottawa," Kamloops B.C., June 1935
        PUBLIC ARCHIVES CANADA/PA-237054
Printed and bound in Canada

This publication was made possible in part through assistance from Welfare Grants, Health and Welfare Canada.

CANADIAN CATALOGUING IN PUBLICATION DATA

Main entry under title:

The "Benevolent" state

ISBN 0-920059-48-1

1. Public welfare – Canada – History. 2. Canada
– Social policy. I. Moscovitch, Allan, 1946–   .
II. Albert, Jim.

HV105.B45 1987   361'.6'0971   C87-093859-2

Contents

Part IV: A Welfare State Established

Contributors

Preface

Canadian social welfare institutions, policies and practices have tended to be commonly understood as having developed in a fashion which parallels the development of similar institutions, policies and practices in Britain, the United States and France rather than in their own terms. Therefore, until recently, less attention has been focussed on the actual historical debates and struggles and on the conditions and the social reform movements (and reformers) which have shaped the timing, scope and type of social welfare measures that constitute the Canadian welfare state. This is not to say that external influences have been insignificant or marginal. This is far from the case. However, it is to say that too often the actual influences have been assumed, rather than investigated.

It has too often been assumed, for example, that if one discussed the English poor laws and the Beveridge Report then one has discussed in large part Canadian social welfare policy development; or that if one discussed Jane Adams, Bertha Reynolds and several other early American social workers then one has discussed the history of social work practice in Canada. Yet as the articles here make clear, there are important major Canadian counterparts: the Marsh Report, the work of J.J. Kelso and of Charlotte Whitton, for example. Thus the colonial heritage often has resulted in the denial of the existence of indigenous Canadian historical development.

In recent years, the re-emergence of historical and contemporary Canadian political economy studies has been an important aspect of the resurgence of Canadian historical writing. However, this resurgence has only just begun to appear in the field of social welfare.

It is arguable that the development of a "welfare state" in Canada represents perhaps the single most important transformation of every-day social life in the past 50 years. Yet it remains virtually unexamined. Only studies of individual constituent parts of this transformation have been undertaken. It remains for others to write studies with the sweep of history necessary to emphasize the magnitude and scope of change leading to and wrought by the coming of welfare state policies. This book is intended as a contribution to this larger project.

The origins of this collection lie in work the editors began several years ago to develop a course for social work graduate students on the origins of the welfare state in Canada. The purpose was to provide them with an opportunity to understand the historical roots of current policies and practices, to better comprehend the unique and the general in what we refer to as the welfare state. It was also to develop a corrective to the blandness of liberal interpretations as the history of "great men doing great things together," with the emphasis on men. An initial project was the preparation of a bibliography, Allan Moscovitch et al., *The Welfare State in Canada*, 1983. It was through this project and the work of course preparation and teaching that we came to appreciate the more recent research on aspects of social welfare history being undertaken in a range of conventional disciplines, and the paucity of books available which address the diversity of the history of the welfare state. From this interest and from necessity came the idea for the present book.

An outline was established, topics and writers identified and a conference organized in April 1981 under the sponsorship of the School of Social Work, Carleton University, and with additional funding provided by Welfare Grants, Health and Welfare Canada. The majority of the articles which appear here were chosen from amongst those presented. These were supplemented by additional material, some previously published elsewhere. The resultant book provides significant insight into the origins, and development of the welfare state.

In any such project there are always many people who have contributed time and effort beyond that of the editors. We are grateful to colleagues in the School of Social work for assistance and encouragement, to Bev Goold, Shirley Clarke, Reta Affleck and Jan Doherty of the School of Social Work for their assistance in the organization of the original Conference, and to Ted Deuling, Dorothy Zaluska, Iris Taylor and Gail Harmer, Graphic Services, Carleton University for their patience and consideration in helping us prepare the manuscript for the book.

We are appreciative of the contributions of Carmen Palumbo who provided editorial assistance, and of Sharon Nelson, who coordinated production. Errol Sharpe of Garamond Press was instrumental in giving us the opportunity to make this book available, and in coordinating the project. Thanks are also due to Evariste Theriault and Esther Kwanvnick, Welfare Grants, Health and Welfare, for assistance. Health and Welfare Canada, through its National Welfare Grants program contributed substantially to this project by providing grants for the support of the original conference, and for the publication of this volume. Lastly, we are grateful to our contributors for their efforts in meeting deadlines and providing us with the material with which to assemble the present book.

Allan Moscovitch
Jim Albert
April 1987

PART I

The Growth of the Welfare State
in the 20th Century

Social Expenditures and the Welfare State:
The Canadian Experience in Historical Perspective

Allan Moscovitch and Glenn Drover

Introduction

While the long-term growth of social expenditures is a common feature of all industrialized countries, the political and economic forces which give rise to these expenditures vary from country to country. In general, one of three theoretical explanations is invoked to account for growth. The most common approach is associated with Wagner's Law.[1] Stated simply, it implies that the level of expenditures results from the level of technological and economic development, the corresponding size of the population, per capita income and urbanization. Some approaches use these and other determining factors to "explain" state expenditures directly; in others, political factors may intervene. In explaining the growth of social expenditures, Wilensky and Lebeaux also emphasize the role of industrial-ization and urbanization.[2]

A second approach, sometimes associated with the work of Anthony Downs, states that politicians spend (or don't spend) to win votes. More generally, in pluralist theory, politicians respond to pressure if they believe this will win them support. There are, of course, a variety of pressures: some from interest groups directly concerned with the plight of the disadvantaged, some from groups fearful of social instability either present or anticipated.[3] An associated explanation sees social expenditures as an extension of political ideology. For example, a proposition common in social welfare is that social expenditures result from the humanitarian concerns of politicians and/or social reformers.

A third explanation, and the one employed in this paper, postulates that expenditures are closely tied to the political economy of the state.[4] In Canada, two interrelated sets of hypotheses are suggested: 1. the necessity of state intervention to assure continued private capital accumulation and profitability, and 2. the necessity of state social intervention, including expenditures on social welfare programmes, to regulate labour in the workplace and at home by diminishing the cost to capital of a mobile, available, and appropriately educated labour force. This is accomplished by maintaining a surplus of workers, particularly women, and by assuring workers of a minimum level of economic security, by maintaining the family and so promote the legitimacy of the social order.

Writers associated with this approach are O'Connor, Gough, and Piven and Cloward.[5] Following these authors, we explore the thesis that increased social expenditures are an essential, though not exclusive, part of the activities of the modern capitalist state. In his book, *The Fiscal Crisis of the State*, O'Connor points out that the state plays two essential roles.[6] First and foremost, it aids private capital accumulation by socializing production costs such as research, education, and providing public infrastructures, or taking over unprofitable sectors such as transportation. Second, it acts to legitimize the social order by promoting social harmony, assuring minimum services to workers, and providing a semblance of justice. Social expenditures are likely to vary depending upon their relationship to primary state functions. Unemployment insurance, for example, tied to unemployment, in turn is closely related to the economic cycle. Therefore, even though unemployment insurance is a primary component of the legitimation activities of the state — in order to assure a reasonable identification of unemployed workers with the capitalist system — it is also tied to capital accumulation.

Expanding this connection, O'Connor argues that economic activity is organized along lines of private and public capital. Private capital is, in turn, subdivided into two categories: competitive industries organized along lines of small scale business and monopolistic enterprises organized along lines of large scale capital. In advanced capitalism, the monopoly sector is dominant, and to assure capital accumulation, accepts state control of unprofitable enterprises in order to retain control of interests that enhance profits and ensure existing social relations of production. In the monopoly sector, the capital/labour ratio is high. Increasing technological improvements result in surplus productive capacity and surplus workers. This expanding surplus population threatens the existing economic structure while still being essential for its continued development. Therefore, unemployment insurance fills an essential gap, assuring at the same time capital accumulation and attachment to the labour market.

By contrast, direct relief, since it supports a relatively smaller proportion of the population not immediately related to the labour market, legitimizes capitalist society in a different way. Because of the market mentality which predominates under capitalism, only those members of society employed by productive enterprises or the state are monetarily compensated. Consequently, there is always a portion of society viewed as unproductive — women doing unpaid work in the home, students, children, the aged, the disabled and people who are for a variety of other reasons unemployable. These groups have no claim to compensation in the market and make varying demands on the state from time to time, whose forms depend upon a variety of historical circumstances. Ian Gough, for example, suggests that wages and government expenditures increased in postwar Britain because the labour movement strengthened relative to the capitalist class. Hence, he concludes that the balance of class forces influences the direction of state expenditures, including funds to support the unemployed and unemployable surplus population.

Seen in this context, the Piven and Cloward study demonstrates the relation between class forces and one form of social expenditure in the U.S. In their book, *Regulating the Poor*, they state that welfare expenditures in the U.S. expand in times of civil disorder as a response to turmoil caused by the poor, and contract during periods of political order to reaffirm an individualistic work ethic.[7] While this theory appears to explain little in Canada, it does highlight the necessity to look at state expenditures in a national historical context. We turn now to that task.

The Beginnings of State Welfarism:
From Preconfederation to 1890

At confederation, the question of the welfare of a growing number of wage workers in urban areas and settlers in rural areas was neither ideological nor political. Social welfare, as noted many times elsewhere, was given only cursory treatment in the British North America Act, which formed the basis of the division of state powers between the new Dominion government and the provincial governments.[8] Before Confederation, there were three different practices in the then existing four provinces. In Lower Canada, following tradition and influenced directly and indirectly by developments in France, welfare institutions for working people, farmers and the indigent, were overseen primarily by the Church and Church-related institutions, orders and committees. While the state conferred on those institutions a charter for their operations, it did not provide a regularized system of grants for their support of charitable activities.[9]

In Nova Scotia and its close relation, New Brunswick, the English poor laws had been in effect as early as 1759.[10] The Nova Scotia, and subsequently, the New Brunswick version of the poor law, conferred on townships and counties the obligation, not simply the right, to collect funds for relief of the indigent and for the provision of asylums and other institutions as needed.[11] In newly founded Upper Canada, the first legislature explicitly excluded the poor laws while in general retaining application of the English common law. This was done on the grounds that Upper Canada had so many opportunities that anyone who wanted could find their living. Subsequently, individuals and municipalities applied to the provincial government for charters and financial assistance to establish specific institutions such as asylums and jails, but it was not until 1849 that municipalities were accorded the right (but not the obligation), to collect funds for the construction and maintenance of local asylums; by 1859 they would provide for the out-of-door relief for the poor.[12]

In 1871, only seven cities had a population of 20,000 or more persons and only twenty with 5,000 or more. Only Montreal had a population in excess of 100,000 persons. Of 3.69 million people registered in the 1871 Census, less than 25 percent lived in urban areas.[13] It is not surprising, then, that in this largely rural, agrarian society with strong beliefs in private charity and individualism, state intervention in the provision of social welfare was not very well developed.[14]

Pre-Confederation provincial expenditures reflect this relatively minor importance of social welfare. At that time, what is referred to as public welfare — certain forms of relief, grants for the construction and maintenance of asylums and other institutions, — represented some 3 percent of total provincial expenditure in 1866 (Table 1). Public education represented 6 percent while the largest single item of the combined total of $15.6 million was debt charges, which amounted to 29 percent. In other words, social expenditures, even making some allowance for jail administration costs, amounted by extrapolation, to about 12 percent of state expenditures.

In the transition to Confederation, a small percentage of social welfare activities were undertaken by the Dominion government, amounting to, in 1871, approximately 1.2 percent of Dominion government expenditures, when total goverment expenditures were $25.2 million (Table 5). With the assumption of provincial debt charges by the Dominion government, combined provincial expenditures in 1871 represented only $4.4 million, of which 9.5 percent was on social welfare and health, 22.5 percent on education and 12.8 percent on protection activities, a total of 44.8 percent for public welfare at the provincial level (Table 6).

The first major shift from a rural based economy occurred during the last third of the nineteenth century. Population increased to 4.8 million by 1891, largely in the urban areas, as the balance began to shift.[15] During this period, the first wave of industrialization took place with manufacturing establishments expanding from 38,898 in 1870 to 69,716 in 1890.[16] While output in general grew from $459 million to $803 million during the period, manufacturing grew from $87 million to $189 million and agricultural output from $153 million to to $217 million. By 1891, there were already 2.7 million acres under wheat cultivation and more than 14,000 miles of railways.[17]

The growth of industry increased the number of wage workers as well as developing a class consciousness among them. However, this growing class consciousness led primarily to work-related demands, not demands for increases in state welfare. The (male) workers in Hamilton and Toronto, who led the fight for a shorter working day, soon found themselves approached by the Conservative Party. This initially resulted in a trade union act providing a form of legal registration and recognition for the trade unions. This period also marked the formation of the first trade union federations, the Canadian Federation of Unions 1873, and subsequently

Table 1

Distribution of Government Functions
Before and After Confederation
1866 and 1874

Government Functions	Provinces %*		Dominion %*	Total %*
	1866	1874	1874	1874
Debt	29	1	27	20
Justice/Gen. Gov't	26	32	21	24
Defence	13	—	6	4
Public Welfare	3	8	1	3
Education	6	18	—	5
Agriculture	2	9	4	5
Transportation	11	15	15	15
Subsidies	—	—	17	12
Other	8	17	8	10
Sinking Fund	1	—	2	2
Total $**	15,558,000	7,986,000	22,485,000	30,470,000

*May not add to 100 percent due to rounding.
**Includes current and capital expenditures.
Source: D. Creighton, *British North America at Confederation*, Background Study for Royal Commission on Dominion-Provincial Relations/Ottawa, 1939, (Adapted).

the formation, in 1886, of the Trades and Labour Congress.[18] Organized labour began to change from the simple object of political attention to a political actor issuing demands; for example, regulations aiding the families of workers injured or killed on the job.[19]

But the new Canadian state remained captive to the economic elite and primarily concerned with assisting economic development by providing infrastructure, capital, and financial backing. Neither economic and social conditions, the nascent working and professional classes, nor the early social reform movements demanded or required significant state intervention for the provision of social welfare. However, the state did begin to play an increasingly important role, both in the provision of financial aid to, and in the regulation and inspection of, welfare institutions and places of work.

While previously, state financial assistance was occasionally provided for specific institutions, to assist with capital cost or maintenance, Ontario moved towards a regularized system of grants-in-aid with the Charity Aid

Act of 1874.[20] Institutions supported included the first institutions for the deaf, the mentally retarded and the blind, the former two opening in Ontario in 1870 and the latter in 1872.[21] Ontario, for example, had begun a system of inspection and regulation of prisons and other institutions as early as 1859, but the provincial governments in general began entering more widely into regulatory activities after Confederation. The regulation of school attendance, public health, hours of work and conditions in the work place (particularly for women and children) and the treatment of children, were all aspects of widening state involvement in social welfare by the end of the nineteenth century.[22]

In the 1880's deteriorating urban conditions in Ontario's industrial cities, especially Toronto, the growing importance of trade unions and the growing number of middle and upper class social reformers, particularly among women, were among the factors in the establishment of a series of public inquiries on social welfare questions; which included the Royal Commission on the Relations of Labour and Capital, and, in Ontario, the Royal Commission on the Prison and Reformatory System (1890).[23] The living conditions of children of the poor were exposed in successive reports of the Ontario Inspector of Prisons and press reports such as those by the young J. J. Kelso.[24] The growing visibility of urban waifs, exacerbated by the growing number of destitute British children being brought to Canada,[25] resulted first, in enacting formal child protection legislation, and subsequently, in chartering a system of semi-public Children's Aid Societies and the appointment of a provincial inspector for children and child welfare institutions.[26]

The trade-off between the needs of capital accumulation and legitimation during this period is shown in the growth of expenditures in Ontario. Initially, social expenditures rose to become relatively significant. The cost of building and maintaining a growing number of asylums, reformatories, jails and other institutions, rose so quickly that by 1893, they represented some 32.4 percent of total provincial expenditures. Yet, this was a relatively insignificant amount of total state expenditures — some $1.3 million. Only about 2.5 percent of provincial expenditures in 1893 supported regulatory and inspection activities with the remainder destined for the support of institutions. By 1911, however, social welfare expenditures in Ontario had fallen to 14.7 percent of the provincial budget, due principally to rising debt associated with development in the productive sector. These changes in social expenditures are detailed in Tables 2, 3, and 4.

During this early period, state intervention in social welfare primarily took the form of legislation to regulate homes, factories, offices, and charitable and public institutions. The regulations concerned women, children, the destitute and the deviant, with enforcement limited and therefore, not costly. At the same time, more state funds were made available to social welfare, health and educational institutions for construction and maintenance, precipitated by both moral and economic

Table 2

Ontario Expenditures On Social Welfare, (dollars)

Item	1868	1878	1888	1893	1911
Office of the Inspector	1,181	8,068	10,739	15,641	48,282
Mental institutions	177,585	457,045	679,940	743,020	1,203,041
Goals, prisons, reformatories	66,992	174,499	224,793	218,109	355,341
Grants to private institutions	39,000	70,673	113,686	164,896	313,925
Deaf and blind institutions	—	103,073	86,130	99,901	6,682
Grant to the industrial school	—	—	1,000	6,500	43,922
Measures for public health	—	—	7,252	10,700	36,358
Inspection of factories	—	—	4,245	4,275	21,760
Protection of children	—	—	—	960	11,106
Total	284,758	13,358	1,127,785	1,264,002	2,040,417

Table 3

Total Provincial Expenditures Compared with Ontario Expenditures On Social Welfare (dollars)

Year	Total Provincial Expenditures	Social Welfare Expenditures	
		Total	Percentage of Total Provincial Expenditures
1868	$ 1,182,386	$ 284,758	24.1
1878	$ 2,784,321	$ 813,358	29.2
1888	$ 3,536,248	$1,127,785	31.9
1893	$ 3,907,145	$1,264,002	32.4
1911	$13,903,207	$2,040,417	14.7

Table 4

Ontario Grants To Private Institutions

	1911 Dollars	Percent
Hospitals	$241,703	77
Children's Aid	14,807	5
Grants to Societies (Houses of Refuge)	9,250	3
Maintenance of Patients	41,465	13
Other	6,700	2
Total	313,925	100

Sources: R. Splane, *Social Welfare in Ontario, 1796 - 1893* (adapted), 62, 83, 85, 232-3 and Ontario, *Public Accounts*, 1912.

pressures, and by specific calamities. No major state social expenditure programmes were instituted or proposed.

Reluctant Welfarism, 1891 - 1940

The twenty-three years from 1891 to 1914 saw not only economic development but also increasing social ferment. A wide range of organizations for political, social, moral and economic reform found their voice during the period: women's organizations such as the Women's Christian Temperance Union, the Dominion Enfranchisement Association, and the National Council of Women; organizations promoting social reform such as the Social Service Council of Canada and the Canadian Conference on Charities and Corrections; movements for broader social concern in the churches, known as the Social Gospel; church and community-based organizations to provide education and charity to poor neighbourhoods, through settlement houses; groups promoting better public health and sanitation, pure water, housing, urban planning, and improved recreational facilities for children in cities and the countryside; and movements for the extension and improvement of education, particularly for women.[27] Radical political organizations, particularly those supported by immigrants and re-established in Canada also began to find more members and a larger voice, from an increasing working class membership.[28] Farmers' and producers' cooperative organizations also developed, and from these organizations sprang the movements and parties of farm protest, during and after the First World War.[29]

Yet this great range of political and social movements still did not exert sufficient pressure to generate the variety of state reforms for which they laboured. Consequently, there was little change in state social expenditures. The better provision of relief through methods of so-called scientific philanthropy, and the more systematic organization of charity, was largely a private undertaking with some municipal assistance. Settlement houses based on the British (Toynbee Hall) and American (Hull House) models, funded by churches and private individuals, began to appear, first in Toronto and then in Winnipeg, Montreal and other centres.[30] Children's Aid Societies spread to other Ontario centres and other provinces, utilizing the model of foster care for children developed by J. J. Kelso, founder of the Toronto Society in 1891, and subsequently, Ontario's superintendent of child welfare. Juvenile courts, recommended in the 1890 Ontario Royal Commission on Prisons and Reformatories, were established in Winnipeg in 1909, after the passage of the Dominion Juvenile Delinquents' Act (1908), to provide separate treatment for juvenile criminals.[31]

By 1911, much of the Dominion expenditure was on war-related pensions (Tables 5, 6), while, as seen at least in Ontario, much of the provincial expenditure was for the maintenance of institutions, asylums, hospitals, schools, and refuges; institutions destined largely for people outside the work force, people who, in the broadest sense, were marginal

Table 5

Federal Social Expenditures (Gross)
1871 - 1977

Year	Social* Welfare	Education	Health	Payments To Other Governments	Total Governmnent Expenditures	
	%	%	%	%	$ million	$ per capita
1871	1.2	-	-	11.5	25.2	6.83
1881	5.5	-	-	10.5	33.4	7.72
1891	2.9	-	-	9.7	40.2	8.32
1901	2.9	-	-	7.2	6.14	11.43
1911	2.5	-	-	7.5	136.0	18.87
1921	13.1	— 0.3 —		2.6	476.3	54.30
1931	25.7	— 0.3 —		3.1	448.7	43.24
1941	5.7	— 0.5 —		1.9	1,807.0	157.03
1951	20.7	0.5	1.2	3.5	3,649.0	260.49
1961	20.2	1.0	4.1	8.6	6,583.0	360.94
1971	28.6	5.6	8.3	8.4	21,377.0	991.14
1977	34.0	4.2	6.8	7.6	45,956.0	1,975.92

*Includes Veterans Pensions
Sources: M.C. Urquhart and K. A. H. Buckley, *Historical Statistics of Canada*, 1965.
Tables G26-44 for years 1871 - 1931, and G128-142 for years 1941, and 1951.
Statistics Canada, *Federal Government Finance: Revenue and Expenditure, Assets and Liabilities*, 68-211, for 1961, 1971, and 1979. Population calculations based on Canadian Tax Foundation, *Canadian Fiscal Facts*, Table I, and Statistics Canada, *Estimates of Population for Canada and the Provinces*, 91-201.

to early Canadian society. However, a significant proportion of the extant social expenditures was devoted to the reproduction of the labour force: through funding for public education and health measures, such as medical officers of health in municipalities. Municipal expenditures, difficult to estimate throughout the period, reached $110 million, of which only 5.8 percent were for social welfare and health (Table 7). Dominion expenditures sextupled from 1871 to 1911, but principal expenditure over this period was used to develop economic infrastructure, such as canals, railroads and other public works, and with servicing government debt.

Before the war, increasing industrial accidents, and in particular, the size and number of court settlements compensating injured workers, led both employers and workers' organizations to press for state intervention. In 1910, the Ontario government set a Royal Commission to report on workers' compensation. The scheme, eventually established on the eve of the First World War, set the pattern for subsequent legislation in Nova

Table 6
Provincial Social Expenditure (Gross)
1871 - 1979

Year	Social Welfare %	Health %	Education %	Protection %	Subsidies To Munici- palities %	Total Government Expenditures $ (million)	$ per capita
1871	—	9.5	—	22.5	12.8	-	4.4**	1.27
1881	—	12.7	—	16.6	8.1	-	8.1***	1.89
1891	—	13.4	—	16.8	10.8	-	11.6***	2.40
1901	—	14.7	—	15.1	8.9	-	14.1***	2.88
1911	—	11.1	—	14.2	7.7	-	43.4	6.02
1921	3.9	8.6	20.0	9.2	-	102.6	11.67
1931	5.8	8.1	18.0	6.2	-	190.8	18.38
1941*	10.8	9.6	13.7	-	1.0	314.0	27.29
1951	14.1	17.1	16.1	5.1	2.1	1257.9	89.79
1961	11.0	24.8	22.9	3.8	1.9	3832.4	210.13
1971	11.3	26.7	26.8	3.4	2.0	17310.0	802.58
1977	14.6	24.3	23.6	3.5	2.6	43585.0	1873.98

*Net Expenditure
**Includes Ont., Que., N.S., N.B. only.
***Excludes Alta. and Sask.

Sources: Provincial Public Accounts, 1871 -1891; *Canada Year Book*, 1901 - 1931; M. C. Urquhart and K. A. H. Buckley, *Historical Statistics of Canada*, G180-191 1941 -1951; *Statistics Canada, Provincial Government Finance: Revenue and Expenditure*, 68-207, 1951-1977.

Scotia in 1915, British Columbia in 1916, New Brunswick in 1918, and Manitoba in 1920.

The Workman's Compensation Act of 1914, eliminated the workers' right to sue the employer directly in court; instead, under the legislation, workers and their families would apply for compensation according to a formula established by the Act. Since all employers risked losing employees or being sued in court before the legislation, all major employers were now required to contribute to the scheme. With hindsight, Ontario's workers' compensation legislation was clearly the first state social insurance scheme established in Canada.[32]

With the First World War, immigration decreased dramatically. The war effort at home and abroad forced the creation of new jobs. Major wartime charities were given a Dominion charter, first to provide help for those in Europe, and secondly, to provide relief to families left behind. As soldiers returned, demands were made to set up pension programmes. A Dominion government commission started early in the war, made recommendations on the size and scope of war pensions and criteria for eligibility. Although the war effort did not initially involve Dominion expenditure for the welfare of soldiers, this being almost entirely in private hands, it did force the Dominion government to establish a war pensions programme which, after the war, generated demands for a major increase in social expenditures.[33]

One result of wartime prosperity was the growth of the trade union movement and interest in radical political organizations. Between 1911 and 1919, union membership almost tripled while the number of strikes and lockouts grew accordingly.[34] Total economic production underwent a major expansion during the war years, particularly in manufacturing, but concurrently, the number of manufacturing establishments fell drastically as capital was further consolidated. Continued pressure from women's organizations led the Dominion government to concede the vote to women during the war,[35] but the wartime response to the trade union movement and the growth of political radicalism, was harsh. Several political organizations were banned under the newly established War Measures Act, while leading trade unionists were put under arrest.[36] The fight in Manitoba over the language question in schools and the imposition of conscription during the latter years of the war exacerbated French-English tensions while the growing demands of western farmers developing

Table 7

Municipal Social Expenditure (Gross)
1913 - 1979

Year	Social Welfare %	Health %	Education %	Protection %	Total Government Expenditure ($ millions)
1913	—	5.8	—	32.8	10.1	110.0
1922	—	7.6	—	35.5	9.3	257.9
1930	—	9.9	—	34.9	9.9	341.6
1941*	7.8	5.4	29.3	-	294.0
1951	5.4	2.7	26.0	11.9	767.0
1961	5.0	2.3	34.8	12.0	2,023.7
1971	3.8	4.9	46.8	6.7	9,439.6
1977	2.8	4.8	42.9	7.4	20,989.3

*Net Expenditures.

Sources: Carl Goldenberg, *Municipal Finance in Canada*, 1913, 1922, 1930; M. C. Urquhart and K. A. H. Buckley, *Historical Statistics of Canada*, G222-230, 1941; Statistics Canada, *Local Government Finance*, 68-204, 1951-77.

their indigenous political voice, exacerbated east-west tensions. To these tensions were added the rising cost of living and, returning at the war's end, the growing number of unemployed soldiers. In this context, the Winnipeg General Strike erupted in the spring of 1919, immediately after the end of the war in November, 1918.

The state's response to these tensions, particularly those involving labour and capital, was to promote a series of task forces, commissions and conferences to air grievances, discuss conflicts and, in general, to promote harmony between them.[37] Concessions to labour, which increased social expenditures, were few and limited. Programmes for soldier resettlement, including land allowances, a housing scheme and Dominion relief grants, were among the few visible signs of Dominion involvement in social welfare at war's end.[38]

One of the few programmes initiated during the period were Mothers' Allowances, first adopted in Manitoba in 1919 and Ontario in 1920. These provinces did so in response to pressure from women's organizations, criticizing the destitution of families without income, particularly fatherless families. After the war, provinces had the additional motivation of inequities caused by war pensions being available for families made dependent by the war, but not others similarly poor. They were also a way of seeming to respond to concerns that the stock of healthy males be replenished after the destruction brought by the war. Lastly, they were a method of encouraging women to leave the workforce and return to the home.[39]

There were other measures taken to buttress postwar child and family welfare. For example, Ontario moved to strengthen its laws regulating adoption and the legitimation of children of unmarried parents, while the Dominion moved to establish a Department of Health and subsequently, a child welfare office.[40] The Quebec government introduced a stronger measure for funding and regulating charities in the 1921 Charities Act, a historic break in the control exercised by the Catholic Church over a major portion of social welfare in that province.

Not surprisingly, postwar Dominion expenditures were largely devoted to covering the now quite extensive debt charges, amounting to more than $139 million, and the cost of public works, railways and subsidies to the provinces. A dramatic shift in expenditures did not occur until the depression.

Recommendations for a range of state social welfare programmes kept appearing in postwar provincial and federal, commission and committee reports into the 1920s. The one most often reiterated was an old age pension. Such a scheme was even included in the 1918 reform platform of the Liberal Party, under its new leader, MacKenzie King. Legislation was passed in 1927, but only as the result of an agreement with J. S. Woodsworth on behalf of the three independent labour members, which had given King votes in the House of Commons in return for old age pensions. Since jurisdiction was unclear, the legislation called for 50 percent Dominion funding if the provinces established a provincially administered, means-tested scheme for people 70 years old or greater.[41]

With the expanding economy of the 1920s, output as measured by GNP rose to $6,046 million by 1928, generating gross profits of $433 million. By 1930, the year after the collapse of stock markets in New York, London and other centres, profits fell to $144 million, and by 1932, in the depths of the Depression, profits completely disappeared with the GNP falling to $3,827 million. The cost of living fell as did income while unemployment rose dramatically.[42] The decline of industrial production, profits and investment in urban areas, was matched by a similar decline in agriculture. Not only did prices fall and markets for agricultural produce decline, but drought compounded the problem, forcing many farmers to leave their homesteads for the cities.

The change in economic conditions brought with it a change of national government. In 1930, the Conservative Party, under R. B. Bennett, was elected to office. The new government faced what was already a major crisis in unemployment, made bleaker by the fact that, at the beginning of the Depression, the Canadian state had few of the pieces of social machinery already in place in other countries. There was the newly created old age pensions, war related pensions, workers' compensation and mothers' allowances in most provinces. However, there was no unemployment insurance; relief was largely a local issue. The new government was quickly forced to increase relief payments. Annual sums were voted for relief in 1930, and for subsequent years of the Depression, such that by 1937, the Dominion government was paying $66.1 million for relief. By this time, the provinces together were spending a further $42.9 million and the municipalities $17.6 million. Bennett was, however, able to resist further extensive federal involvement in social welfare until his new deal reforms of January, 1935.

Even though state involvement expanded during the period, much of it was devoted to restructuring capital and developing state institutions such as the Bank of Canada, to further preserve and stabilize Canadian capitalism. Bennett and the Conservative Party's response to growing demands from the organized trade union movement and to the fears of employers, as well as the pleading of social welfare reformers, was again largely repressive. Political organizations, including the Communist Party of Canada, were suppressed, and large numbers of suspected organizers and radicals were deported from Canada. The Department of National Defence, under General McNaughton, was authorized to establish relief camps in various isolated areas throughout the country, offering employment at minimal rates to single, able-bodied men as a means of keeping them from congregating in the urban streets.[43]

In January 1935, Prime Minister Bennett took the unprecedented step of bypassing parliament and making a direct public appeal through a series of radio broadcasts, during which he presented his "New Deal" reform proposals. Strongly influenced by the style and substance of American

President Roosevelts' New Deal, Bennett presented a number of reforms, principal of which was unemployment insurance. The government argued that it had the authority to institute this and other labour related reforms due to being signatory to international labour agreements committing Canada to such reforms. The legislation was challenged in the courts by the provinces, and eventually (1939) declared to be a provincial, not a federal responsibility.

The New Deal reforms were not enough to sustain Bennett in office; in the autumn election of 1935, the Liberals, under MacKenzie King, were elected. It was King who appointed the Royal Commission on Dominion-Provincial Relations — to examine the division of powers in regard to both expenditures and revenues — which reported back in 1939.

It was, however, under wartime conditions that agreement between the provinces and the Dominion government was reached for a constitutional amendment allowing it to establish an unemployment insurance plan, put in place in 1941, and the tax agreement through which income tax was transformed into a major source of wartime and postwar revenues.[44]

By 1941, in the early years of the war, the Dominion government had cut relief expenditures drastically. Only 5.7 percent of total government expenditures, which by this time had burgeoned considerably, were spent on social welfare (a considerable drop from 25.7 percent in 1931) and a further .5 percent on education and health combined (Table 5). Provincially, social welfare expenditure rose to 10.8 percent by 1941, from 5.8 percent in 1931, largely due to maintenance of provincial relief programmes, while expenditures on health had risen to 9.6 percent, as some provinces had introduced reforms for medical assistance for the indigent (Table 6). By 1941, municipalities had reduced social welfare expenditures to 7.8 percent while health expenditures accounted for an additional 5.4 percent. In fact, from 1930 to 1941, municipal expenditures *fell* from $341.6 million to $294 million (Table 7).

The changes in federal social expenditures from 1891 to 1941, reveals considerable absolute growth but less dramatic relative growth. Social expenditures grew from $1.2 million in 1891 to $103 million by 1941, but only from 2.9 percent to 5.7 percent of total federal government expenditures over the same period (Table 5). The combined social welfare and health expenditures of all the provincial governments grew from $1.6 million in 1891 to $64.4 million in 1941 (Tables 6), rising from 13.4 percent to 20.4 percent of all provincial expenditures. Available municipal data suggest an absolute growth from $6.4 million to $38.8 million and a relative growth from 5.8 percent to 13.4 percent, over the period 1913 to 1941 with social welfare and health expenditures taken together (Tables 7). Only during the Depression did state social expenditures approach the relative importance they reached in the 1960s and 1970s. After the Depression, social expenditures receded, even though state expenditures continued to expand rapidly in the subsequent thirty-six year period, as we shall see.

The preceeding data and brief review of economic and political conditions relative to state social programmes suggest that state expenditures developed primarily to provide a wider range of initiatives assisting capital accumulation, *other than* by socializing labour costs. The maintenance of labour supply was still largely a private matter; organizations and funding established or expanded in the Depression were run down or eliminated as unemployment abated in the early years of the war.

Four major peacetime social programmes were put in place in the period. Workers' compensation and mothers' allowances were introduced randomly by the provinces, roughly between 1914 and 1930, while old age pensions and unemployment insurance were introduced by the federal government, but not resulting in a major expansion of social expenditures. Federal old age pension contributions did not reach $30.0 million until 1939; war pensions ranged between $55 million and $60 million throughout the depression years.[45] A permanent system of relief funding was not established, despite the circumstances.

The response of the state to economic conditions and demands for change from the union movement, social reformers, and businessmen was to use a variety of means *of avoiding* social reform. The use of the military to control strikes and demonstrations, deportations of suspected leaders and sympathizers, and the banning of organizations were not uncommon. The promotion of company unions and welfare schemes was another approach. Committees of inquiry proved to be another effective method of delaying and deflecting demands for reform.[46] Lastly, as the question of reform became an urgent political and economic necessity, the question of the level and sphere of state authority became manifest. The longstanding quarrel over revenues and expenditures between the federal government and the provinces, played out in the 1930s (and subsequently), further stalled social reforms.

The Establishment of a Welfare State, 1941-1974

In order to meet the requirements of war and the production of war materials, the Canadian state was forced to take an ever-growing role in wartime economic and social life. Wage, price, rent and materials controls were introduced as were a range of crown corporations to run the war effort. With a wider array of state activity came broader public acceptance of state intervention. Demands for a better life led to widening support for the CCF, which won important federal bi-elections (1942), became the opposition party in Ontario (1943), and was the elected government of Saskatchewan (1944).

The labour movement grew both in membership and militance during wartime as well. After a major series of strikes, the federal government legalized trade unionism and contract bargaining to avoid protracted conflicts over employee rights to a union. One consequence of increased support for the CCF and the labour movements was renewed interest by MacKenzie King and the Liberal government in social welfare.[47]

At the beginning of the war, King had appointed an Advisory Committee on Reconstruction to make regular reports on problems of reconstruction. The director of research for the Committee, Leonard Marsh, was asked in December 1942 to prepare a report on social security, which was released publicly in March, 1943.[48] Marsh's report, calling for a comprehensive program of social insurance and social expenditure, appeared only months after the British Beveridge Report, which was of wide influence in Canada, the United States and other countries. On the same day as the Marsh Report's release, the Heagerty Report on public medical care was also released. A later Advisory Committee report, prepared by Marsh, called for large-scale housing construction, including public housing.[49]

Yet, this social reform climate produced few social reforms. Though a major recommendation of the Marsh Report, the federal governments' primary concern in legislating Family Allowances, in 1944, appears to have been to deflect trade union pressure to lift wartime wage controls and allow wage increases for low-paid workers. Nonetheless, family allowances for 1945, at $172.6 million, represented a substantial expansion of social expenditures, although considerably less than the $401.7 million spent by the federal government on veterans' benefits that year.[50]

Most other federal proposals for social reform were postponed until after the reelection of the Liberal Party, in 1945. The Green Book proposals on social assistance, health insurance and old age pensions, presented to the provinces at the postwar Dominion-Provincial Conference, in 1945, were linked to provincial agreement ceding income, corporate and estate taxes to the federal government. The meeting ended quickly, with the Quebec and Ontario Premiers opposed to such an arrangement.

With hindsight, the postwar compromise between labour, capital and the state was reached at a relatively low cost to the latter. The trade union movement, growing in political strength and number, was concerned with establishing legalized trade union rights. Politically, the coalition within the Liberal Party held power, as the party moved to accept several elements of the social welfare programme offered by its nearest and principal wartime rival, the CCF. While state expenditures expanded enormously due to the war effort, the expansion of the state during the war was matched by a managed contraction of the state after 1945. Most of the Crown Corporations established to produce war materials were run down, or sold to private corporations.

One such corporation, Wartime Housing Limited, set up to build housing for workers (and later for veterans) in war-related industries, had, by the end of the war, accumulated a major portfolio of rental housing. These assets were transferred to the newly formed Central Mortgage and Housing Corporation (CMHC) with a mandate to sell this considerable stock of public housing. In addition, government effort was fostering private construction; funds for public housing were purposefully restricted until the 1960s.[51]

The 1945 White Paper on Employment declaration of permanent government involvement maintaining full employment did not represent, as in Britain and Europe, social democratic ideology and initiative, but rather liberal ideology. It was therefore, a statement of a circumscribed role for the state in the provision of social welfare. Unlike many European countries, where legislation was implemented in the 1940s and the early 1950s, the fiscal structures of the Canadian welfare state were not in place before the mid-1960s, for reasons both economic and political. On the one hand, postwar expansion was an immediate concern of the federal government. Except for a temporary slump in 1946, the Canadian economy grew rapidly in the 1940s and early 1950s, and unemployment declined. On the other hand, the primary focus of the state, at all levels, was strengthening private enterprise; interest in social reform was more limited, except in specific circumstances.

Despite the failure of the 1945 Dominion-Provincial Conference, and the mood of the times, reform of the old age pension remained on the political agenda. Both the trade union movement and the CCF organized campaigns opposing the means test; in the 1949 federal election, all three major parties were committed to its elimination. After the Liberals' reelection, a 1950 House of Commons Committee reported in favour of a universal pension at 70, and a means-tested plan at 65, a compromise allowing them to stay between proposals for a complete universal scheme and a contributory scheme. This position, linked to a special social security tax, was accepted by the government and the provinces who acceded to a constitutional amendment, in 1951. In its first full year of operation, 1952, $323.1 million were spent on the universal pension. In the early 1950s, the federal government followed this change with improved benefits for veterans, the blind and the disabled.[52]

However, growing unemployment in the mid-1950s led to steadily rising pressure on the resources of private welfare organizations, and on provincial and municipal governments. An agreement between the provinces and the federal government, preceded the passage of the 1956 Unemployment Assistance Act, the first modern legislated responsibility for relief. It was a conditional grant programme requiring provincial opting-in legislation. As a result, both New Brunswick (1958) and Nova Scotia (1960) finally took the Poor Law off their books. The new legislation also set the stage for the Canada Assistance Plan, because it provided shared-cost funding only for those deemed "unemployable," creating an incentive to the provinces to redefine recipients into this category in order to claim federal funds.[53]

Of the three main areas covered in the 1945 federal Green Book proposals, old age pensions had been revised in 1951, and social assistance in 1956. In regard to health insurance, no plan was instituted until the 1960s. In 1948, the federal government instituted the health grants programme for hospital construction, and in 1957, after protracted bargaining sessions and much studied political delay, a national funding programme providing hospital care came into being. Only the CCF in Saskatchewan went further, when, in 1962, they introduced the first medical care insurance programme, after a compromise with the doctors.[54]

In the mid-1950s, a major downturn in the Canadian economy produced growing dissatisfaction with the Liberals and led the Conservatives to victory under Diefenbaker, in the 1957 federal election. The economy slumped even further, a result of declining world trade and restrictive and inept economic policies of the Conservatives. The recession from 1957 to 1963, forced the federal government to increase expenditures on unemployment assistance and direct relief.[55]

By 1961, federal social welfare expenditures had risen to roughly $1,329 million, still a smaller proportion of the budget than in 1951, when 20.7 percent was spent in the same category. In 1931, just over one-quarter of federal funds had been spent primarily on relief and pensions. Provincial social welfare expenditures, at $421 million, had also fallen, from 14.1 percent in 1951. The main increases between 1951 and 1961 social expenditures, were in provincial expenditures on health and education (Tables 5,6).

Events changed in the early sixties, as the American economic position improved and a ten-year phase of renewed expansion began. While out of office, the Liberals constructed a social reform platform. In 1963, reelected under Pearson, they headed a reform-oriented minority government. A unified labour movement (1956), now formally allied with the CCF (1961) in the New Democratic Party (NDP), called for further social reform. In addition, there was a growing awareness of poverty in a period of relative affluence, particularly of disparities between the French and English in Quebec.[56] The pressures coalesced, causing the creation of a wide range of federal programmes aimed at equalizing opportunities, rather than substantially reducing inequality.

The renegotiation of the Unemployment Assistance Act resulted in the passage of the Canada Assistance Plan, a cost-sharing agreement eliminating the distinction between employable and unemployable recipients. Social assistance was to be made available on the basis of "need" alone, although it was the provinces which would determine the meaning of the term. The revived debate over pensions resulted in enacting the contributions-based Canada Pension Plan, applicable to nine provinces, and the Quebec Pension Plan (1965).

Revisions to the old age pension made it universal at age 65, but a new, supplementary means-tested scheme was also introduced, the Guaranteed Income Supplement (GIS), in 1967. Lastly, following a Royal Commission on Health Insurance report, agreement was reached between the federal government and the provinces to institute a national medical insurance programme. Based on Saskatchewan's example, the plan left doctors as entrepreneurs whose fees would be covered by public, rather than private, insurance.[57] Administratively, hospitalization funding, federal contributions to post-secondary education and the new medicare programme were linked together in one fiscal instrument. First passed in 1964, the Established Programmes Financing Act was renegotiated in 1967, and every five years since.

Two other changes of note were introduced during the Pearson years. A 1964 National Housing Act amendment provided loans to provincial housing corporations for public housing at reduced interest rates, and, the same year, extended a new Youth Allowance to families with children between 16 and 18.

By the end of the Pearson years, therefore, the essentials of the Canadian welfare state were in place. The total package, coupled with Unemployment Insurance amendments in 1971 and Family Allowances in 1972, led to rapidly increasing social expenditures. Including social welfare, health and education, they grew from 4 percent of GNP in 1946 to 15 percent by the mid-1970s (Table 8).

The structure and function of Canadian social expenditures can be better appreciated if we look more closely at postwar trends. Table 8 shows the ratio of total government expenditures and social expenditures (transfers and social services) to GNP from 1946 to 1978, in constant dollars. In 1946, government expenditures accounted for 32 percent of GNP but fell quickly; by 1951, they were down to 24 percent. Thereafter, they increased about 1 percent per year until the period between 1966 and 1971, when they increased about 1.4 percent per year. Spending at all levels of government accounted for about 42 percent of GNP by 1978, whereas transfers and social services were about 16 percent. By 1978, GNP had increased fourfold over 1946, while total government expenditures increased sixfold and social expenditures eighteenfold. The most dramatic change occurred in the ten-year period from 1966 to 1976, which more or less follows the period of social reform and precedes restraint.

One way to judge changing priorities in social expenditures during the postwar period is to examine cumulative percentage increases in each programme relative to GNP (Figure 1). Doing this, clearly shows family allowances and adult occupational training increasing more slowly than the GNP from 1946 to 1977. Education, unemployment insurance and personal social services were considerably above GNP increases, while welfare, workers' compensation, pensions and health had cumulatively increased roughly on an equivalent basis.

When social expenditures are compared with economic growth and unemployment over the postwar period (Figure 2), three characteristics stand out. First, social expenditures vary more inordinately than economic growth; also variations in social services are greater than transfers, suggesting that social expenditures are very sensitive to economic fluctuations. Secondly, there is frequently, though not consistently, a trade-off between transfers and social services. Sometimes they move in opposite directions; at other times there is a lag. To keep total social costs

Table 8
Relation of Expenditures to G.N.P.
(Constant 1971 Dollars)
$ (Millions)

Year	GNP	Gov't Expenditure (GE)	Transfers (TR)*	Social Services (SDE)**	Proportion GE to GNP	Proportion TR to GNP	Proportion SOC to GNP
1946	26,411	8,335	897	157	32	3	1
1951	32,787	7,919	980	259	24	3	1
1956	46,800	12,005	1,738	550	26	4	1
1961	52,861	16,266	2,620	2,065	31	5	4
1966	74,045	22,875	2,990	3,661	31	4	5
1971	93,462	35,207	5,071	7,924	38	5	8
1976	128,385	51,768	8,997	10,498	40	7	8
1978	131,510	55,213	9,892	10,614	42	8	8

* Transfers: includes unemployment insurance, family allowances, pensions, welfare and workers' compensation.

**Social Services: includes health, education, social welfare services, adult occupational training.

Sources: Statistics Canada, *System of National Accounts*, *National Income and Expenditure Accounts*, 13-201, various years. The method of calculation is based on Michel Bergeron, *Social Spending in Canada*, Ottawa, 1979, 86.

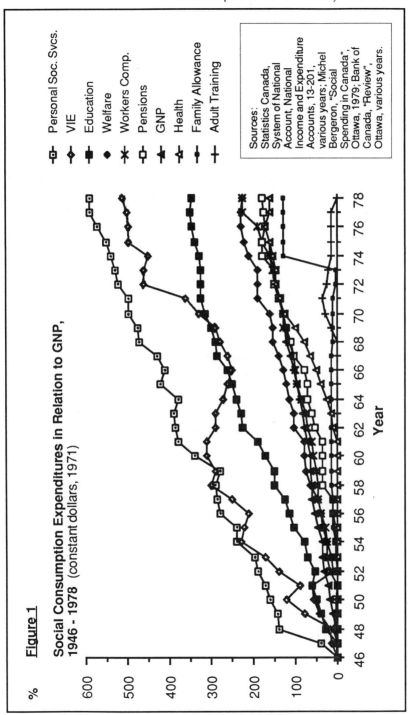

Figure 1

Social Consumption Expenditures in Relation to GNP, 1946 - 1978 (constant dollars, 1971)

Legend:
- Personal Soc. Svcs.
- VIE
- Education
- Welfare
- Workers Comp.
- Pensions
- GNP
- Health
- Family Allowance
- Adult Training

Sources:
Statistics Canada, System of National Account, National Income and Expenditure Accounts, 13-201, various years; Michel Bergeron, "Social Spending in Canada", Ottawa, 1979; Bank of Canada, "Review", Ottawa, various years.

down, one set of programmes is played against another. Thirdly, transfer payments are more likely to be countercyclical than social services expenditures. In fact, excepting more recent cutbacks, social services have increased as frequently during upturns in the economy as downturns. However, a distinctive element of recent cutbacks differing from earlier periods is that, despite high unemployment, transfers and services are not being used to offset the recent downturn in the economy.

In Table 9, we have used James O'Connor's approach to examine trends in postwar expenditures, comparing what O'Connor calls social consumption expenditures to two other categories — social investment and social expenses. Social consumption includes those state expenditures intended for the social reproduction of the labour force, including health, education and social welfare expenditures. Social investment refers to government spending that primarily assists capital accumulation while social expenses refers to state spending on social control and social order. Clearly, one difficulty with this approach is that many expenditures classified in one category could also be in others because they have a wide effect. We have allocated expenditures according to the primary function of each. The data confirm that social consumption expenditures have been

Table 9

Canadian Government Expenditures by Social Function Percent Distribution 1946 - 1977

Year	#	1946	1951	1956	1961	1966	1971	1976	1977
Social Expenses	1	15	30	27	19	15	10	10	10
Social Consumption	2	40	29	33	39	43	50	51	51
Social Investment	3	13	14	17	17	17	15	15	15
Other	4	22	27	23	25	25	25	24	24

1. Protection of persons and property, defence, foreign affairs.

2. Health, Education, Social Welfare.

3. Transportation, Communication, National Resources, Primary Industry.

4. General Government, National Debt, Leisure, Misc.

Sources: M.C. Urquhart and K.A.H. Buckley, *Historical Statistics of Canada*, Table G83-95, for 1946-56; Statistics Canada, *Consolidated Gov't. Finance, 68-202, for 1961-77.*

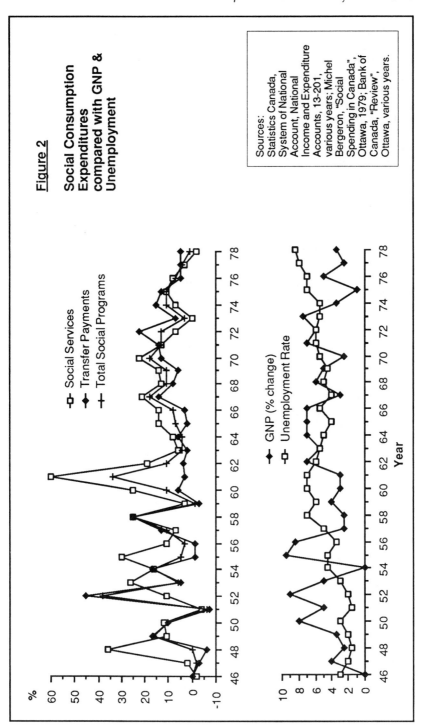

Figure 2

Social Consumption
Expenditures
compared with GNP &
Unemployment

Sources:
Statistics Canada,
System of National
Account, National
Income and Expenditure
Accounts, 13-201,
various years; Michel
Bergeron, "Social
Spending in Canada",
Ottawa, 1979; Bank of
Canada, "Review",
Ottawa, various years.

largely responsible for increases in postwar government expenditures while social expenses declined over the same period. Social expenses did climb as high as 30 percent of government expenditures, due mainly however, to defense costs associated with the Korean War. Social investment varied somewhat, but remained between 13 percent and 17 percent of total expenditures.

From this brief review, the appearance and nature of postwar social welfare reforms and the consequent expansion in state expenditures, clearly show significant changes during the period 1941 to 1974. Though the process of social reform is rooted in the long history of the relations of class, gender and the state, a substantial number of reforms were put in place in the 1963-1968 period. Thus, at the end of this period, Canada can be seen as a developed welfare state in the sense that social welfare programmes, or social consumption, enters the daily lives of a majority of the population.

Further, social consumption expenditures grew to more than 50 percent of total Canadian state expenditures in the mid-1970s. Such expenditures, however, have a two-sided purpose and impact: they increase economic and social security for the mass of people who claim the benefits offered — to workers in the home and in the labour market, they have become a part of the social wage, a publicly provided counterpart to the private wage. However, to employers, they socialize some of the costs of the labour force. Health and education programmes constitute the major part of social consumption expenditures, since they are intended for the general social reproduction of labour. Unemployment insurance and workers' compensation socialize the cost of market fluctuations and accidents, while programmes like the Canada Assistance Plan, Old Age Pensions, and Family Allowances, socialize the costs of maintaining a surplus population. Consequently, social expenditures legitimize capitalism as a social system, growing in size and scope relatively and absolutely. At the same time, by socializing labour costs to a large degree, they play an important role in the accumulation of capital in contemporary capitalism.

The Appearance of Fiscal Crisis, 1974-78

The rapid rise in expenditures is a frequently given reason for the cuts in funds for state social programmes initiated in the mid-1970s, during the Trudeau years. For many observers of government, the cutbacks simply follow from expenditure increases in the postwar period and the tendency of Canadians to live beyond their means, pushing the Robin Hood principle beyond economic rationality. Right-wing critics and economists argue that state expenditures have gone too far in the direction of give-aways; others argue for the necessity of temporary retreat. One difficulty with these responses, however, is that social expenditures are not particularly high by postwar international standards — there is little evidence of a Robin Hood in our midst.[58]

Even with significant increases in its social expenditures, Canada still ranked behind the Netherlands, Sweden, Norway, Denmark, Germany, Belgium and France in total government expenditures, ranking *well* behind many.[59] Since Canada also has a higher per capita income than many of these countries, the restraint of the mid-1970s onward is evidently not just related to affordability.

It does not appear to be high expenditures *per se*, which explain the restraint initiated in the mid-1970s, but a crisis in profitability resulting from conflict between labour and capital.[60] With slow growth, there was a general downturn in investment. Consequently, business organizations exerted pressure on the state to minimize the economic decline and fluctuations in profit while increasing demands for government to lessen borrowing from the money market and cut its spending, so that the private sector could regain its position. As the downturn continued into the 1970s, this crisis further aggravated the demands on government. At the same time, faced with rising unemployment, the state was pressured to offset the decline of private wages with increased social wages in the form of social expenditures.

This pressure, from both capital and the working class (not simply rising expenditures), creates what O'Connor calls the fiscal crisis of the state arising from a shortfall in revenue at the same time expenditures rise. The state was pressed to assume greater responsibility for underwriting high risk in the capital intensive resource sector while gains accrued to private investors.

Moreover, when social expenditures rise, there is no evidence they fundamentally change the structural basis of Canadian society.[61] This is one contradiction of the welfare state. While government increasingly assumes the costs of reproducing labour, the welfare state does not appreciably redistribute income from rich to poor, guarantee full employment, or assure equality in health, education and social services. Cutbacks, on the other hand, are a short-term solution to the longer-term problem of the crisis in profitability. As seen in earlier periods, cutbacks are not new. The difference between the present period of restraint and previous ones, is that government now accounts for a larger percentage of the GNP and the labour force, at the very time it receives a declining revenue from the productive sector, thus leading to the now widely-recognized revenue squeeze.

During downturns in the economy, the private sector pressures government for assistance. The state, under this pressure, redirects expenditures to aid capital or reduces taxation. Both actions have the effect of squeezing social expenditures and increasing deficit financing. Typically, there is a trade-off between transfers to persons and aid to business and industry. In the postwar period, when transfers to persons increased, spending on capital declined. Conversely, when spending on capital increased, transfers to persons declined.

Increased aid to capital can be achieved directly by subsidies or taxation expenditures. Taxation expenditures affect the government purse in a way similar to direct subsidies, but are not directly recorded in public accounts. A Federal government study showed that corporate tax expenditures amounted to almost $14 billion in 1976 and $18 billion in 1979, considerably in excess of direct government spending on capital which was $10 billion and $11 billion respectively.[62] During a downturn, it has become easier for government to reduce taxes on capital than to increase public expenditures, producing the net effect of continuously shifting the tax burden from corporations to persons (Figure 3). At the end of the war, the corporate sector in Canada accounted for 17 percent of tax revenue, increasing to 23 percent by 1951. Thereafter, it gradually declined until, by 1979, it was 8 percent. By contrast, direct taxation on persons increased from a postwar low of 20 percent of government revenue in 1951, to 29 percent in 1979. A consequence is that the rate of growth in services has been increasingly supported by deficit financing. Faced with mounting debt, the state has eroded social expenditures on programmes where political resistance was least likely to occur.

Conclusion

The Canadian state, from the time of confederation, was perceived to be crucial to the development and survival of the country, both economically and culturally. As a consequence, policies by the Canadian state to encourage and fund accumulation of capital were manifest from the beginning. The legitimating activities of the state were also fully recognized at Confederation but required few social expenditures. Instead of expanding social programmes in this early period, the state expanded its regulatory activities. Nevertheless, some of the legal foundations of the welfare state were established during this same period.

In the phase of reluctant welfarism, some important social welfare programmes were put in place, but social expenditures remained relatively insignificant until the 1930s. Social reforms were strongly resisted by the state, but the demands of war and its resultant social impact opened the way for reforms long advocated by labour, women and social organizations. It took the Depression of the 1930s, however, to force expansion of social expenditures and, although World War II temporarily curtailed their growth, by 1940, the principle of major state involvement was established.

The past forty-five years, therefore, have seen social reforms and social expenditures begin to directly affect the social welfare of the majority of the population and expand to the point of becoming a significant part of state activity. While plans were laid in bureaucracy and government during the 1940s, there was resistance within the state to many social reforms eventually instituted over the subsequent 30 years. In contrast to the previous period, the economic buoyancy of the 1960s, demands from labour, women's and social organizations, combined with a minority federal reform government, paved the way for significant social reform. The programmes put in place expanded social expenditures dramatically between 1965 and 1974.

Figure 3
Direct and Corporate Taxes
as Proportion of Government Revenue

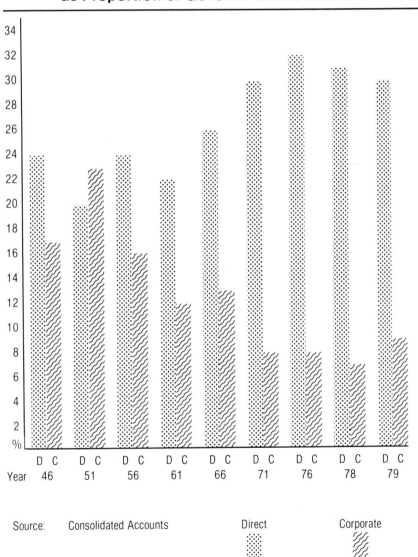

Source: Consolidated Accounts   Direct   Corporate

In the most recent phase of fiscal crisis, the state has increasingly been squeezed for revenue because of a crisis of profitability. In the 1960s, the state offset the growth of social expenditures by borrowing against the future, as well as shifting the revenue burden from corporate to income taxes. With the economic downturn since 1974, borrowing has become increasingly costly. Many business organizations have amplified their demands to shift the balance from social consumption to social investment, and simultaneously, for cuts in taxes and the deficit. Hence, the pressure on the state to reduce social expenditures.

NOTES
1. For a discussion of Wagner's law, see Alan Peacock and Jack Wiseman, *The Growth of Public Expenditures in the United Kingdom*, Princeton, 1961, 40 ff. or Richard Musgrave, *Fiscal Systems*, New Haven, 1969, 73-75. See also Richard M. Bird, *The Growth of Government Spending in Canada*, Toronto, 1970, 69-88.
2. Harold L. Wilensky and Charles N. Lebeaux, *Industrial Society and Social Welfare*, New York, 1958, Part One.
3. Anthony Downs, *An Economic Theory of Democracy*, New York, 1957, 3-76.
4. James O'Connor, *The Fiscal Crisis of the State*, New York, 1975; Ian Gough, "State Expenditures in Advanced Capitalism," *New Left Review*, 92, 1975.
5. Frances Piven and Richard Cloward, *Regulating the Poor: The Function of Public Welfare*, New York, 1971.
6. James O'Connor, *Fiscal Crisis*, Chapters 4-6.
7. Piven and Cloward, *Regulating the Poor*, Chapter 1.
8. Elisabeth Wallace, "The Changing Canadian State," Ph.D., Columbia University, 1950, Chapter 2.
9. B. L. Vigod, "The Quebec Charities Act Controversy, 1921," *Histoire Sociale*, 1978 and Esdras Minville, *Labour Legislation and Social Services in the Province of Quebec*, Ottawa, 1939.
10. Nova Scotia, and subsequently New Brunswick incorporated many of the provisions of the English Poor Laws. See K. de Schweinitz for an outline of the development of the English Poor Laws, *England's Road to Social Security*, New York, 1975.
11. R. B. Splane, *Social Welfare in Ontario, 1791-1893*, Toronto, 1971, Chapter 2.
12. Chester Martin, *"Dominion Lands" Policy*, Toronto, 1973, Chapter 13; Gustavus Myers, *A History of Canadian Wealth*, Chapters 9-17; Robert Chodos, *A History of the CPR*.
13. M. C. Urquhart and K. A. H. Buckley, *Historical Statistics of Canada*, Toronto, 1961, Series AIS-19; *Census of Canada, 1871*.
14. See Wallace, "The Changing Canadian State," 25-101; Allan Smith, "The Myth of the Self-Made Man in English Canada, 1850-1914," *Canadian Historical Review*, 59:2, June, 1978, 189-219.

15. Urquhart and Buckley, *Historical Statistics*, Series AIS-19.
16. Ibid, Series Q1-11.
17. Ibid, Series, E202-213, E214-244, L125-138, S24-38.
18. Charles Lipton, *The Trade Union Movement of Canada, 1827-1959*, Montreal, 1968, Chapter 2.
19. See Ontario Bureau of Industry, *Annual Reports*, 1882-1900.
20. R. B. Splane, *Social Welfare*, 43-64.
21. Ibid, Chapter 5.
22. A summary of developments may be found in R. B. Splane, *Social Welfare*, Chapters 2, 3, 4, and in Elisabeth Wallace, "The Changing Canadian State," Chapter III.
23. Splane, *Social Welfare*, 265-277; G. Kealey ed., *Canada Investigates Industrialism*, Toronto, 1973, Part 1.
24. Andrew Jones and Len Rutman, *In the Children's Aid*, Toronto, 1981.
25. Len Rutman, "Importation of British Waifs into Canada: 1868 to 1916," *Child Welfare*, 53:3, March, 1973, 158-66; P. T. Rooke and R. L. Schnell, *Discarding the Asylum: From Child Rescue to the Welfare State in English Canada 1800-1950*, Lanham, U.S.A. 1983, Chapter 7. Joy Parr "Transplanting from Dens of Iniquity: Theology and Child Emigration," in Linda Kealey ed. *A Not Unreasonable Claim*, Toronto, 1979, 169-84.
26. Neil Sutherland, *Children in English-Canadian Society*, Toronto, 1976, 91-123.
27. No single volume can, nor does, adequately review these developments. See for example, V. Strong-Boag, *The National Council of Women, 1893-1929*, Ottawa, 1976; Richard Allen, *The Social Passion: Religion and Social Reform in Canada, 1914-28*, Toronto, 1971; John C. Weaver, "Tomorrow's Metropolis Revisited: A Critical Assessment of Urban Reform in Canada 1890-1920," in G. A. Stetler and A. F. J. Artibise eds. *The Canadian City*, Toronto 1977, 393-418; Paul Rutherford, *Saving the Canadian City*, Toronto, 1974; "Fire, Disease and Water in the 19th Century City," *Urban History Review*, VIII:1, June, 1979, Special Issue; P. A. Bator, "Public Health Reform in Canada and Urban History: A Critical Survey," in *Urban History Review*, IX:2, October 1980, 87-102.
28. N. Penner, *The Canadian Left*, Toronto, 1977, Chapter 2.
29. Ian MacPherson, *Each for All: A History of the Cooperative Movement in English Canada, 1900-1945*, Toronto, 1979, Chapter 3; W. L. Morton, *The Progressive Party in Canada*, Toronto, 1967.
30. Richard Allen, *The Social Passion*, Chapter 1.
31. N. Sutherland, *Children*, Chapter 9.
32. Theresa Jennissen, "The Development of the Workman's Compensation Act of Ontario, 1914," *Canadian Journal of Social Work Education*, 7:1, 1981, 55-71; Michael J. Piva, "The Workmen's Compensation Movement in Ontario," *Ontario History*, 67:1, March 1975, 39-56.
33. J. Castell Hopkins, "Voluntary Contributions to War Funds," *Canadian Annual Review*, Toronto, 1914, 222-35; R. C. Brown and R. Cook, *Canada 1896-1921*, Toronto, 1976, 212-27. For details on the pension scheme see Walter S. Woods, *Rehabilitation (A Combined Operation)*, Ottawa, 1953, Chapter 24.
34. Urquhart and Buckley, *Historical Statistics*, D412-413, D426-433.
35. Carol Bacchi, "Divided Allegiances: The Response of Farm and Labour Women to Suffrage," in Linda Kealey ed. *A Not Unreasonable Claim*, Toronto, 1979, 89-108; Catherine Cleverdon, *The Woman Suffrage Movement in Canada*, Toronto, 1950; Brown and Cook, *Canada 1896-1921*, 294-9.
36. Martin, Robin, *Radical Politics and Canadian Labour*, Kingston, 1968, 151-77.

37. See Brown and Cook, *Canada 1896-1921*, 231-38; T. Traves, *The State and Enterprise*, Toronto, 1979, esp. Chapter 8; Victor Levant, *Capital and Labour: Partners?*, Toronto, 1977.

38. Wallace, "The Changing Canadian State," Chapter 5; A. Moscovitch, "Canadian Federal Housing Policy 1867-1975," paper presented to CPSA, 1981; James Struthers, "Prelude to Depression, The Federal Government and Unemployment 1918-1929," *Canadian Historical Review*, 53:3, September, 1977.

39. Dennis Guest, *The Emergence of Social Security*, 48-63; Enrique Romo, "The Origins of Mothers' Allowance Legislation in Ontario," MSW Research Paper, School of Social Work, Carleton University, 1979; Ceta Ramkhalawansingh, "Women During the Great War," in J. Acton et al eds, *Women at Work, 1850-1930*, Toronto, 1974, 261-308; V. Strong-Boag, "Mothers' Allowances and the Beginnings of Social Security in Canada," *Journal of Canadian Studies*, 14:1, Spring 1979, 24-34.

40. Richard Allen, *The Social Passion*, Chapter 15; L. Hamlet, "Charlotte Whitton and the Growth of the Canadian Council on Child Welfare 1926-1941," MSW Research Paper, School of Social Work, Carleton University, 1978; Tamara Harevan, "An Ambiguous Alliance: Some Aspects of American Influences on Canadian Social Welfare," *Histoire Sociale*, 1969, 90-96; P. T. Rooke and R. L. Schnell "Making The Way More Comfortable: Charlotte Whitton's Child Welfare Career," *Journal of Canadian Studies*, 17:4, Winter 1983.

41. K. Bryden, *Old Age Pensions and Policy Making in Canada*, Montreal 1974, 51-59, 61-101; Roger Roome, "Ideology and Social Welfare Legislation in Canada — A Case Study of the Government Annuities Act of 1908," MSW Research Paper, Carleton University, 1986. See also Wallace, "The Changing Canadian State," 120-21 on the commissions and 113-21 on the Liberal Party platform; on the latter see also H. Ferns and B. Ostry, *The Age of MacKenzie King*, Toronto, 1976, Chapter 9, 10.

42. Urquhart and Buckley, *Historical Statistics*, E1-12, D238-253, C47-55.

43. A. E. Grauer, *Public Assistance and Social Insurance*, Ottawa, 1939; James Struthers, *No Fault of Their Own: Unemployment and the Canadian Welfare State 1914-1941*, Toronto, 1983.

44. For reference sources on this period see Grauer, *Public Assistance and Social Insurance*; Carl Cuneo "The Canadian State and Unemployment Insurance," *Studies in Political Economy*, Spring 1980, 37-65; Royal Commission on Price Spreads, Report, 1935; J. R. H. Wilbur, *The Bennett New Deal: Fraud or Portent?*, Toronto, 1968, 80-93; J. R. H. Wilbur, "H. H. Stevens and R. B. Bennett, 1930-34," *Canadian Historical Review*, 43:1, March 1962, 1-16; Alvin Finkel, *Business and Social Reform in the Thirties*, Toronto, 1976, Chapter 7. On the constitutional issues see Brooke Claxton, "Social Reform and the Constitution," *Canadian Journal of Economics and Political Science*, 1:3, August 1935, 409-35; C.A. Curtis, "Dominion Legislation of 1935: An Economist's Review," *Canadian Journal of Economics and Political Science*, August 1935, contains an outline of Bennett's New Deal programme. An article by L. Richter, "The Employment and Social Insurance Bill," 436-48, contains a review of the proposed unemployment insurance.

45. Urquhart and Buckley, *Historical Statistics*, G26-44.

46. King established not only The Royal Commission on Dominion-Provincial Relations, but the National Employment Commission (1938) under Arthur B. Purvis. Bennett established Commissions to deal with the Bank of Canada, (Macmillan) and Price Spreads (Stevens). Provincial governments also established a range of commissions in the 1930s. For a review of the Report on Dominion

Provincial Relations and the background studies in social welfare see Harry Cassidy, "Social Services in a Federal System," *Social Service Review*, 14:12, December 1940, 678-709.

47. Robert Bothwell and William Kilborn, *C. D. Howe*, Toronto, 1979, Chapters 10, 11; Royal Commission on Prices, *Report*, Ottawa, 1948; J. L. Granatstein, *Canada's War, 1939-45*; L. S. MacDowell, "The Formation of the Canadian Industrial Relations System during World War Two," *Labour/Le Travailleur*, 3, 1978, 175-96.

48. L. Marsh, *Social Security for Canada*, Toronto, 1975, (reprint).

49. Advisory Committee on Reconstruction, Housing and Community Planning, Ottawa, 1944. For a study of Marsh's life and work see A. Moscovitch ed, *Journal of Canadian Studies*, Special Issue on Leonard Marsh, 21:2, 1986.

50. Urquhart and Buckley, *Historical Statistics*, 626-44; B. Kitchen, "Wartime Social Reform: The Introduction of Family Allowances," *Canadian Journal of Social Work Education*, 7:1, 1981, 29-54.

51. See for example, Jill Wade, "Wartime Housing Limited 1941-1947," UBC Planning Papers, November 1984.

52. Bryden, *Old Age Pensions*, Chapter 6.

53. James Struthers, "Shadows from the Thirties: The Federal Government and Unemployment Assistance, 1941-1956," Unpublished, 1986.

54. M. Taylor, *Health Insurance and Canadian Public Policy*, Montreal, 1979.

55. Peter C. Newman, *Renegade in Power*, Toronto, 1963, chapters 9, 21; H. Scott Gordon, *The Economists Versus The Bank of Canada*, Toronto, 1961.

56. Economic Council of Canada *Fifth Annual Review* Ottawa, 1968, chapter 6; Privy Council, Special Planning Secretariat, *Profile of Poverty in Canada*, Ottawa, 1965; Tom Kent, *Social Policy for Canada: Towards a Philosophy of Social Security*, Ottawa, 1962. Henry Milner and Sheila Hodgins Milner, *The Decolonization of Quebec*, Toronto, 1973.

57. Taylor, *Health Insurance*,

58. W. Irwin Gillespie, *In Search of Robin Hood*, Montreal, 1978; See for example L.B. Smith, *Anatomy of A Crisis*, Vancouver, 1977; A.G. Grubel, *Unemployment Insurance: Global Evidence of Its Effects on Unemployment*, Vancouver, 1976.

59. *Economic Review*, April 1979, Table 10.3; see also Ross Stanford, *Social Security in a Changing World*, U.S., HEW, 1979.

60. David Wolfe, "The State and Economic Policy in Canada" in L. Panitch ed. *The Canadian State*, Toronto 1977, 251-288; Bert Young, "Taxation and The Capitalist State," in A. Moscovitch and G. Drover, *Inequality* Toronto, 1981, 227-248.

61. Allan Moscovitch and Glenn Drover, *Inequality: Essays on the Political Economy of Social Welfare*, Toronto, 1981, 18.

62. Department of Finance, *Tax Expenditures Account*, Ottawa, 1979.

PART II

Origins

Preconditions of the Canadian State: Educational Reform and the Construction of a Public in Upper Canada, 1837-1846

Bruce Curtis

Recent work in the social history and political economy of North American educational reform has been situated to a large extent in a "social control" paradigm. In this paradigm educational reform is treated as a response on the part of élite groups or ruling classes to the social unrest associated with industrial capitalist development. Depending upon the particular version of the "social control" thesis one encounters, educational reform is seen as an attempt to control urban poverty and crime, an attempt to repress the menace of class struggle on the part of the working class, or both.

"Revisionism" in social history and "reproduction" theory in neo-Marxist political economy — the two main versions of the social control thesis — have produced major advances over earlier models of the nature of educational development and the role of educational institutions in capitalist societies. Revisionism opened enormous new fields of investigation for educational history, including the study of literacy and rates of school attendance, and the investigation of reform ideologies.[1] Neo-Marxist reproduction theory, which in North America was very much affected by revisionism in social history, produced thorough refutations of many propositions and conceptions derived from liberal educational theory.[2]

Yet the social control thesis has tended to mystify educational development. In exlaining the transformation of capitalist societies, the social control approach has tended to abstract in a misleading manner from the concrete political contexts in which actual educational reforms were made. The assumption — sometimes quite valid — that key social groups agitated for educational reform in an effort to control or repress workers has led to a failure to investigate historically the educational activities of workers themselves.[3] The view of educational reform as an essentially repressive process aimed at the control of the "poor" or the working class by an "élite" or bourgeoisie has directed attention away from both the political conflict and struggle over education, and from an analysis of the content of educational reform. In fact, as I will argue, far from simply aiming to repress or neutralize the political activities of certain classes in society, educational reform in mid-nineteenth-century Upper Canada sought to reconstruct political rule in society by reconstructing the political subjectivity of the population. Reforms sought to do this not simply by repressing consciousness, but by developing and heightening consciousness within newly constructed state forms. Educational reform sought to build political subjects, and in so doing also furthered construction of the state.

The popularization of a social control approach to educational reform owes a great deal to the influential early work of Michael Katz — especially his work, *The Irony of Early School Reform*. In part, what Katz did was take the methodological imperative of the new social history — "let people speak for themselves" — and apply it to educational reform in mid-nineteenth-century Massachusetts. Katz investigated the conceptions and arguments of school reformers, taking their conceptions more or less at face value in the sense that he refused to organize their conceptions in terms of any structure not immediately present in their discourse. This led to an inadequate conception of social class and social structure.[4] Having begun with ideology, rather than with the conditions of its production, Katz was forced to attempt to locate that ideology in social structure *post festum*. Having restricted his conception of social class to that current in the discourse of educational reformers and in his documentary sources, Katz could not come to grips with the real conditions of the production of educational reform. To connect the ideology of reform to social organization, Katz was forced to rely upon motives which he imputed to school reformers — specifically a desire, stemming from a fear of social unrest, to control and repress workers.[5]

In the literature of Upper Canadian educational development, a clear version of the social control approach can be found in Alison Prentice's *The School Promoters*. Prentice attempted to let school reformers speak for themselves and accepted that social class should be considered as school reformers had themselves considered it. Prentice attempted to treat the statements of educational reformers as a consistent universe of discourse, containing within itself a perfect logic of educational reform. This approach enabled her, to a certain extent, to elucidate the world view of school reformers; but, as in Katz's case, it also confronted her with certain methodological limitations.

Prentice, like Katz, was forced to connect in some manner the discourse of school reform with the concrete context of school reform. For her, the connection was a fear of urban crime and poverty on the part of school reformers. She argues that this fear propelled the process of school reform. By emphasizing this, Prentice elevates what I will suggest was a relatively minor theme in the discourse of school reform into a major explanatory principle.[6] She was to neglect the political struggles over education which characterized Upper Canadian society and to portray educational reform as a largely repressive process.

Furthermore, in trying to treat the statements of school reformers as an internally consistent universe, Prentice encountered the methodological problem of the inconsistent statement. For example, in speaking to farmers in defence of centralized education under state auspices, the reformer Egerton Ryerson glorified and lauded his audience. Farmers were described, more or less, as the backbone of the nation, and it was educational reform that would gain them the recognition they deserved while keeping their sons at home and transforming their daughters into piano-playing domestic appurtenances.[7] On the other hand, farmers were denounced by Ryerson in a report to the colonial parliament. Here the same people were portrayed as ignorant, degraded, and politically dangerous.[8] How was one to make sense of this "inconsistency"?

Had Prentice balanced her historical meticulousness with a political-economic approach she would have seen that Ryerson was quite consistent. The consistency lay, not directly in his statements, but rather in his structural location. Ryerson was a state agent agitating for state control over education. This position and the interest it embodied remained constant across Ryerson's statements and allows some sense to be made of them.

For Prentice, however, the attempt to treat the discourse of reform as a self-contained universe produced an inability to make sense of this sort of inconsistency. Prentice concludes that Ryerson made inconsistent statements because of a personality defect.[9] Without an analysis of the political-economic context of discourses, letting "people speak for themselves" may well produce an inability to understand what they say.

The neo-Marxist approach to educational reform in North America has largely been conducted within the same social control paradigm, with a few changes of a largely terminological nature. Bowles and Gintis,[10] for instance, take Katz's study as the basis of their examination of educational reform in the United States in the middle of the nineteenth century. In their version, educational reform is a response of a class-conscious bourgeoisie to capitalist industrialization. This class-conscious bourgeoisie is held to have designed the educational system in the face of the menace of class struggle and in order to control workers. No examination of the educational activities of workers in the same period is made, and indeed, this class is reduced to the role of an anonymous menace. No struggle over education itself is apparent and, once in place, the educational system seems to function with the well-oiled smoothness sought by the bourgeoisie.[11]

A replica of this approach has appeared in Schecter's treatment of Canadian educational development. The Canadian case, as I have argued elsewhere, presents a notable peculiarity with which, to his credit, Schecter attempts to deal.[12] This peculiarity resides in the fact that the Upper Canadian system, as organized in the 1840s, was a specifically capitalist or industrial school system, while capitalist industrialization in Upper Canada was only slightly developed. The Upper Canadian educational system, in part, presents an instance of educational autonomy in which educational development cannot be seen as a purely indigenous product.

However, despite his awareness of the uneven institutional development of Upper Canada in this regard, Schecter maintains that educational reform in Upper Canada was motivated by the necessity of "social control of an emerging working class."[13] The Canadian bourgeoisie in Schecter's account, was a farsighted group which realized before the development of the Canadian working class, that the school system and its practices would be "as indispensable then as they are now to the effective subordination of the working class."[14] The educational reforms of the 1840s were apparently motivated by a desire for social control.

What constituted social control in education? In Schecter's account, there seem to be two major components:

The social control functions of schooling were twofold. On a specific level the reforms were designed to discipline the nascent labour force for industrial capitalism. On a general level they were designed to legitimate that social order in such a way that the upheaval it brought about could be dealt with without questioning the social order itself.[15]

Despite Schecter's attempt to elucidate the subtleties and ambiguities of educational reform, his account essentially portrays the process as repressive, in which "workers" were trained in the habits of industry and pumped full of ideology to legitimate new social relations of production.

While Schecter is quite correct in connecting Upper Canadian educational development to international capitalist development, I think that the attempt to treat educational development as an *anticipation* of capitalist development is essentially incorrect. The relative autonomy of education in the case of Upper Canada should alert us to the disjuncture here of education from economic development. Educational reform, I will argue, did not seek to discipline workers not yet in existence. On the contrary, educational reform was promoted in Upper Canada for its political promise to the Tory Party and to the imperial state. The disjuncture between educational and economic development in the case of Upper Canadian school reform points to the dominance of political struggles. While these struggles certainly had a political-economic foundation, they are not reducible to struggles between a bourgeoisie and a working class.

The models for the educational reforms adopted in Upper Canada were indeed historically specific. The curriculum and pedagogy both embodied relations peculiar to an industrial capitalist education.[16] However, one must remember that plans for educational reconstruction in Upper Canada were made in 1845-46, well before the Irish famine migration placed the first substantial proletariat in Canadian towns.[17] The political promise of educational reform must be sought elsewhere.

The political context of educational reform in Upper Canada in the period after the Rebellion of 1837 will set the stage for an exegesis of the content of the proposed Upper Canadian school reforms, as they were expressed in Egerton Ryerson's seminal *Report on a System of Public Elementary Instruction for Upper Canada*.[18] I will argue that political reconstruction of a definite sort was implied in educational reform that, in itself, was an important mechanism for state-building.

Political Crisis, Political Reform
and Education in Upper Canada

The 1840s in the Province of Canada was a decade of statebuilding. In the wake of the rebellions of 1837-38 and Lord Durham's critical report on colonial government, the imperial state undertook to reconstruct the colonial administration. The question of the form of the Canadian state and the nature of this colonial administration dominated the political life of the Canadas for a decade. To the extent that colonial history can be read from the colonial side of the Atlantic, it can be read largely as a history of conflict and struggle over this question.

Educational reform, which especially characterized the 1840s in Upper Canada, was inextricably connected to questions of the form of the colonial state. All the fundamental questions concerning educational organization — who could educate, who was in need of education, what was necessary to know, how should it be learned, who should pay for it — these and others were answered only by answering at the same time questions concerning the state: who would rule, how, of what would rule consist, how would it be financed. The struggle over education was at once a struggle over political rule.

Debates over educational reform in Upper Canada had characterized the political development of the colony from the first decade of the nineteenth century.[19] After the Rebellion of 1837 and the Act of Union, these educational conflicts acquired a heightened importance. To many conservative elements, especially those in the Tory Party, the Rebellion of 1837 showed that "in the bosom of this community there exists a dangerous foe."[20] The colony had been polluted by its proximity to the United States, "that arena for the discussion of extreme political fantasies,"[21] and by the presence of an unassimilated American population interested in democracy and republicanism. In the view of R.B. Sullivan, later president of the Legislative Council of Upper Canada, the Rebellion pointed to the existence of a crisis of government. Sullivan claimed that the existing school system had been infiltrated by American adventurers. The propagandistic activities of American tractarians had undermined the loyalties of Canadian youth to the point where their minds were

> only accessible to motives of adherence to the Government by means of terror and coercion, or through the equally base channel of personal and pecuniary advantage.[22]

In Sullivan's view — one typical of colonial conservatives — the Rebellion of 1837 was in large part the result of an educational failure. The school system and religious institutions had failed to shape the "youthful mind" of the colony adequately and to instruct people in their political duties. This meant rule could proceed only by coercion or bribery — unstable mechanisms in light of the rebellion. The political/ educational problem for conservatives was one of fixing the "good and noble sentiments" of the population on the proper objects. They were joined in this concern by the Lieutenant-Governor.[23] A major assault upon prevailing community-controlled education was launched by conservatives in the late 1830s, and this assault resulted in the production of a draft school act in 1841.

Before the Union of 1840, the Reform Party in Upper Canada had consistently championed local control in educational matters. The struggles over the state church, the colonial lands, and the powers of the elected assembly itself placed the Reform Party in a position of opposition to executive control over education and support for local autonomy.[24] After the Union, the struggles over "responsible government," struggles in which members of the Reform Party sought parliamentary autonomy for Canada within the colonial connection, also placed Reformers in a position to support decentralized, locally-directed education.

Until the political crisis of 1843-44, a version of Reform educational policy prevailed in Upper Canada. The miserably inefficient School Act of 1841 was a version of the Tory-inspired draft legislation based on the Education Commission of 1839, as amended by Reformers in committee. In 1843, under the Reform ministry of Baldwin and Lafontaine, this act was replaced by one which extended local control over educational matters while increasing the funds available. Both the acts of 1841 and 1843 required localities to raise matching funds through a combination of property taxes and fees for state educational grants. The 1843 act placed the management of education in all its important aspects in the hands of school trustees elected by the parents of school children. Local trustees controlled curriculum, pedagogy, the internal management of the school, teacher evaluation and working conditions, hours of attendance and so forth.[25] Reformers publicly vaunted the act as one which placed control over educational matters in the hands of the people directly.[26]

The School Act of 1843 was a success in practice. It increased local educational funds, legitimized local practice in educational matters, and restricted central influence over the system to one of information-gathering and coordination. Taxation for educational purposes in some instances far exceeded the legal minimum, and the number of children enrolled in the schools increased markedly.[27] However, the Tory Party objected in principle to local control over education. The political crisis of 1843-44, which brought the Tory Party to power, led to a major reorganization of the Upper Canadian educational system.

Political Crisis and the Rise of Ryerson

Late in 1843, the Reform ministry of Baldwin and Lafontaine resigned over the reservation of the Secret Societies Bill and the refusal of the Governor-

General to distribute governmental patronage along lines determined by the ministry. The ministry expected fresh elections, but these were not called. Instead, for several months, the colony was ruled more or less directly from the office of the Governor-General with the aid of three parliamentary ministers. A political furor ensued involving, in part, serious public agitations in favour of colonial political autonomy.[28] After some time, a nominally Tory ministry was constructed by the Governor-General and, in elections held in 1844, this ministry won a small majority centered in Upper Canada. This electoral victory was in part a product of the activities of the Reverend Egerton Ryerson.[29]

An able propagandist, professional cleric and controversial but influential leader of the moderate Wesleyan Methodist population in Upper Canada, Ryerson undertook to debate the Reformers in the press in a lengthy and much-publicized series of letters. Ryerson's political biography was a chequered one, characterized by frequent shifts in position and party alliance. A vocal opponent of executive control over education in the 1830s, Ryerson had become convinced that, while a moderate degree of political liberalization in Canada was desirable, any such project demanded a reform of popular education. Ryerson supported "responsible government" in the sense of government by people educated to act responsibly. This was a matter upon which he had communicated at length with public officials.[30]

Ryerson also agreed more or less completely with the attempts by the imperial state and its first Canadian Governors-General to de-politicize the colony by replacing "factionalism" with "sound administration." This policy involved an acceptance of the legitimacy of protestant religious sects and encouraged protestant social experimentation. Protestant religion was in some ways particularly well-fitted for social reconstruction in Canada and for the continuation of British imperialism which that reconstruction implied. It put forward a vision of political universality in which social harmony, compromise, and the high moral character of social leaders would guarantee political justice.[31]

Ryerson wrote to the Governor-General, as he prepared to engage the Reformers in the press, that

> In the present crisis, the Government must of course, first be placed upon a strong foundation, and then must the youthful mind of Canada be instructed and moulded in the way I have had the honor of stating to your Excellency if this country is long to remain an appendage to the British Crown.[32]

After the success of the Tory Party in the elections of 1844, Ryerson was named Assistant Superintendent of Education for Upper Canada and charged with formulating a plan for educational reconstruction.

The reform of education which followed was an attempt on the part of the Tory Party to deal with a two-fold political problem in Canada: the maintenance of the colonial connection in the face of political disloyalty, demonstrated by sections of the population in 1837 and again in 1843-44, and the creation of forms of rule which would work without bribery or coercion.

The Planned Educational Reconstruction

To the Tory Party, the School Act of 1843 left control over education precisely in the hands of those most in need of instruction by the state in their political duties. In the crisis of 1843-44 and in their rather shaky response to appeals for loyalty to the Crown, sections of the rural population had shown this to be the case. Education, Ryerson wrote, had to be reorganized so as "to render the Educational System, in its various ramifications and applications, the indirect, but powerful instrument of British Constitutional Government.[33] Ryerson and the Tory administration set out to transform education into a state-directed political socialization.

To this end, Ryerson embarked upon an educational tour to collect information about educational systems in the United States and Europe. This trip produced an extensive educational report and draft school legislation which formed the basis for educational organization in Upper Canada until 1871 (if not later). Ryerson's *Report on a System of Public Elementary Instruction for Upper Canada*, printed by order of the legislature in 1847, provided the blueprint for educational reconstruction in the late 1840s.

Ryerson was by no means the first person interested in educational experimentation aimed at transforming schools into instruments of state policy. In his travels, he encountered the fruits of many initiatives undertaken by members of different social classes in various countries. He also encountered, assimilated and reproduced in his report various attempts to produce efficient and effective pedagogies and curricula. The conditions under which Ryerson's report was produced and the solutions it proposed consisted of responses to common problems faced by liberal reformers in all capitalist societies in the middle of the nineteenth century.

In general, Ryerson's *Report* suggested that the aim of education was the successful training of the forces possessed by each individual. A successful training of these forces would create habits of mind and body conducive to productive labour, Christian religion and political order. The report was shot through with a concern for the efficient training of human energy.[34] Ryerson sought to make education *practical*; not in the sense of training people for particular occupations or teaching particular skills, but in the sense of creating habits, predispositions and loyalties in the population which would then *practically* guide action. Ryerson agreed with Archbishop Whately, one of the architects of the Irish national system of education, that successful governance in representative institutions required the creation of "rationality" in the population.[35]

There were three parts to this rationality-producing education. Ryerson wrote:

> Now, education thus practical, includes religion and morality; secondly, the development to a certain extent of all our faculties; thirdly, an acquaintance with several branches of elementary education.[36]

Religion and morality were to provide the political/habitual/attitudinal content of education. The cultivation of "all the faculties" was the method of instruction, and the several branches of education were the specific contents and devices used to transmit religious and moral training. I will consider Ryerson's pedagogy before discussing the religious and moral conceptions which his reforms embraced.

Inductive Education and Pedagogical Humanism

Ryerson's *Report* was in large measure a critique of a system of education common in Europe and North America in the first decades of the nineteenth century: rote learning. In the monitorial schools, common in working class districts of English cities, students were taught by rote in groups of as many as six hundred under the direction of a single teacher. Monitorial education was developed more or less simultaneously in the 1790s by Andrew Bell in Madras, India, and by Joseph Lancaster, a Quaker schoolmaster, in London. Monitorial schools were run using simple principles of the factory division of labour. The teacher was assisted by groups of child monitors, each monitor being in charge of a group of younger children. Simple bits of information passed by rote, from teacher to monitor to student.

This system was extremely inexpensive to run. Also, in an age when ruling classes regarded popularization of the ability to read with a considerable amount of political suspicion, monitorial education eliminated the need for books by having children gather around large printed cards.[37] In the first two decades of the nineteenth century, monitorial schools were quite common in England and the United States, and an attempt was made in the 1820s to introduce them into Upper Canada by the first General Board of Education.[38]

By the time Ryerson wrote, the critique of monitorial education was well developed. Spokespersons for the English workers' movement, like the radical Ricardian, William Thompson, denounced rote learning for its sacrifice of all human intellect to the memory and for its inhumanity.[39] In working class districts of English cities, monitorial schools were poorly attended and teachers were often the victims of violence.[40] The failure of monitorial education in part contributed to the development of an independent English workers' educational initiative.

To middle class school reformers — particularly the Secretary of the Massachusetts Board of Education, Horace Mann (whose writings influenced many nineteenth century reformers, including Ryerson) — rote learning was rejected primarily for its inefficiency as a means of moulding the subjectivity of the student. Ryerson accepted and elaborated this criticism in his *Report*.

In this view, rote learning was seen as incapable of training the "faculties." It addressed only the memory. It did not penetrate beneath the surface of the mind to the psyche or character and for that reason could not form human energy in a lasting and comprehensive manner. An efficient education, on the contrary, would involve "the cultivation of all our mental, moral, and physical powers."[41] An education which successfully formed human energy in a durable manner would engage as many faculties of human perception as possible:

> Our senses are so many inlets of knowledge; the more of them used in conveying instruction to the mind, the better; the more of them addressed, the deeper and more permanent the impression produced.[42]

In a technical sense, one can see, Ryerson rejected rote learning for its failure to penetrate to the core of the human subject's consciousness. Ryerson's alternative to rote learning was not simply a form of ideological repression aimed at controlling or neutralizing the political energies of students. Rather, Ryerson's pedagogy sought to generate self-regulating subjects by expanding the capacity of individuals to feel and to reason within definite forms and conceptions.

In place of rote learning, Ryerson proposed the "inductive" method of education.[43] The emotional susceptibility of the child as well as his or her simple pleasures, were enlisted in the service of instruction. This has frequently been described as "humanistic" education and Ryerson himself drew attention to its "humanizing" result.

Inductive education proceeded by creating in the child an emotional dependency upon the teacher so that the teacher could govern the child with the utmost economy by means of looks, gestures, expressions and qualities of voice. Once such a connection was established, once the "human" qualities of students were developed to a certain point, the teacher could, by his own mobility, deployment and display of energy, draw out the energy of his students in a pleasing and economical manner.[44] This pedagogy offered several advantages from the perspective of education as state-directed socialization.

In such a system, order could be maintained by the manipulation of characteristics developed by pedagogy in the student population. Violence and coercion — the physical display of brutality — would become unnecessary as elements of rule. Rather, rule would proceed through reason and sentiment. Ideally, no teachers would waste energy in physical discipline. Also, no negative experiences would take place which would provide students with grounds for resisting the process of education or forming alternative grounds of self-definition. The subjectivity of the student would be completely captivated by pedagogy and his or her energy made readily accessible to the ends of education.[45] Rule would proceed without appearing as rule. The later consequences of this pedagogical transformation were enormous.[46]

"Humanization" was a pedagogical device which involved the development of the capacities for feeling and moral behaviour. While these capacities were ethically and aesthetically pleasing to school reformers, they were also political instruments for the development of new modes of self-regulation. The "moral" attitude which this pedagogy sought was a way of relating to others and also an ethically-founded acceptance of and affection for existing political forms.

The "humanistic" pedagogy contains, to a large degree, the key to the explanation of Ryerson's curricular reforms — especially his adamant opposition to that instrument of rote learning *par excellence*, the spelling book.[47] The thrust of pedagogy upon curriculum is perhaps nowhere more evident than in the matter of vocal music. "All men," Ryerson quoted in his argument for teaching vocal music in all the elementary schools, "have been endowed with a susceptibility to the influence of music."[48] Vocal music was an important and intrinsically pleasing avenue to the faculties. Teaching children moral songs could displace the ribald and frivolous amusements they pursued, while turning their recreation into a means of instruction. "Music," if correctly used, could "refine and humanize the pupils."[49] Ryerson approvingly quoted the English Privy Council Committee on Education which claimed that since the common schools of Germany had begun to teach workers to sing, "the degrading habits of intoxication" so common there had been much reduced.[50]

Ryerson's humanistic and inductive pedagogy was an instrument and tactic aimed at developing the senses so that they could be enlisted to make contact with human energy. Humanistic education was not a form of social control in any simple sense. It sought not to repress workers or students by feeding them doses of propaganda or ideology, but rather to develop their capacities for feeling and moral behaviour. Students were to become self-disciplining individuals who behaved not out of fear or because of coercion, but because their experience at school had created in them certain moral forms for which they had a positive affection. In Ryerson's pedagogy, the student would have no desire to oppose the process of education and no grounds upon which to do so. Education would be intrinsically pleasing to the student and in consequence he or she would *become* the character sought by pedagogy. Education would produce in the population habits, dispositions and loyalties of a sort congenial to the state and to representative government. The problem of governance faced by generations of conservative educational critics would vanish: political rule would no longer be dependent upon "social control," coercion, terror, or bribery. One would be able to appeal to the "higher sentiments" of the subject formed by education; the state would rule by appeals to the emotions and intellect of the educated population.

Our Common Christianity

Educational reform, in Ryerson's view, was "justified by considerations of economy as well as of patriotism and humanity."[51] By forming the habits and attitudes of individuals, education would eliminate poverty and crime. It would prepare individuals for their "duties and employments of life, as Christians, as persons of business, and also as members of the civil community in which they live."[52] However, the basis of the new system of education was to be what Ryerson called "our common Christianity," a subject to which his *Report* devoted thirty pages (in contrast to a few throwaway lines at the outset on poverty and crime). Ryerson repeatedly stressed the *"absolute necessity of making Christianity the basis and cement of the structure of public education."*[53] Without Christian education there would be no "Christian state," and since Canadians were Christians, their educational system should also be Christian.[54]

The question of what, for Ryerson, constituted "our common Christianity" is essential to understanding the nature of educational reform. The development of the faculties and several branches of education were the methods and devices of a Christian education. Its content was to be found in religion and morality.

On its face, the notion of a common Christianity in Upper Canada is chimerical. Sectarian squabbling was general, and the Wesleyan Methodists were no exception. Protestants of various sects struggled against the predominance of the Church of England. Orange and green regularly smashed each other's heads in the streets. Ryerson himself belittled someone like the Reverend Robert Murray, a Presbyterian who dared to oppose the Temperance positions.[55] Absolute renunciations of Christianity were rare but certainly not unknown.[56] Despite a rather desultory replication of Archbishop Whately's list of common beliefs of all Christians, Ryerson's *Report* did not devote much energy to attempting to demonstrate that common Christianity had an empirical content.[57]

In practice, common Christianity meant a kind of political behaviour and made reference to certain contradictory political ideals. These ideals were characteristic of an urban professional clergy attempting to articulate through Christianity a new form of social and political universality. It was through the language and discourse of protestantism in Upper Canada that the transition from social universality as membership in the state church to universality as citizenship in the political state was made. Protestantism was well-fitted for the political reconstruction being attempted in Canada during the 1840s.

At the heart of the notion of a common Christianity was a desire to create in people a predisposition to act in accordance with principles. This meant that people would accept the legitimacy of, and govern themselves rationally in keeping with certain social postulates. Our common

Christianity was a conception which both specified and gave divine sanction to the principles in question. These were, generally speaking, principles concerned with the relation of self to self and self to others. They involved toleration, meekness, charity, and a respect for the rights of others — including established authority. Common Christianity excluded reciprocal principles such as an eye for an eye and a tooth for a tooth, did not counsel turning the money-lenders out of the temple, and made no mention of the sanctity of struggle against slavery or debt. On the contrary, it involved turning the other cheek, meekly accepting abuses from others, being kind to those in error, and refusing to oppose actively those who caused one harm. These were principles to be posted in all the schools.[58]

Common Christianity involved, first of all, the creation of a form of social order in which subjects would willingly accept political forms, would respect political authority even if it appeared to be unjust, and would reject violent political activity. This did not exhaust the content nor the efficacy of the form of rule Ryerson saw emerging from educational reorganization.

Our common Christianity and common schooling (as it was called) both expressed and embodied a limited democratic content and much of its efficacy was based upon this content. Ryerson, following Horace Mann of Massachusetts, advocated common schooling as (in Mann's words) "the great equalizer of the conditions of men — the balance wheel of the social machinery."[59] Ryerson's reforms sought to overcome class antagonism in civil society by creating harmony and personal contact between members of all social classes at school. "Common" as an educational adjective came to mean "in common" in the 1840s rather than "elementary" or "rudimentary" as it had in the 1830s. Common schooling meant placing "the poor man on a level with the rich man."[60] It meant providing common intellectual property to members of all social classes and, in part, this conception arose out of attempts in Europe and the United States to compensate for the urban proletariat's lack of real property with a common intellectual property. In Upper Canada, this property was to be appropriated only in state institutions, and in the process of intellectual appropriation, members of all social classes would come to occupy a common position in relation to the state.

This phenomenon in Upper Canada was part of an attempt by protestant religion to create forms of civil and religious universality through educational forms of classlessness. Educational classlessness to some extent was advocated as a means to substantive classlessness, thereby saving civil society from itself.[61] Educational reform sought to create new forms of governance. It sought to obviate the necessity of governance by suppression of the individual will. Instead, it sought to shape and develop individual will so governance could proceed by individual self-repression, without actually being experienced as such. It sought to replace the naked exercise of coercion by the rational economy of administration.

Despite serious opposition from the Reform Party and some organs of local government (which produced alterations) the educational reforms of this alliance between the Tory Party, the imperial state and protestant religion went forward in Upper Canada. The durability of the humanistic and classless discourses can be seen by their presence in educational training manuals well into the twentieth century.

Educational Reform and State-Building

Educational reform cannot be seen as a process of social control, in the sense in which that term has been used in the literature, without distorting our understanding of social development. Significantly, the leading authors in the social control approach neglect almost entirely the role of the state in educational reform and the consequences for the state of this same process.

Educational reform in Upper Canada should be seen as a dialectical process in which a state educational administration was created out of conflict in civil society and in which, once created, this educational administration set about reconstructing the conflicts of which it was itself a product. The self-generation of an administrative logic can be clearly seen even in the incomplete recent histories of educational administration.[62]

There are several components to this process of the creation of an educational administration, of this process of state building. In the most obvious sense, educational reform (to the extent that it is merely contiguous with earlier forms) embodied a new division of labour in which part of a state structure was constructed through the appropriation of functions formerly carried out communally. The state grew visibly in this process through the appropriation of a part of the social product for educational purposes, through the multiplication of individuals employed by it, and through the construction of buildings and the accumulation of other elements of educational technology.[63]

Educational reform built state knowledge as well, and in a double sense. In the first place, the school curriculum became a state property. Knowledge of and about social organization, knowledge of and about the state itself, developed under state auspices. In Canada, educational reform meant the expulsion from the elementary schools of privately produced curricula and the substitution of state curricula. Initially in Upper Canada, the curriculum after reform was comprised of books produced by the Irish National Board of Education, but increasingly after 1865, books commonly written by members of the Education Department displaced these.[64] The appropriation of state-generated knowledge came to be an important dimension of citizenship.

In the second place, the state created a new field for information gathering in the administrative organs of education. Systematically-designed school reports had to be completed by school officials as a condition of state financing and these reports constituted a body of knowledge about the nature and condition of the educational population, local policies, local conflicts, solutions and so forth. This development of knowledge about the field that was to be administered was in part a condition of the legitimacy of administration itself. "Fair" and "rational" administration demanded a knowledge of "both sides" of questions, as well as a "larger view."

A detailed investigation of the processes involved in the construction of the state educational domain is beyond the scope of the present article. These are numerous and potentially illuminating for those interested in documenting the growth of the state. However, one of these processes — the complement to the construction of administrative mechanisms — must be noted. One might argue that the state grew most importantly through educational reform where it did so least visibly. Foucault has argued that political power is most effective where it vanishes.[65] Power operates most effectively, Foucault suggests, by forming the subjectivity of the ruled in such a way that rule becomes internalized. Educational reform sought to transform the subjectivity of the body politic. It sought to transform the nature of the individual's relation to himself/herself and others such that governance could proceed by dealing with sentiments and reason. It sought to make the individual a willing participant in his or her own governance, giving that person a "Chrisitian character" so that there could be a "Christian nation." Insofar as this exercise succeeds, it appears to the individual only as the self he or she lives, as the elemental force of a natural law. It may not appear as a form of governance at all. This is precisely its power.

The Construction of a Public

Educational reformers in Canada, and elsewhere in the initial period of reform, frequently described their activity as one of "public instruction." They were somewhat mistaken. Reformers did not confront a ready-made public, a population existing on a terrain of universality and classlessness. Rather, they attempted to *construct* a public, to create and to extend a sphere of classlessness in which the state could rule through impartial administration.

Common schooling was to place members of all social classes in a common relation to each other and the state. Schools, scattered throught civil society, were to be (if you will) "pure state spaces," places purged of the conflicts, struggles and stresses of civil society. In the "republic of letters" the poor man and the rich man would be social equals.[66] Schooling would create a real commonality on a national scale.

The failure of educational reform to create substantive universality is obvious and well documented by neo-Marxist political economy. The success and significance of this transformation of popular socialization is less well charted and indeed cannot be exhaustively treated here. Two final points can be made in this regard.

First, the educational reforms of the 1840s in Upper Canada transformed the nature of educational struggle. Very soon after the construction of a state educational administration, serious questions about the *form* of education ceased to be widely posed. The creation of a "sphere above politics," as Ryerson liked to call the school system, transformed the debate over education from one over competing and conflictual forms of education into one over the management of a state form. The construction of a public sphere transforms questions of form into questions of administration. In the process, possibilities not contained in the public domain itself tend to vanish.

Secondly, with the creation of public education on a wide scale, the conception of the state and civil society as separate realms seems seriously inadequate. The social control thesis in neo-Marxism portrays the state as a repressive force located outside civil society. In fact, through educational reform the state was placed in key ways in a dialectic in which civil society and itself were reconstructed through the creation of social forms. This conception of separate spheres of state and civil society becomes difficult to sustain since the conduct of "private" activities goes forward increasingly in state forms. If the state in fact successfully shaped the subjectivity of the population as a whole (an untenable proposition at this level), in a sense all of the life of civil society would be conducted in state forms. The present article suggests, at least, that the relation of state and civil society is not that presented by the social control thesis, a relation of externality and repression. Rather, the state and civil society interpenetrate; the struggles and class antagonisms which are structurally based are, in a crucial sense, conducted in state forms. This process of what one might tentatively and hesitantly call the "colonization of civil society" demands more attention from Marxist writers.

Educational reform was part of the process of creating a domain in which the state could rule and of creating the mechanisms of rule. As such, it constituted at the same time a process of state development and the preconditions for state development.

NOTES

This paper has been previously published in *Studies in Political Economy*, 10, Winter, 1983. The paper has gone through a number of versions and in the process I have received invaluable assistance from a large number of people. Jim Albert and Allan Moscovitch provided a first opportunity to present the paper. Barry Wellman and Bob Brym encouraged me to produce it as a working paper and Susan Haggis was an excellent editor. Raymond Murphy provided a useful commentary. I am especially indebted to Robert Gidney, Jud Purdy, and the other members of the History Research Group at the University of Western Ontario. The detailed criticism offered to me by these people was perceptive, unrelenting, and encouraging at the same time. Reg Whitaker's insightful comments led to serious improvements in the final version, as did the editorial suggestions of the board of *SPE*. While the article had benefited substantially from the efforts of these people, all errors are my responsibility alone.

1. A good example of this approach can be found in M.B. Katz and P.H. Mattingly, eds., *Education and Social Change: Themes from Ontario's Past*, New York, 1975.
2. The concept of "reproduction theory" comes from Paul Willis's address to the American Sociological Association in Toronto in August 1981. I have in mind here especially, S. Bowles and H. Gintis, *Schooling in Capitalist America*, New York, 1976, although other works could be mentioned.
3. This critique is extended in my Ph.D. dissertation. See Curtis, "The Political Economy of Elementary Educational Development: Comparative Perspectives on State Schooling in Upper Canada," University of Toronto, Department of Sociology, 1980, chap. 1.
4. M.B. Katz, *The Irony of Early School Reform*, Boston, 1968, esp. 22n.
5. Curtis, "Political Economy," 15-25. (See n.3 above.)
6. Alison Prentice, *The School Promoters: Education and Social Class in Mid-Nineteenth Century Upper Canada*, Toronto, 1977, 22. To foreshadow briefly, Ryerson's *Report on a System of Public Instruction for Upper Canada*, Montreal, 1847, a crucial source for a work like Prentice's which bases itself on an exegesis of the discourse of reform, devotes a few lines to this question of poverty and unemployment. For Ryerson this was an almost obligatory genuflexion towards what had become an official idol in the discourse of reform. But Ryerson's actual concerns were much different. It was to religion and morality that Ryerson's *Report* attended closely.
7. See Egerton Ryerson, "The Importance of Education to an Agricultural People," 1847, in J.G. Hodgins ed., *The Documentary History of Education in Upper Canada...*, Toronto, 1894-1910, vol. 7, 141ff.
8. See the Report of the Chief Superintendent of Education for 1847, reprinted in Hodgins, *Documentary History*, vol. 7, 104ff. (See n.7 above.)
9. Prentice, *School Promoters*, 182-3. Prentice denies here that the discourse of the school promoters comprised a monolithic universe with a definite and unchanging objective. However, her avowed and actual method of investigation is to seek the logic of reform in the statements of reformers. If she took literally her own conclusions in this study, she would begin, not as she does, by trying to make the logic of school reform emerge out of the statements of reformers, but by making the logic of these statements emerge out of the conditions of their utterance.
10. *Schooling*, chap. 6 (See n.2 above.) See also Curtis, "Political Economy," chap. 1.
11. Curtis, "Political Economy," 27-35.
12. Stephen Schecter, "Capitalism, Class and Educational Reform in Canada," in Leo Panitch, ed., *The Canadian State: Political Economy and Political Power*, Toronto, 1977, 373-416, esp. 379. Schecter is at his strongest in his elucidation of the internal connections among the parts of the Upper Canadian reforms. With respect to the question of uneven development see also Curtis and Edginton, "Uneven Institutional Development and the 'Staple' Approach: A Problem of Method," *Canadian Journal of Sociology*, 4:3, 1979, 257-73; and Curtis, "Political Economy."
13. Schecter, "Capitalism," 378. (See n.12 above.)
14. Ibid, 378.
15. Ibid, 379.
16. See Curtis, "Political Economy," chap. 2.
17. For the famine and its impact on Canada: Kenneth Duncan, "Irish Famine Immigration and the Social Structure of Canada West," in Horn and Sabourin, eds., *Studies in Canadian Social History*, Toronto, 1974, 140-63. Of course the debates and struggles over educational organization had been going on long before even an

imaginative researcher could find a "nascent working class." The logic of educational reform in Upper Canada is not an economistic logic.

18. See note 8 above.

19. Curtis, "Political Economy," chap. 4.

20. "Mr. Sullivan's Report on the State of the Province 1838," in *The Arthur Papers....* ed. C.R. Sanderson, Toronto, 1943, pt. 1, 134.

21. Ibid, 134.

22. Ibid, 151

23. Arthur to the Bishop of Montreal, 18 December 1838, in Sanderson, *The Arthur Papers*, pt. 1, p. 465. (See n. 20 above.)

24. Curtis, "Political Economy," chap. 4.

25. For the text of the Act of 1843, see Hodgins, *Documentary History*, vol. 4, 251ff.

26. See Hincks' after-dinner speech in Toronto in 1843, quoted in Sir Francis Hincks, *Reminiscences of his Public Life*, Montreal, 1884, 177.

27. The Midland District Council, for instance, raised over two thousand pounds by a rate on property. See Hodgins, *Documentary History*, vol. 5, p. 127. For school attendance: *Documentary History*, vol. 5, 267-8.

28. As Dent points out in *The Last Forty Years: Canada Since the Union of 1841*, Toronto, 1881, vol.1, 372, the instability of the Canadian administration and the public furor over responsible government also had their echoes in the imperial parliament.

29. There is an enormous literature on the question of Egerton Ryerson's influence in the elections of 1844. In fact, we have no real means of measuring exactly how influential he was. Those who try to claim he had little influence contradict themselves. For example, C.B. Sissons, "Ryerson and the Elections of 1844," *Canadian Historical Review*, 23, 2, June, 1942, 157-76, argues that Ryerson's admittedly substantial public influence temporarily declined before these elections. It is likely, but by no means certain, that his influence was large. In any case, his influence was large enough in the eyes of the administration for it to appoint him Assistant Superintendent of Common Schools. For other contributions to the debate see J.M.S. Careless, *The Union of the Canadas*, Toronto, 1967, 86-8; P.G. Cornell, *The Alignment of Political Groups in Canada, 1841-1867*, Toronto, 1962, 14-5; Dent, *Last Forty Years*, vol. 1, 362, (See n.28 above); R.D. Gidney, "The Rev. Robert Murray: Ontario's First Superintendent of Schools," *Ontario History*, 63, 202-3.

30. Egerton Ryerson, *The Story of My Life*, ed. J.G Hodgins, Toronto, 1883, 284. See here the text of Ryerson's letter to Sydenham urging the publication of a monthly periodical "in order to mould the thinking of public men and the views of the country in harmony with the principles of the new Constitution and the policy of Your Excellency's administration." Ryerson claimed after Sydenham's death that Sydenham had been about to appoint him to the office of Assistant Superintendent. Ryerson was convinced that the office could be used to produce peace and loyalty to existing institutions "upon high moral principles." See Ryerson to Secretary Murdoch, 14 January 1842, *Public Archives of Ontario (PAO)*, RG2, C-6-C.

31. And Lord Stanley had already written to Bagot in his special instructions of October 1841: "You will give every encouragement in your power to the extension, within the Province of Religious Education, and of Secular Instruction, and you will not fail to bear in mind, that the habits and opinions of the People of Canada are, in the main, averse from the absolute predominance of any single Church." G.P. de T. Glazebrook, *Sir Charles Bagot in Canada: A Study in British Colonial Government*, Toronto, 1929, 126. The connection between protestantism and the processes of the

political transformation from loyalty to the state church to citizenship in the national state is little explored, relatively, and demands more attention. A useful introductory work is E.R. Norman, *The Conscience of the State in North America*, Cambridge, 1968.

32. Ryerson, *Story of My Life*, 321. (See n.30 above.)

33. Hodgins, *Documentary History*, vol. 5, 240.

34. I am indebted to Michel Foucault's *Discipline and Punish: The Birth of the Prison*, New York, 1979. This is a reformation of the Marxist conception of abstract labour, or at least in my opinion Foucault must be read with the theory of abstract labour firmly in view. Perhaps nowhere is the historically specific character of Ryerson's educational reform more evident than in this conception of individuals as fundamentally undifferentiated bundles of human energy — the educational form of the reality of labour power as a commodity.

35. Ryerson, *Report*, 20. (See n.6 above.)

36. Ibid, 22.

37. See J.M. Goldstrom, "The content of education and the socialization of the working-class child, 1830-1860," in *Popular Education and Socialization in the Nineteenth Century*, ed. Phillip McCann, London, 1977, 93-109; Brian Simon, *The Two Nations and the Educational Structure*, 1780-1870, London, 1974, 148-9. For the general question of literacy and politics, in addition to Simon, see R. Altick, *The English Common Reader*, Chicago, 1963.

38. For details of the attempt, see Curtis, "Political Economy," chap. 4. The first General Board of Education subsidized the printing, by James McFarlane of Kingston, of 2000 (or more) copies of Mavor's *Spelling Book* on large paste board cards and distributed these to the district boards of education in 1828 and 1829. See *Minutes of the General Board of Education*, 6 May 1828; the annual report for 1829; and 13 May 1829 in *PAO*, RG 2, A.(See n.30 above.)

39. Brian Simon, *The Radical Tradition in Education in Britain*, London, 1972, 11.

40. See Phillip McCann, "Popular education, socialization and social control: Spitalfields, 1812-1824," in McCann, *Popular education*, 29. (See n.37 above.)

41. Ryerson, *Report*, 57.

42. Ibid, 75.

43. See Ibid, 131. To date I have been unable to find a systematic exposition of the source of this conception. The documents of Upper Canadian education make very occasional mention of a pedagogy called "inductive" or "induction." It appears in Dr. Duncombe's *Report on Education of 1836*, Hodgins, *Documentary History*, vol.2, p.308, but in a different sense than that used by Ryerson, a sense much closer to the classic theory of associationism. In the school reports for 1842, pedagogies were described variously as "Lancastrian," "Monitorial," "Intellectual" and "Analytic." Parents and school trustees and commissioners were clearly concerned and acting before Ryerson to regulate the education of their children in such a way as to make it gentle and also interesting. There was certainly no "rote" learning of the sort Ryerson was criticizing in general use in Canada. See "Miscellaneous School Reports," *PAO*, RG 2, F2, especially George Elmslie, Bon Accord, Nichol Twp., 10 November 1842; Isaac Denike, No. 3 Huntingdon Twp., 12 October 1842; School Commissioners, Pakenham to Mr. And Dickson no.4, 7 June 1842.

44. Ryerson, *Report*, 120.

45. Ibid, 168-9.

46. For instance, the general transition from the maintenance of order in the school by means, ultimately, of the physical force of the teacher to the maintenance of order backed ultimately by the administrative power of the state was one of the

crucial preconditions for the successful feminization of the teaching labour force which went forward rapidly between 1850 and 1900.

47. See the interesting exchange in Ryerson to Thomas Donnelly, Bloomfield, 21 December 1846, in Hodgins, *Documentary History*, vol. 6, 285.

48. Ryerson, *Report*, 129.

49. Ibid, 126.

50. Ibid, 131.

51. Ibid, 10.

52. Ibid, 11-4.

53. Ibid, 32. (Ryerson's emphasis.)

54. Ibid, 50-1.

55. See Gidney, "Rev. Robert Murray." (See n.29 above.)

56. Sanderson, *The Arthur Papers*, pt. 3, pp. 1-2. Arthur to the Archbishop of Canterbury, January 1, 1839: "Instruction after incursion has been made by a lawless gang of Ruffians from the American States....On being questioned by the Court what was the Religion they professed will your Lordship believe it the Answer *generally* has been 'None'!"

57. Robert Gidney was kind enough to point out to me that this was a matter upon which Ryerson had elsewhere written and published a significant number of pieces.

58. See for example Ryerson, *Report*. pp. 44-5n.

59. Quoted in H.S. Commager, ed., *The Era of Reform, 1830-1860*, Toronto, 1960, 134.

60. Hodgins, *Documentary History*, vol. 7, p.192.

61. Again, the role of protestant religion as a bridge leading to this conception of civil universality is crucial.

62. See the four articles by R.D. Gidney and D.A. Lawr which deal with the development of educational administration. The best is perhaps "Bureaucracy vs. Community? The Origins of Bureaucratic Procedure in the Upper Canadian School System," *Journal of Social History* 13:3, 1981, 438-57. See also: "Egerton Ryerson and the Origins of the Ontario Secondary School," *Canadian Historical Review* 60:4, 1979, 442-65; "Who Ran the Schools? Local Influence on Educational Policy in Nineteenth Century Ontario," *Ontario History* 72:3, 1980, 131-43; and "The Development of an Administrative System for the Public Schools: The First Stage, 1841-50," in N. McDonald and A. Chaiton, eds., *Egerton Ryerson and His Times*, Toronto, 1978, 160-84. It is significant commentary on contemporary Marxist scholarship in Canada that much of the debate over the development of the state goes forward in isolation from the actual investigation of the development of the state. It is left to social historians to do the necessary research to inform the debate.

63. The state also grew through the physical reconstruction of the school, through the transformation of the relation of pedagogical space to the community, and inside the schools, through the transformation of the relations of teachers and students in pedagogical space.

64. See Viola E. Parvin, *Authorization of Textbooks for Schools of Ontario, 1846-1950*, Toronto, 1965. There is quite a deliberate and demonstrable campaign to transform the curriculum from a community property into a state property, a campaign that transforms both form and content of the schoolbook. A detailed investigation by me of this process is forthcoming.

65. *Discipline and Punish*, 194. (See n.34 above.) Foucault argues that this is always

the case. Such a position underestimates the effectiveness of naked brutality under certain circumstances.

66. Ryerson's vision was one of social harmony, a sphere of universality safe from social conflict. The teachers generally wanted reliable pay, a clear set of rules for the schools, enough schoolbooks of the same sort to go around, protection from local officials and generally, those things which would relieve the "drudges in the Republic of letters usually called Teachers of Common Schools." James Finn, London District to Murray, 29 May 1843, *PAO*, RG2, C-6-C.

J.J. Kelso and The Development of Child Welfare

Leonard Rutman

This paper presents the developments in child welfare practice in Ontario during the late nineteenth century by focussing on the career of J.J. Kelso. Kelso is one of Canada's most widely recognized social reformers, having been involved in the formation of the Toronto Humane Society, the Children's Fresh Air Fund, the Santa Claus Fund, and the Toronto Children's Aid Society. Between 1893 and 1934 he served as Superintendent of Neglected Children. In this capacity, he guided the development of Children's Aid Societies across Ontario and played an important role in their spread throughout other English Canadian provinces. Within this context of services to children, developments in social work practice will be discussed.[1]

This paper will describe briefly the social conditions in Toronto when Kelso became involved in social welfare reform. There will also be some discussion of the types of services for children in this period.

The main focus is on the specific movements with which Kelso became involved: the development of the Toronto Children's Aid Society; the implementation of the 1893 Act designed to protect neglected children; the lobbying for separate trials for juveniles; the closing of institutions for juvenile delinquents; and the emigration of British waifs to Canada.

Background

Industrial development in Toronto accelerated during the 1870s and 1880s with the population almost doubling in the decade between 1880 and 1890. Despite increased employment opportunities through the opening of new factories, unemployment and poverty were still widespread while housing conditions deteriorated. The response to these conditions was from private and voluntary organizations. Goldwin Smith estimated that 5 percent of the city's population relied on charity in 1890.[2]

The British poor laws at least recognized the existence of poverty as they reflected public responsibility for the poor. In most of Canada there was no corresponding public acceptance. Instead, the prevailing attitude was that the poor should fend for themselves and the idea of providing relief received little support. This viewpoint is reflected in this extract from The Globe which warned in 1874 that:

> Promiscuous alms giving is fatal....it is the patent process for the manufacture of paupers out of the worthless and improvident. A poor law is a legislative machine for the manufacture of pauperism. It

is true mercy to say that it would be better that a few individuals should die of starvation than a pauper class should be raised up.[3]

During the twenty years after Confederation, the Ontario government became more active in providing social services because the municipalities, who supposedly had this responsibility, were unwilling or unable to do so. Provincial mental hospitals were expanded, institutions for the mentally retarded were established, and there was the development of schools for the deaf and blind, homes for the aged, and a refuge for girls. The Factories Act passed in 1884, outlining standards for manufacturers regarding safety and child labour, and in 1887, the Workmen's Compensation for Injuries Act was passed, providing for the possibility of compensation to victims of industrial accidents through the courts.

Private charity developed alongside government programs. Starting in the mid-eighteenth century, charities and other non-governmental bodies established a wide range of welfare services: hospitals, orphanages, asylums, houses of industry, refuges, reformatories and hostels. The passage of the Charity Aid Act of 1874 spurred the growth of private institutions since the Province of Ontario was then able to financially support privately operated institutions.

There were four major types of services for children during this period: apprenticeship, special institutions, adoption, and industrial schools. From the early nineteenth Century, the apprenticeship system was the primary means of dealing with orphans and abandoned children. Children were placed mainly with farmers and were expected to work on the farm. Supplying families who could benefit from such placements seemed to be the major purpose of the program and the child's welfare in these placements was of secondary importance.

In the mid-1850s, special institutions for dependent children developed. Young or handicapped children who could not easily be placed in homes could be sent to these special institutions, which were a back-up for the apprenticeship system. Adoptions took place, although there was no legal status for such arrangements. The adopted child was without special rights or protection.

The final arrangement, the establishment of industrial schools, was based upon the Industrial Schools Act of 1874, the first legislation directly concerned with neglected children. This Act gave public schools the right to establish residential, custodial and educational institutions for certain categories of problem children:
1) children under 14 convicted by magistrates because they were found begging, homeless or destitute
2) children considered in the category of "unable to control," committed by their parents or guardians and children believed to be growing up without parental control.

J.J. Kelso and Early Reforms
J.J. Kelso's family immigrated to Canada from Ireland in 1874. From the age of ten he worked at various day jobs and studied at night. He joined a

newspaper as a typesetter, later became a proofreader, and at the age of twenty-one, he began his career as a journalist with the *World*. He later moved to the *Globe* where he became a police reporter.

Kelso regularly covered the meetings of the Canadian Institute. At one meeting, he was asked to make a presentation and used this opportunity to speak about the need for preventing cruelty to animals, a need identified by a reader in a letter sent to him. The meeting of the Canadian Institute gave him the forum for proposing the establishment of an organization which would have among its objectives the prevention of cruelty to animals as well as "rescuing children from vicious circumstances." Kelso pursued the idea by calling a public meeting. Prominent Torontonians were invited and from this group of influential people a committee was established to spearhead the formation of a Toronto Humane Society. Mechanisms were established for fundraising and organizational responsibilities were assigned. Kelso used the Humane Society as a vehicle for carrying out other reform activities. He and Beverly Jones drafted a Children's Protection Act which the government of Ontario passed in 1888. There were two major points related to this Act: 1) the establishment of public responsibility for the maintenance of neglected children by giving courts the authority to commit children to recognized institutions; and 2) allowing the Lieutenant Governor at the request of any municipal council to appoint a commissioner to deal with juvenile offenders.

Kelso became involved in other reforms which had children as their focus. He helped organize the Children's Fresh Air Fund in 1888, which involved the business community in making donations so that children from poor families could take outings. Later that year, he helped organize a Santa Claus Fund to provide a Christmas party for children from families living in poverty.

Kelso's involvement in these reforms reflected his essential concern with the well-being of children from families living in poverty. Moreover, these reforms reveal Kelso's preference for involving wealthy and middle-class Torontonians — those relatively well off were asked to be more charitable to the poor. The attack was not against the roots of poverty; rather, the reforms aimed at providing some amenities to children from poverty-ridden backgrounds.

Neglected Children

The need for a Children's Aid Society emerged from the experiences of the Toronto Humane Society. It became evident through the work of the Humane Society that there was a lack of authority to protect children in situations where action was resisted by parents. Kelso became convinced that an organization with greater powers was needed to protect children from neglectful and cruel parents, and believed that this power should be granted to responsible members of the community. He expressed these concerns in testimony before the Ontario Prison Reform Commission whose final report in 1891 supported Kelso's views. With support from this important Commission, Kelso began to organize a Children's Aid Society.

Repeating his earlier approach, he invited two hundred prominent people to a public meeting which focussed on the theme that child neglect was related to crime. All of the speakers emphasized this particular concern in supporting the development of a Children's Aid Society. The need for such a society was unanimously accepted and a motion was passed to form one with Kelso serving as President. The theme emphasized to initiate the society was repeated in the appeal for funds, including the motto: "it is wiser and less expensive to save children than to punish criminals."

The main effort of the Children's Aid Society was toward the establishment and operation of a Children's Shelter. In addition, the provincial government was pressed for improved legislation to deal with the problem of child neglect. Rev. Starr, who was to be the first Executive Director of the Toronto Children's Aid Society, headed the committee concerned with this legislation. The Children's Protection Act passed in 1893 and Kelso was appointed by the Ontario Government as Superintendent with responsibility for administering the new act.

The provisions of the Children's Protection Act reflected Kelso's views about child neglect and how social services should be organized to address this problem. The Act provided for punishment of persons found guilty of neglecting or exploiting children, with fines of up to $100 and imprisonment for up to three months. Children found to be neglected could be placed under the charge of any duly authorized Children's Aid Society. These agencies had authority to apprehend children, supervise them in the children's shelter, and carry the prerogatives of legal guardians for the children committed to their care by the court. There were provisions for Children's Visiting Committees to select foster homes, visit children in the foster home placements, remove children from one home and place them in another if it was found necessary. The muncipalities were held liable for the foster home costs ($1.00 per week) and for maintaining children's shelters.

The major accomplishment following the passage of the Act was the growth of Children's Aid Societies, twenty-nine societies being established by 1895. This involved organizing people in the various communities to participate on a voluntary basis with an agency dedicated to the protection of children.

Several issues arose in implementing the Children's Protection Act. Municipalities were not making payments for the care of children, which reflected an unwillingness on their part to assume responsibility for neglected children. The thrust toward the use of foster homes created conflict with existing institutions because of the threat which foster homes posed to the survival of the institutions. Therefore, the extent of reliance on institutional care continued to be a contentious issue during the early development of child welfare services. The arrangement of having visiting committees did not prove successful either. The role of the visiting committees overlapped with the Children's Aid Societies and this caused some confusion and animosity within the societies. Another criticism of these committees was that they lacked the professionalism considered important in dealing with situations of child neglect. The dilemma the visiting committees found themselves in is reflected in comments Kelso made several years later:

> . . . those societies that have tried visiting committees find that the volunteer is not experienced or tactful enough, is spasmodic in services, and is liable to do as much harm as good. They do not, as a rule, study the work sufficiently to be experts, nor do they know the homes where great care has to be exercised to avoid giving offence. Foster parents object to a local visitor, perhaps a neighbour, calling to see the child as an inspector, whereas someone coming from a distance and knowing all about the work is received on an entirely different basis.[4]

Clearly the thrust of the Children's Protection Act was to rely upon voluntary effort in dealing with the problem of child neglect. The Children's Aid Societies were essentially run by volunteers and the day-to-day practice was carried out by volunteers as well. Voluntary effort continued to be a preference of Kelso's even though he reluctantly hired salaried people to assist in the work. In 1896, Kelso appointed an assistant to visit children in foster homes and other salaried people were subsequently appointed.

There are several important philosophical underpinnings in relation to the early development of child welfare services. The preference was for foster care over institutions, reflecting the viewpoint that a loving, Christian family environment was important for dealing with neglected children. Preferring to use volunteers over paid officials, assistants were hired only in those situations where voluntary efforts were not sufficient. There was also general support for keeping children in natural homes. However, if separation was needed, it was absolute. There was little effort devoted to maintaining contact between the child and the natural family and little attempt at working towards the return of the child to the natural parents.

Juvenile Delinquents
The Act of 1888 referred to above permitted the appointment of a magistrate to hear charges against juveniles. This was the first formal recognition of the need to deal with juveniles in the criminal justice system quite separately from adults. However, it was only in Toronto, in 1890, that a commissioner was finally appointed to do so. However, since the most common charge, larceny, was under the Criminal Code, the commission concluded that a municipal magistrate had no jurisdiction over Dominion Law, and only a minority of juvenile offenders could be dealt with in a separate manner.[5]

Kelso advocated the separate trial of juveniles even while he was with the Toronto Children's Aid Society in 1892. He submitted a brief to the Federal Minister of Justice, proposing such an arrangement. The Dominion Minister, Sir John Thompson, expressed support and inserted the following clause in the Criminal Code: "the trials of all persons apparently under the age of 16 years shall, so far as it is expedient and practicable, take place without publicity, and separately and apart from that of other accused persons, and at suitable times to be designated and appointed for that purpose."

This clause inserted in the criminal code appeared to overcome the constitutional impediment in regard to the separate trial of juveniles. The problem was that magistrates decided whether or not it was expedient and practicable to hear the cases of juveniles separately and therefore the intent of the clause was not realized. Kelso's main concern was for the best interest of the child to be adequately represented in court. He felt that this could not occur in the regular adult court, and in his position as Superintendent, led the campaign for separate trials for juveniles in many ways. He wrote articles for newspapers, advocating the separate trial of juveniles, and he personally intervened during the trial of two girls, arguing that it was improper and detrimental to their well-being to be tried in adult court. This received extensive publicity. He also prepared a petition which was circulated and received one thousand signatures in support of separate trials.

In 1894 a Dominion Youthful Offenders Act was passed providing for the separate trial of juveniles. However, it was ignored by magistrates and judges in Ontario for over a decade. Kelso continued to agitate for the separate trial of juveniles and for a probation system which would supervise them in the community as opposed to dealing with them through institutions. Kelso's viewpoints were incorporated in the Juvenile Delinquent's Act of 1908. Its philosophy stated: "each child was to be treated not as a criminal, but as a misdirected and misguided child, and one needing aid, encouragement, help and assistance". It was not until 1911 that a commissioner was appointed in Toronto, the Reverend Starr, formerly the Director of the Children's Aid Society in Toronto. It would be an exaggeration of Kelso's influence to suggest that he was responsible for the passage of the various pieces of legislation, including the Juvenile Delinquent's Act, which led to the separate trial of juveniles. Kelso was however, a prominent individual who, among others, pressed for such changes.

Reformatories
The Province assumed responsibility for boys under thirteen who were sent to a reformatory for supervision and upkeep. Kelso had a negative view of such institutions, preferring the general use of foster homes, and he undertook action which resulted in the ultimate closure of the reformatory for boys.[6] Kelso, and the Warden of Central Prison, where juveniles spend

some time before going to the reformatory, came to an agreement whereby the boys would be placed in homes supervised by the Children's Aid Society. These boys did not get transferred to the reformatory and nobody appeared to show interest in them or enquired about their whereabouts. Over a four-year period there were about forty children who were intercepted in this manner. When it came to the attention of the Attorney General, he agreed to shut his eyes. The impact of this action resulted in a declining number of boys in the Penetanguishene Reformatory, and this, combined with the growing cost, resulted in the decision to close it. Several years later there was a similar closure of the Mercer Refuge for Girls.

The closure of these reformatories put greater reliance on the use of Industrial Schools. This created problems as children considered to be quite serious offenders were placed within the more open setting of Industrial Schools. Kelso and others changed their position on the use of reformatories and, later, such facilities were used again.

Child Immigration

Beginning in 1869, British children were brought from the work houses in England to Canada. Numerous agencies emerged to carry out this work and by 1892, there were 28,935 children brought to Ontario this way. About 75 percent of the children came from private or church orphanages and rescue homes, the remainder were wards of the Poor Law workhouse.[7]

The agencies involved in this work viewed it as an effective means of rescuing dependent children from their deprived surroundings in the British industrial cities. Canadian farmers tended to see these children as a source of labour. Between 1870 and the turn of the century, the demand for child workers outstripped the supply.

The agencies took responsibility for receiving the children, making placements and ensuring that they were properly treated. However, there was continual public concern about the treatment and overworking of the children placed with the farmers. The public began to show concern about the expense these children created for Canada because it was felt that many of them would become part of the criminal class. There was little evidence to show that these children were in fact swelling the ranks of criminals but this nevertheless continued to be a major public concern. Another issue was whether these children were detrimental to the employment of Canadian workers. The Toronto Trades and Labour Congress felt that juvenile immigrants would flood the Canadian Labour market and thereby drive down wages.

Some supported the child immigration movement as a humanitarian effort while others viewed it as a means of satisfying the demand for labour, which existed because of the urbanization taking place at this time. The great public concern about this movement led to an investigation and resulting legislation entitled an Act to Regulate Juvenile Immigration. The provisions of the Act were expected to protect the children who were being imported and placed with farmers. Kelso, as Superintendent of Neglected

Children, was given responsibility for this movement. The provisions of the Act included a requirement for agencies to be licensed and inspected four times a year. These agencies were expected to supervise juveniles until they reached the age of eighteen. It was an offence for an agency to bring "any child who, from defective intellect or physical infirmity, is unable to follow any trade or calling or any child of known vicious tendencies or who has been convicted of a crime." If a child became dependent on the municipality or province within the first three years in Canada, the agency could be required to pay the cost of maintenance. The right of these children to attend the province's public schools was affirmed, and a post of overseas examiner was created to examine children in England before they left.

In 1900, the Federal Government assumed the responsibility for the importation of British waifs. This ended Kelso's responsibility for supervising the movement. The numerous issues discussed above continued to surface during the remainder of the movement, which ended around the first world war.

Reform Tactics

Kelso's involvement in the various movements reflects a particular approach to reform. He dealt with civic leaders and wealthy individuals who could lend support to and financial backing for the organizations he established. Having received some commitment from influential Torontonians, he invited them to a public meeting where they could speak in favour of the particular cause. The climax of the meeting was a motion by one of the prominent members to take action by establishing an organization. Kelso would then be appointed to a senior position within the organization and his activities would be carried out in the name of the particular organization. In this way, he led deputations, organized conferences, wrote submissions, addressed meetings, raised funds, and wrote letters and articles to the newspapers.

Underlying the reforms which Kelso initiated was the belief that societal improvements could be produced through concerted action by committed private individuals motivated by concern for public welfare. According to Kelso, reform required politicians, officials, employers, parents and the general public to act in a more humane and moral manner. He did not relate to the structural divisions within society and the institutional inequality. Rather, he felt that those who are in an advantaged position could be convinced to help those less fortunate. This viewpoint reflected the manner in which social problems were analyzed and the types of approaches implemented to address those problems.

There were four sectors of society which had a role to play in reform. First was the social and economic elite, who provided public support for the cause and contributed funds to the organizations; this group gave legitimacy to the many reforms which Kelso implemented. A second group comprised the middle-class participants who provided the human resources for the Children's Aid Society, the visiting committees, and other efforts directed toward poor and neglected children. The middle-class also served as the role model which parents from the poorer classes were expected to emulate. Their morals, standards of behaviour, and religious involvement were held out to the poor to follow. Thirdly, the professionals; who were viewed as carrying out relatively minor roles in the provision of social services. By the turn of the century, there was a growing recognition of the need for professionals. However, Kelso did not favour the substitution of skills and techniques for benevolence and compassion. Fourth, the government; expected to provide voluntary agencies with statutory authority, funds, and regulations for supervision of voluntary agencies. There was clearly a preference for using voluntary organizations to carry out the work and government was expected to facilitate these voluntary initiatives, not to supplant them.

Conclusion

Social reforms in which Kelso became involved after the turn of the century included: support for Mother's Allowance, development of playgrounds for children, improvement of housing conditions, and the settlement house movement. It was during this period that more attention was paid to the social and economic conditions of the poor rather than simply providing some amenities for them. Also during this period, social work practice was becoming increasingly professional. Kelso contributed toward this development by advocating the need for university courses in the field of social services. In 1914, such a programme was established at the University of Toronto. Despite his longstanding support of both the scientific study of social conditions and a professional approach to practice, the professionalism of social work returned to haunt Kelso when, toward the end of his career, there was criticism of his role as Superintendent on the grounds that he had not kept pace with current social work practice.

NOTES

1. For a more complete and detailed discussion, see Andrew Jones and Leonard Rutman, *In the Children's Aid: J.J. Kelso and Child Welfare in Ontario*, Toronto, 1981.
2. Elizabeth Wallace, *Goldwin Smith: Victorian Liberal*, Toronto, 1957, 104-7.
3. Richard B. Splane, *Social Welfare in Ontario, 1791-1873: A Study of Public Welfare Administration*, Toronto, 1965, 16.
4. Jones and Rutman, *Children's Aid*, 79.
5. Secondary sources dealing with the background to the Juvenile Delinquents' Act are found in Ian Bain, "The Role of J.J. Kelso in the launching of the Child Welfare Movement in Ontario," M.S.W. Thesis, University of Toronto, 1955; Neil Sutherland, *Children in English-Canadian Society: Framing the Twentieth Century Consensus*, Toronto, 1976; and Phyllis Harrison, *The Home Children*, Winnipeg, 1979.
6. Kelso's involvement in the closure of the reformatories is covered in Splane, *Social Welfare*, and Sutherland, *Children*.
7. For an overview of the movement, see Leonard Rutman, "Importation of British Waifs Into Canada: 1868 to 1916", *Child Welfare*, 1973, 159-166; Kenneth Bagnell, *The Little Immigrants*, Toronto, 1980; Joy Parr, *Labouring Children*, Montreal, 1980.

Early Women's Organizations and Social Reform:
Prelude to the Welfare State

Wendy Mitchinson

The history of social welfare in Canada has concentrated its attention on the twentieth century. We do know, however, that the groundwork for state intervention was being laid in the closing decades of the nineteenth century. Governments were slowly beginning to link their subsidies to orphanages, refuge homes, and hospitals to the standard of care being provided by them. The state was also intervening in areas of life which, earlier in the century, Canadians had considered inviolable. The most obvious example was in the power of Children's Aid Societies to assume guardianship of children over that of the natural parents. But why were Canadians willing to accept this new turn of events? This paper examines one group of citizens who helped prepare the way for state involvement in the social welfare area. They are the middle class women who belonged to the myriad of women's reform organizations which emerged in the last three decades of the nineteenth century. Through their participation in these organizations, tens of thousands of Canadian women and their families were exposed to the problems of Canadian society and the difficulty of coping with those problems.

Canadian women's involvement in reform really began with charitable endeavours in the early part of the nineteenth century.[1] At first these usually took the form of voluntary contributions on a personal level or through the church. When women attempted to form more structured and permanent societies which would do more than momentarily alleviate a problem, they focused specifically on the needs of women and children which the governments at that time seemed unwilling to meet. In one form or another, they helped to found or administer orphanages, asylums, and refuge homes for destitute infants, children, and women.[2] In some, women had complete control, as in the Protestant Orphan Asylum in Montreal. In others, although women essentially ran the particular institution and did the necessary work, an advisory board composed entirely of men oversaw their activities.[3] In still others, control rested primarily in a committee composed of both men and women.[4] But whatever the pattern, the women involved were not figureheads. they ran the homes, raised the necessary funds for the day to day operations, and hired the personnel necessary to help run them.

By the end of the century, women's organizational activity had increased tremendously. It no longer was restricted to local community activity but was national in scope. It was no longer dominated by the social elite but attracted a wide spectrum of middle-class women. And no longer were the interests charitable in nature but rather reformist in orientation.

Four organizations typify this new direction — the missionary societies of the Protestant churches, the Young Women's Christian Association (YWCA), the Woman's Christian Temperance Union (WCTU), and the National Council of Women (NCW). Of the four, the first two were closest to the traditional involvement of women in society. Women had always belonged to the church and were encouraged to participate in it. Mission work was simply a natural extension of that. The YWCA continued women's participation in charitable activities by trying to help working women, although striving to eliminate the charitable overtones of its approach. The WCTU and the NCW, on the other hand, represented more significant departures from earlier activity, for both were very public in their work and in their demand for government assistance.

In some respects, these organizations and their members were the precursors of the social welfare mentality. Both the social welfare state and the reform-minded women based their activities on the perception of the needs of citizens in society, needs which were a result of problems not always of a person's own making. The women were largely motivated by a sense of Christian concern which, in the state, became a secular sense of responsibility.[5] They expressed that concern through intermediaries, just as the state in its developing bureaucracy looked to the expert or the professional as the means of fulfilling its responsibility. Service was a major part of the commitment, although its aim was not the personal gratification of those being helped. The goal for both reformers and the state was and still is objective; that is, the creation of a stable, ordered, and peaceful society — a society where the needs of those being served were and are secondary to those of the society as a collective entity.

The Religious Influence on Reform
The women who joined the missionary societies, the YWCA, the WCTU and even the nominally non-sectarian NCW were strengthened and encouraged in what they did by a quiet confidence that what they were doing was right — not simply socially right but morally right. Their work was God's work. Of course, other factors were significant: the rise of urban centres, the obvious need for reform which accompanied them, and the desire to protect the family from many urban problems. However, without the security provided by the belief in a caring God, without a sincere commitment to the Christian ideal of the 'Good Samaritan', it is unlikely that women's reform organizations would have attracted the number of women they did. After all, women had long been involved in charity, but reform was a much more public enterprise and could lead to confrontation with those interests opposing their specific reforms. When coupled with

the fact that the dominant ideology of the day insisted that a woman's place was in the home, it becomes evident the members of these organizations needed all the support they could get just to form such women's groups. Their religious beliefs provided that support.

Church Missionary Societies
In the case of the church missionary societies, it was the only justification needed for their work. Church societies concentrated their efforts on the conversion of heathen women to Christianity as part of their own responsibility to Christ. The focus of all the groups, whether Anglican, Presbyterian, Baptist, or Methodist was on foreign mission work. Believing that Christianity recognized women as equal to men, heathen women would be uplifted spiritually but also temporally through the efforts of the women missionaries these societies were supporting.[6] To them, Christianity and civilization went hand in hand. The Woman's Foreign Missionary Society of the Presbyterian Church in Canada (Western Division) believed its purpose was "through the education and conversion of heathen women and girls, to assist in opening to civilization, and its handmaid, Christianity, the dark places of the earth."[7] They emphasized temporal change in the lives of the heathen through religious conversion. Their conviction that they were following God's will gave them a security which cannot be overestimated. It justified their involvement and provided them with a feeling of accomplishment. They had stepped out of their world, into one finer.[8] Eventually that commitment led them to look at their own society when they became involved in home mission work.

The Young Women's Christian Association
While the YWCA was not a church organization, the religious influence was still significant. In fact, the evangelical nature of the Y attracted many women to it who otherwise might have shied away from a purely secular endeavour.[9] The Saint John Association insisted when it formed that its members be in good standing with a church, and the Toronto Y, in turn, proposed that ministers' wives be honourary members of the Board.[10] This connection made the secular work of the YWCA respectable as well as possible. For example, the Toronto Y received most of its revenue from the thirty-seven churches endorsing it.[11] In return, the word Christian in the Young Women's Christian Association was more than a gesture, rather a commitment to Christian work within a specific Protestant evangelical framework.

The Toronto Y made this very clear. Although interested in helping provide cheap and respectable accommodation for young women in the city, it was equally interested in "securing their attendance at some place of Worship and ... surrounding them with Christian associates."[12] It was felt that young working women would benefit from being surrounded by Christian souls, ensuring they were made spiritually strong and hence morally strong.

The importance of this religious aspect was revealed in the YWCA's refusal to join the National Council of Women. The Association was not hostile to the work of the Council or its president, Lady Aberdeen. In fact, it had asked her to become patroness and honourary president of the Association to which she had consented.[13] Nevertheless, at the first annual meeting of the YWCA, affiliation with the Council was rejected because of the use of silent prayer by the Council in lieu of audible prayer.[14] The YWCA with its strong evangelical base found this unacceptable.

Woman's Christian Temperance Union

The WCTU as well found the silent prayer unacceptable.[15] Like the YWCA, the WCTU's reform work and religious commitment went hand in hand and it was difficult to separate the two. The WCTU did not insist on church affiliation as a condition of membership, but it would have been awkward for anyone of non-Protestant persuasion to join. The Union patterned itself after the church, opened its meetings with a prayer and a hymn, and ended them with a benediction. During the meeting there was further hymn singing, a collection, and often an address by a minister.[16]

Similar to the Y, the WCTU used religion as part of its reform approach. It believed that drunkards could only be reclaimed through Christ.[17] By attempting such reform, WCTU members were working for Christ.[18] This belief added a moral rightness to their efforts, comforted them, and gave them assurance when faced with opposition.[19]

The commitment of the WCTU was directly linked to religion. The executive of the WCTU by and large represented the more evangelical or active Christian churches. Forty-three percent were Methodist and Methodists had long disapproved of the consumption of alcohol and had been active in their condemnation of its use.[20] The Methodist Church was also the most active of the Protestant denominations in its social involvement and strongest in its encouragement to women to participate in that involvement.[21]

Perhaps for that reason WCTU members felt religion was important to them as women. The church was the one institution that late nineteenth-century society had encouraged women to participate in, even if only in a subordinate role. But the women did not feel subordinate. They believed that Christ's birth had redeemed all women from the curse of Eve. They were convinced that Christianity more than any religion accepted equality between the sexes.[22] By doing so it bound women closely to its side. Consequently, when the Methodist Church encouraged women to become involved in temperance work as part of their religious commitment, it is not suprising that they believed such involvement was a fulfillment of their Christian responsibility and that this would overcome any reluctance they might have about public activity.

The National Council of Women

The NCW, unlike the church missionary societies, the Y, and the WCTU, did not align itself with any specific religious belief. Its president, Lady Aberdeen, hoped by eschewing any denominational affiliation and any overt religious adherence to attract those women's societies which would have been alienated by such an avowal.[23] Its desire to do so was quite unique among women's organizations and to a certain degree it succeeded.[24] At the same time the NCW did not reject the importance of religious belief. If the NCW did not want to publicly associate itself with any denomination or faith it was still the religious ethics of the 'Golden Rule' which dominated it.[25] As well, it did institute silent prayer, not as a denial of the importance of religious belief but as a recognition of it. In this way the NCW hoped all faiths and creeds would feel comfortable within its ranks. But as already noted, this was not enough to gain the immediate support of the YWCA and the WCTU. Audible prayer to these two organizations was a positive commitment to Christianity. Silent prayer was viewed as a negation of this.

Without its acceptance, however, the NCW would have been weakened, especially in the Catholic province of Quebec.[26] In the eyes of Catholic Quebec, audible recitation of the Lord's Prayer would have made the NCW simply another Protestant organization, similar to the Y and the WCTU. With its acceptance, all creeds could now feel welcome within the organization and pray to their God in their own way. The success of the NCW was not in bringing together Protestant women of one church — that had been done by the missionary societies — nor bringing together Protestant women of different denominations —that had already been done by the YWCA and the WCTU. Its success was rather in bringing together Catholic and Protestant. As a result, a common religious faith was not an assumption the NCW could make of its members. It could be a devisive issue rather than a unifying factor as it was with the church societies, the YWCA, and WCTU.

Summary of the Religious Influence
The religious faith of their members was important for all four organizations but in different ways. For the missionary societies, it accounted not only for their motivation but for their very existence. Their activities, helping heathen women whether abroad or at home, were dictated by their belief that Christianity and civilization went hand in hand. The local YWCA's, by aligning themselves directly with evangelical Protestant churches, attracted members and received financial support. As well, religion was an essential part of the Y's effort to help working women. The WCTU also used religious faith as a reform tool in its efforts to reclaim drunkards. Nevertheless, the WCTU did not directly connect itself with any organized church, although it was greatly influenced by the outward form of religion. The NCW went one step further. It neither accepted any ties to organized religion, nor overtly used the trappings of religion in its meetings. Silent prayer was a practical response to the problem of making the NCW acceptable to women of all faiths. That some form of prayer was

deemed necessary suggests the importance religious faith had for these women, although the inability of the NCW to emphasize faith to the extent of the other two secular organizations did eliminate evangelical techniques as a possible reform approach. However, the morality of all these organizations was Christian, and often defined as such; to ignore it is to overlook an important aspect of their reform orientation.

Women's Organizations and Secular Reform

Church Missionary Societies
The church missionary societies attracted many women still unsure of themselves outside the domestic sphere. The church lent respectability to their efforts and shielded them from public scrutiny. Although the societies appear extraordinarily conservative, they were a step forward for many church women who, until the advent of missionary societies, had been limited to local charitable activities and being the homemakers of the church.[27] Missionary societies were fundamentally different. They were national in organization and international in scope. They were great money raisers[28] and they provided that first step necessary to further women's involvement in society.

Their primary focus was the conversion of heathen women overseas, a rather safe endeavour in that it did not challenge the existing value system in Canada since foreign missionary societies concentrated on trying to persuade non-Western nations and peoples to adopt Western religious values. Neither were the problems such attempts entailed faced by the membership of the missionary societies but rather by the missionaries they supported.

Home mission work, however, could pose a challenge. It brought women face to face with problems of Canadian society which persisted despite the acceptance of the religious and cultural values which missionary societies believed would work wonders among heathen people. Solutions to these problems might necessitate reform of accepted values, and consequently, most missionary societies were reluctant to get involved in this issue. The Woman's Foreign Missionary Society of the Presbyterian Church in Canada (Western Division) felt home mission work was a "radical change."[29] The Baptist women, when they became involved in home mission work, did so with Canadians of non-Anglo Saxon heritage — the native peoples and the French. They believed the latter were "willing prisoners to the fascination of a tyrannical fanaticism" and "bound in the chains of Romanism."[30] The Methodists, too, seemed to concentrate on non-Anglo Saxons.[31] However, unlike the rest, the Methodists were willing to support secular reform as a means of bringing about religious conversion. They eschewed alcohol as part of their religious beliefs, and thus were willing to support the WCTU in its endeavours. They also supported the NCW.[33] They were concerned about the treatment of Chinese girls in B.C. and "memorialized the Dominion Government to take such steps as shall prevent the importation into British

Columbia of Chinese women for immoral purposes."[33] They worried about the effects of cigarette smoking, disapproved of the raising of revenue from the liquor and opium trade by the Anglo-Indian government, and in 1896, expressed to the government their horror at the Armenian atrocities.[34]

The Methodists were atypical among the church women in this regard. But what all the groups had in common was the distance they placed between themselves and those they were trying to help; that is, they worked through an intermediary, the missionary, or in the case of the Methodists and their secular work, appealing to the government for action. Unlike the charity societies, they did not make any distinction between the deserving and the undeserving. All souls were in need of and deserving of Christ. They could believe this since they were not dealing, for the most part, with the temporal sphere but with the spiritual, where equality was easier to accept since it did not have to be faced immediately.

The YWCA

The YWCA, unlike the church missionary societies, was founded to respond to a secular need — to help working women by providing them with a cheap and respectable place to live.[35] Various YWCA's also organized classes in nursing, dress making, millinery, domestic science, photography, stenography and typing to help more young women develop skills with which to obtain better employment.[36] YWCA representatives even met in-coming trains so that those working women newly arrived in the city would have a safe place to stay. The Y reflected the changing role of women within Canadian society, that is, their increasing number in paid employment.[37] By helping them, it gave guarded acceptance to that change, reflecting a new perspective. The destitute and helpless had long received assistance through charity associations. Now, working women struggling for economic independence, received assistance as well. Although many Canadians believed that the helpless and destitute would always be with them, the position of the working poor was somewhat different. Their poverty, after all, did not stem from their inability or disinclination to work but rather from conditions in society. Perhaps their position could be altered. This could only be done through reform of the social and economic system. By inadvertently bringing attention to the working woman, the YWCA helped lay the groundwork for such reform, although not fully participating in it.

Restricting the Y's reform impulse was the attitude of the Y members. There was little feeling of affinity between them and the boarders in their homes. They provided a service and the boarders accepted it. For example, at the inaugural meeting of the Toronto Y, the Ladies Committee had discussed "who should be objects for 'the Home.'" These women obviously believed they were providing assistance, which made those who accepted it less than equal to themselves.

Boarders had to supplicate to the Board for privileges, not rights. In 1874, boarders were permitted to invite *one female friend* for Christmas dinner.[39] In 1896, at the meeting of the Toronto Directresses, complaints concerning the "incessant" calls at the telephone had been received. As a result telephone privileges were removed; boarders now had to pay five cents to use the phone, no one could receive calls and all messages were taken by the secretary or matron.[40] In a multitude of ways, those using Y homes had to ask for every freedom and favour. The Y ladies realized these young women were not charity cases but obviously had difficulty acting on that perception.

In addition, the Y's interest in working women extended only to their private lives, that time spent away from their jobs. The YWCA never became involved in trying to ameliorate the conditions under which these women toiled. One exception occurred in 1881, when the Toronto Association approached the Bell Telephone Company and requested it not to compel its employees to work on the Sabbath.[41] The Y believed Sabbath Observance and morality went hand in hand. As well, the Y's evangelical beliefs supported the keeping of the Sabbath. Only such a strong motivation could make the Y speak out. Generally, it was not interested in becoming involved in the public aspect of the lives of working women, i.e. their working conditions, only in making it easier for them to cope with existing conditions. It provided cheap and respectable living accommodation for the working woman, but apparently it did not ask why it was so difficult for her to find such accommodation without help. The ladies of the YWCA treated the symptom, not the cause, which in most cases was low wages. As long as reform remained in the private sphere, that is, the home life of working women, the Y had no difficulty. Involvement in their public life, that is, their work situation, would have necessitated Y involvement in the public sphere, and this was a move the members of the Y were reluctant to take.

The WCTU

The WCTU had no such reluctance. It made by far the most radical demands of any women's organization. It wanted to eradicate intemperance. Spurred on by its Methodist members, the WCTU believed that the consumption of alcohol was morally wrong. To eliminate it, the WCTU could either direct its energies toward the reformation of drunkards or the acceptance of prohibition by the state. The first approach was that of the YWCA, working directly with those who were experiencing the problem. While the WCTU engaged in this to a limited extent, it concentrated most of its efforts on prohibition. Working with drunkards was not the same as working with respectable working women and the WCTU members may have been reluctant to become involved with individuals who, in the view of the Union, caused their own problems. The WCTU was more concerned with helping those deserving of aid, specifically the wives and children of the drunkards, the innocent victims of intemperance. As women, WCTU members could easily sympathize with them.

Like the Y, the WCTU's aim was to help the deserving of society to the point where they could help themselves. While Y members could do this or felt they could through private effort, the WCTU believed only prohibition could overcome the problems caused by intemperance. It was an immediate and complete solution.

Prohibition, however, required society to change in order to create an atmosphere of temperance for the individual. This was an interesting change in focus. Other organizations such as the YWCA had emphasized the adjustment of the individual to the existing norms of society. In most areas the WCTU agreed with this approach; but, because of the harm caused by intemperance, it was willing to invoke the power of the state to change the norms of society since it believed only legislation could ensure a temperate society. The WCTU perceived that governments responded best to public pressure. Consequently, to persuade Canadians to bring such pressure to bear, the WCTU became much more actively involved in the public sphere than most women's organizations. Unlike the YWCA, the WCTU supported public agitation. Yet the aim of the WCTU's public involvement was the same as the Y's — to protect the private sphere, the home life of Canadians that was being disrupted through intemperance.

Unfortunately, the government refused to implement prohibition and the WCTU had difficulty understanding why. After all, it believed the state was an active agent in society and as such had a responsibility to do "not what shall punish wrong-doing so much as what shall tend to right doing."[42] Instead of this, the Canadian government legalized the liquor trade and as the WCTU put it, "for a price, for revenue, makes the whole nation, women and all, party to its own degradations."[43] The Union's vehemence reflected its conviction that it was right and the government was wrong, a conviction reinforced by the religious beliefs of many of its members.

The WCTU felt few inhibitions or restrictions on its reform impulse, unlike the church missionary societies which were restricted by the conservative nature of their focus and by that of the churches with which they were affiliated, and the YWCA, which was limited by the charitable orientation of its members. Its support of prohibition was a comfortable belief for intemperance endangered its members' way of life. Husbands of the executive were in law, business, medicine and journalism. The husbands of twenty-one percent of the executive were members of the clergy.[44] Considering the association the temperance women made between crime, immorality and intemperance, it is not surprising that they saw in intemperance a challenge to the middle class virtues of thrift and Christian morality.[45] It was the foreign element in an otherwise ordered society, and they believed that endless blessings would accrue to society once liquor was prohibited. For the WCTU, prohibition complemented its members' religious beliefs, helped those in need, and protected their members' own interests. It is no wonder that the Union was determined to achieve it.

The NCW

The NCW was not as single-minded. Its specific aim was to bring together a wide variety of women's organizations, reform and non-reform alike, so that the women of Canada could speak with one voice. Thus its reform activities had to be carefully chosen so as not to alienate any of its disparate affiliated organizations. It was similar to the church societies in that respect. As a result, it rejected the two most controversial reforms of the nineteenth century — prohibition and woman's suffrage. This careful approach was a reflection of the type of women who joined the NCW. They were women of moderation who understood the niceties of a 'civilized' existence and basically accepted life as they found it, although wanting to leave it somewhat improved.[46] To attract such women, the NCW appointed as honourary vice-presidents, the wives of the provincial lieutenant-governors, and as president, the wife of the Governor General.

Despite the limitations on reform presented by the type of women the NCW tried to attract and the necessity of catering to a wide spectrum of women's organizations, the NCW was able to reach decisions on a wide variety of concerns. By 1901, it had fourteen standing committees on such topics as the Law for Better Protection of Women and Children, Pernicious Literature, Custodial Care of Instruction, Furtherance of Election or Appointment of Women on School Boards, and the Raising of a Loan for the Doukhobor Women.[47] These committees reflected the concern of women for other women, something which all these women's organizations expressed. They did not demand that women work outside their traditional role, but rather through it for the well-being of society.

The Council's interests were similar to those of the YWCA and WCTU, that is, to help those who were deserving. Council members were sometimes able to do this through their own efforts, such as raising money to help Doukhobor women, but more often they placed pressure on government to implement relevant legislation. More than the YWCA, the NCW looked to the government for aid, perhaps because it could engage in individual reform neither through faith due to its non-sectarian nature nor through the personal involvement of its members; like the WCTU, the Council did not often work with individuals but rather with the 'problems' abstracted from the individuals who experienced them. Only the power of the state could exert any influence in such a situation.

One example of the type of effort the NCW engaged in was lobbying the various provincial governments to introduce domestic science training in schools. The NCW's support of this reflects not only its dependence on institutional means of reform but also the way in which the needs of its own members often determined the policy it would pursue. In this specific instance, the lack of domestic servants led the NCW to espouse domestic science training.

Girls no longer entered domestic service as they had in the past.[48] Many preferred to work in the newly opened factories where, if they were not better paid, they at least enjoyed more independence. This scarcity of servants aggravated the situation of the middle class woman who was able to afford a servant but could not hire one. In 1891, the ratio of female servants to households was 1 to 11.3. By 1901, it was only 1 to 13.[49] Some women believed one factor which contributed to the scarcity of domestic help was the lack of domestic training. Because girls no longer learned to do housework, they could not consider it a means of employment.

Interest in domestic science education was, in part, a reaction to a class-oriented need. Discussions within the NCW gave little consideration to the servant girl but emphasized the difficulties faced by the women without one. Some observers believed the bias was so great that "Cooking being taught in the schools...was an effort by 'the classes' to foist an inferior education on the 'masses.'"[50]

The NCW was also concerned that women be properly trained for their role in life. The NCW believed the home was an important and integral part of society and woman's role was to care for it properly. It feared many girls were not learning domestic skills from their mothers, undermining the ordered system in which role division between the sexes was clear. With more and more women entering the work force and fewer of them going into domestic work, the fear existed that those women were rejecting the home and the 'natural' division between the sexes. To ensure that women did not reject domestic life because of inadequate training was the responsibility of the educational system.[51]

Domestic science education was typical of the kind of change in society that the NCW was willing to endorse. It stressed care of the home, something on which all women's organizations affiliated with the NCW could agree. It would benefit the members of the NCW through providing a more abundant supply of servants and it would benefit society through the training of future wives and mothers. It could conceivably even provide employment for the increasing number of women entering the work force.

Summary of Reform Approaches

The four organizations revealed a variety of perceptions and approaches to solving societal problems. Although many women probably belonged to more than one of these organizations at the same time, they did so for different reasons. The YWCA and church societies stressed the role of a woman as a Christian, believing a woman had a Christian duty to help others. While the missionary societies did not come into contact with the women they were trying to help, the missionaries they supported did. Their attitude tended to be maternalistic, although softened by the recognition of spiritual equality. The Y, too, was limited by the attitude of its members to the working women it was trying to help. It saw a woman as part of a family and in its desire to recreate a home environment for the working woman the Y acted as a surrogate parent, which meant the boarders were treated as children. Another inhibiting factor for the Y was its refusal to become involved in the working conditions of women. It did not believe women had the right to demand better treatment from society in the public sphere, for themselves or for others. The WCTU did. More than the Y, it was balanced in focus. Christian idealism underlay the Union's motivation and efforts; concern for domestic stability directed it to the families of drunkards, the innocent women and children who were victims of the liquor traffic; and belief in the rights and responsiblity of women led it to demand prohibition from the state. The NCW made equally strong demands upon government to implement its reforms. As well, the traditional view of women and class need often determined what those demands were as in the case of domestic science instruction. Because of its non-sectarian nature, the NCW could not stress woman in her Christian role. Nonetheless, the morality behind its concerns was often religious.

Because the focus of each organization differed slightly, each appealed to women in various stages of social consciousness. The church societies and the YWCA demanded little beyond financial support from its general membership. The WCTU and the NCW demanded more than fund raising from their members. They investigated problems, found solutions, and then tried to get those solutions implemented. Such activity necessitated public attention which many Canadian women found repugnant. Through its size, prestige, and avoidance of controversial reforms such as prohibition, the NCW was able to overcome this and create an acceptable forum for women reluctant to strike out in new directions with little support. The WCTU, because of its refusal to compromise, never received the wide support which the NCW did.

Conclusion

The organizational movement which emerged in late nineteenth-century Canada was obviously not a monolith. It appealed to middle class Canadian women but that was never enough to bring them together, as evidenced by the refusal of the YWCA and WCTU to join the NCW and the inclination of the missionary societies, by virtue of their religious affiliations, to remain separate. Issues such as religion kept them apart. Yet faith also prodded them in the same direction, for the God of most reformers was an active God who demanded activity.[52] Church women felt Christ had given them an obligation to spread his word. To pray and be devout was not enough. The YWCA and WCTU shared this motivation. Even the NCW was affected; it was a non-sectarian organization, not a non-religious one.

All four of these organizations increased women's awareness of the problems facing Canadians in society. The church missionary societies concentrated on the religious diversity of Canadians and, while their focus was always on the spiritual, they could not help but become aware of secular needs. Their members helped to provide schooling for young children and orphanages where needed, especially among the native peoples. Although they worked through others, they were nevertheless important as fund raisers and administrators. While they may not have been reformers *per se*, their work raised their sensitivity to problems in

Canadian society and this often led many to seek activity in secular areas outside the church. Thus the missionary societies were a training ground for other women's organizations. The YWCA focused on a secular need in society and like the church groups accepted personal responsibility for meeting the needs of the people they had identified as in need of help — working women. However, they too worked at a distance, seldom coming into contact with the women boarding in their homes, preferring to work through a matron. The WCTU, unlike the church societies and the Y, was a new departure for women in that it focused on a secular need but did so in a public way by insisting that the state accept responsibility. But like the previous two organizations, it seldom worked directly with those people it was trying to help. Neither did the NCW, which, with the WCTU, concentrated on institutional solutions as the goal of secular reform.

All four organizations emphasized meeting the various needs of people but the goal behind this was the stability of society. The church missionary societies believed that helping the heathen convert to Christianity could only lead to temporal peace. Within Canada, this conversion meant making Canada into a Protestant country which, as a consequence, would eliminate those divisions of religion which so often dominated the political scene of the nineteenth century. The YWCA believed that by protecting and helping working women they were keeping them off the streets and preventing a social evil from occurring. The WCTU truly believed prohibition would eliminate the major problems of society — crime, poverty and immorality — and in so doing, protect the home. The NCW, by focusing its activities on the home, was protecting that very unit which Canadians believed was the foundation of social stability.

It is in the three areas of their religious motivation, awareness of secular problems in society and desire for a stable social order that these women's organizations prepared Canadians for the welfare state and perhaps even directed the shape it took. The distance between contemporary governments which initiate social programmes and the people these programmes actually help is very similar to the gulf between these organizations and the people whose conditions they wished to see improve. As well, the present day welfare state, as were these organizations, is concerned with society as a collective, not with the rights of any one individual. And underlying the work of the state is a belief in the responsibility it has to meet the basic needs of Canadians. This responsibility is no longer expressed in religious terms but it is based on the religious heritage of past generations and the morality that it engendered in subsequent generations.

NOTES

Parts of this paper have appeared in a slightly different form in "Woman's Missionary Societies in Nineteenth Century Canada: A Step Towards Independence," *Atlantis*, II: 2 Spring, 1977, 57-76; "The YWCA and Reform in the Late Nineteenth Century," *Histoire Sociale* 1: 24, Nov. 1979, 368-84; "The WCTU: For God, Home and Native Land: A Study in Nineteenth Century Feminism," in L. Kealey ed., *A Not Unreasonable Claim*, Toronto, 1979, 151-68; and "The Woman's Christian Christian Temperance Union: A Study in Organization," *International Journal of Women's Studies*," 4: 2, Mar./Apr. 1981, 143-56.

1. For further discussion of charitable endeavours in which women were involved see Susan E. Houston, "The Impetus to Reform: Urban Crime, Poverty and Ignorance in Ontario, 1850-1875," Ph.D., University of Toronto, 1974, Chapters VI, VII; Judith Fingard, "The Winter's Tale," Canadian Historical Association, *Historical Papers*, 1974, 65-94; M. Angus, "Health, Emigration and Welfare in Kingston, 1820-1840," in D. Swainson ed., *Olivers Mowat's Ontario*, Toronto 1972, 120-36.

2. The Catholic Orphanage, Montreal, 1832; the Protestant Orphan Asylum, Montreal, 1822; the Harvey Institute, Montreal, 1847, which cared for half-orphan girls and trained domestic servants; the Montreal Ladies' Benevolent Society, 1833, which was to "lessen pauperism and fit children for honourable and useful lives"; the Female Orphan Asylum, Quebec, circa 1830; the Orphan's Home, Kingston, 1857; the Orphan's Home of the City of Ottawa, 1865; the Girl's Home, Hamilton, 1862; the Girl's Home, Toronto, 1850; the Infants' Home, Halifax, 1875; The Working Boys' Home, Toronto, 1867; the Protestant Home for Women, Quebec, 1859; the Home of the Friendless, Hamilton, 1859; plus many more. National Council of Women, *Women of Canada*, Montreal, 1900, 324-91.

3. The Girls' Home, Hamilton.

4. The Working Boys' Home, Toronto.

5. In her book, *The Remembered Gate: Origins of American Feminism*, New York, 1978, 152-55, Barbara Berg maintains that religion has been overemphasized as a factor in the woman's organizational movement in the U.S. She argues that the clergy were not interested in encouraging female philanthropy and she is doubtful that many of the early women's organizations formed in the United States were influenced by the religious fervour of the Second Great Awakening. Berg's manner of measuring religious influence does not seem to apply to the Canadian context. The clergy by the end of the nineteenth century did not criticize women's involvement in philanthropy or reform to any great extent. Most women involved in reform were also very careful not to alienate the church. As well, religious belief does not have to be linked to religious fervour in order to be strong.

6. *Annual Report*, Woman's Missionary Society, (WMS), Methodist Church, 1892-93, 22; *Annual Report*, Woman's Baptist Missionary Union, (WBMS), Maritimes, 1890-91, 24; *Annual Report*, Woman's Foreign Missionary Society, (WFMS) Presbyterian Church, Western Division, (WD).

7. *Annual Report*, WFMS, Eastern Division (ED), 1889, 12.

8. Isabel Hart, "Woman's Work for Heathen Women," *Canadian Methodist Magazine*, 12, 1880, 266-67; *Annual Report*, WFMS, ED, 1889, 13.

9. Many women had received their first experience in group activity through the church and carried its influence with them as they became more involved in secular activity.

10. Mary Quayle Innis, *Unfold the Years*, Toronto, 1949, 10; Toronto YWCA, August

22, 1873.

11. Minutebook, Toronto YWCA, Sept. 5, 1873.

12. Minutebook, Toronto YWCA, Oct. 31, 1873.

13. Minutebook, Toronto, YWCA, Feb. 3, 1893.

14. "Minutes", National Executive Committee, YWCA, May 30, 1895; *Annual Report*, National Council of Women of Canada, (NCWC), 1895, 207.

15. *Annual Report*, WCTU, Canada, 1894, 28.

16. *Annual Report*, WCTU, N.B., 1896, 14.

17. *Annual Report*, WCTU, Quebec, 1884-84, 70.

18. *Annual Report*, WCTU, B.C., 1893, 23.

19. *Annual Report*, WCTU, Ontario, 1884, 71; *Annual Report*, WCTU, Quebec, 1884-85, 16-17.

20. Minutebook, WMS Methodist Church, London Branch, 1899, 69; Marion Royce, "The Contribution of the Methodist Church to Social Welfare in Canada," MA University of Toronto, 1940, 147.

21. In 1898 the General Conference of the Methodist Church discussed supporting woman's suffrage.

22. *Annual Report*, WCTU, Ontario 1887, 25.

23. Such societies would have been those which had strong representations of Jewish, Roman Catholic and Unitarian members.

24. Roman Catholics and Unitarians were represented on the executive of the Council, as well as members of the Church of England, Baptist, Presbyterian, Methodist, and Congregational Churches.

25. *Annual Report*, NCWC, 1894, 22.

26. Lady Marjorie Pentland, *A Bonny Fechter*, London, 1952, 112.

27. It was through the work of the Ladies' Aid Societies that women received their reputation as homemakers of the church since it was the responsibility of these societies to see that the church was kept beautiful. Mary McKerihen, *A Brief History Relative To The Growth and Development of Women's Associations 1913-1943*, Toronto, 1944, 4.

28. In 1885 the Woman's Baptist Missionary Union (WBMU) in the Maritimes raised $5,000. In 1899 the WFMS, WD, raised $45,513. In 1901 the WMS, Methodist Church raised $50,972. *Between 1892-1895 the Woman's Auxiliary of the Church of England had raised $50,155. Mary Cramp, *Retrospects: A History of the Formation and Progress of Women's Missionary Aid Societies of the Maritimes Provinces*, Halifax 1893, 18; National Council of Women, *Women of Canada*, 305-06; *Annual Report*, WMS Methodist Church, 1901-02, XXIX; Emily Cummings, *Our Story 1885-1928*, Toronto, 1928, 47; *Report* of the Triennial Meeting of the Woman's Auxiliary to the Board of the Domestic and Foreign Missionary Society of the Church of England in Canada, 1895.

29. *Annual Report*, WFMS, WD, 1889, 9.

30. *Annual Report*, WBMU, Maritimes, 1891-92, 87; 1894-95, 93-94.

31. *Minutebook*, WMS, Methodist Church, Nov. 8, 1881, 8.

32. *Annual Report*, WMS Methodist Church, 1892-93, 22; *Minutebook*, WMS, Centenary Church Hamilton, April 3, 1882; *Minutebook*, London Conference, WMS Methodist Church, 1899, 69.

33. *Annual Report*, WMS, Methodist Church, 1890-91, XV.

34. *Minutebook*, WMS, Methodist Church, London Branch, 1896, 22-23; *Annual Report*, WMS, Methodist Church, 1892, 11.

35. Innis, *Unfold the Years*, 19.

36. National Council YWCA, *The Story of the YWCA in Canada*, Toronto, 1933, 1-2.

37. In 1891, 111 women per 1000 (ten years of age and over) were employed. By 1901 this had risen to 120, representing an increase of 41,959 workers or 21.4%. *Sixth Census of Canada*, 4, 1921, xii-xiv.

38. *Minutebook*, Toronto YWCA, May 9, 1873.

39. *Minutebook*, Toronto YWCA, Dec. 21, 1874, emphasis mine.

40. *Minutebook*, Toronto YWCA, Dec. 3, 1896.

41. *Minutebook*, Toronto YWCA, Dec. 2, 1881.

42. *Annual Report*, WCTU, NS 1897, 24. Letitia Youmans, "Haman's Licence," in Rev. B.F. Austin, ed., *The Prohibition Leaders of America*, N.P., 1895, 36.

43. *Annual Report*, WCTU, Canada 1892, 53.

44. WCTU Executive:

Occupation of Husband:		
Business	19%	8 members
Law	14%	6
Ministry	21%	9
Medicine	9.5%	4
Journalism	12%	5

These figures represent only the professions with the largest representation.

45. *Annual Report*, WCTU, Ontario 1898, 96; *Annual Report*, WCTU, Dominion of Canada 1891, 77; *Annual Report*, WCTU, Nova Scotia 1897, 28; Agnes Machar, "Cholera and Alcoholic Stimulants," *The Woman's Journal*, Dec., 1884.

46. Lady Aberdeen, in J.T. Saywell, ed., *The Canadian Journal of Lady Aberdeen*, Toronto, 1960, entry for April, 1894. For a definitive look at the NCW see Veronica Strong-Boag, *The Parliament of Women: The National Council of Women in Canada 1893-1929*, Ottawa, 1976.

47. *Annual Report*, NCWC, 1901.

48. D.S. Cross, "The Neglected Majority: The Changing Role of Women in Nineteenth Century Montreal," *Social History/ Histoire Sociale*, 6, Nov. 1973, 208.

49. Genevieve Leslie, "Domestic Service in Canada, 1880-1920," in *Women at Work: Ontario 1850-1930*, Toronto, 1974, 75.

50. Aberdeen, in *The Canadian Journal of Lady Aberdeen*, 3 Oct. 1897, 417.

51. *Annual Report*, NCWC, 1894, 117.

52. Christopher Lasch, *The New Radicalism in America, 1889- 1963*, London, 1965, 29.

PART III

The Transition from the Private to the Public

"A Children's Bureau For Canada":
The Origins Of The Canadian Council On Child Welfare, 1913-1921

R.L. Schnell

The establishment of the United States Children's Bureau in 1912 occasioned a flurry of interest in Canada that laid the groundwork for federal and voluntary initiatives in child welfare at the end of World War I.[1] The American impetus for a federal Children's Bureau originated in the anti-child labour organizations. The National Child Labor Committee (NCLC), organized in 1904, formally endorsed the idea in April, 1905. In January 1909, a Conference on the Care of Dependent Children, meeting in Washington, D.C., at the invitation of President Theodore Roosevelt, recommended "the establishment of a permanent organization to undertake, in this field, work comparable to that carried on by the National Playground Association, the National Association for the Study and Prevention of Tuberculosis, the National Child Labour Committee, and other similar organizations in their respective fields." The Conference also suggested the passage of "a bill pending in Congress for the establishment of a federal Children's Bureau to collect and disseminate information affecting the welfare of children." President Roosevelt was persuaded to send a personal message to Congress in support of the bill.[2]

On April 9, 1912, President William Howard Taft signed into law the bill establishing the Children's Bureau, with authority to investigate and report "upon all matters pertaining to the welfare of children and child life among all classes of our people."

The agency was located initially in the Department of Commerce and Labour. With the creation of the Department of Labor in 1913, the Children's Bureau found a new home that lasted until its transfer in 1945 to the Federal Security Agency. The United States Children's Bureau (USCB) included a chief, assistant to the chief and directors for the six divisions of social service (which included children in need of special care), child hygiene (staffed with physicians and public health nurses), recreation, industrial, statistical, and editorial. These developments in the U.S. supported efforts in Canada to develop a similar Bureau in this country, but to date these efforts have not been seriously explored.

Public and Private Responses in Canada

Canadian responses came almost simultaneously from both the federal government and voluntary social services. In October 1913, E.L. Newcombe, Deputy Minister of Justice, appointed R.H. Murray, Secretary of the Nova Scotia Society for the Prevention of Cruelty to Children (SPCC), and Ernest H. Blois, Superintendent, Nova Scotia Department for Neglected and Dependent Children, to investigate and report on the establishment of a children's bureau.[3] During their visit to the United States, Murray and Blois attended the annual meeting of the American Humane Association in Rochester, New York, where they interviewed such notable child savers as Peter G. Gerry, vice-president of the New York SPCC, Robert W. Kelso, secretary of the Massachusetts State Board of Charities, Robert Parr, director of the National SPCC of England, and met Julia Lathrop, USCB chief in New York, and C.C. Carstens, secretary of the Massachusetts SPCC. In their report of 31 January 1914, Murray and Blois recommended the establishment of a Canadian Children's Bureau to counteract the forces "militating against the proper development of child life." The Bureau would be a research department with advisory powers in the areas of juvenile courts and probation, institutions for dependent and neglected children, legislation affecting children, and child labour.[4]

In 1913, the Moral and Social Reform Council of Canada, which had grown out of the successful conclusion of the Lord's Day Campaign in 1907, was transformed into the Social Service Council of Canada (SSCC). Although largely an inter-church organization, the SSCC, by placing a greater emphasis on general social reform, served as a half-way house for those social reformers moving from church-based to secular social action.[5] The renamed Council successfully staged a major Social Service Congress in Ottawa on March 3-5, 1914. Child welfare interests were ably represented by such notables as J.J. Kelso, Superintendent of Neglected and Dependent Children of Ontario, R.L. Scott, KC, Dr. Helen MacMurchy, Judge L. Choquet, and Rose Henderson, who spoke on the significance of child welfare, the role of juvenile courts, the problems of defectives, physical and mental, and the value of pensions for mothers, respectively. One of the resolutions passed by the Congress called for "the creation of a Canadian Department of Child Welfare."[6]

Although this early momentum was diverted by the First World War, women's groups such as the National Council of Women (NCW) and the Imperial Order Daughters of the Empire (IODE) continued to advocate a Children's Bureau.[7] Moreover, just as the demands of the war effort would ultimately force the federal government to reconsider its responsibility for public health and welfare, the campaigns for greater efficiency and productivity on the home front and the War Elections Act of 1917 which gave the vote in federal elections to female relatives of service men demonstrated the need for programs that would attract women voters. A notable example of political interest in women as citizens was the Women's War Conference. The War Committee of the Cabinet called a Women's War

Conference for Ottawa on 28 February - 2 March, 1918, as part of its campaign to obtain "the wider participation [of women] in war work." Although the War Committee's call emphasized "increased agricultural production, commercial and industrial occupations, the compilation of the national register, conservation of food, and the further development of a spirit of service amongst the Canadian people," the women established a section on national health and child welfare as well as those recommended by the Committee. Chaired by Helen R.Y. Reid, the section on national health and child welfare recommended the establishment of a federal Department of Health and further, "that immediate steps be taken by the Government to conserve infant life and to deal with the problem of venereal disease." These recommendations were adopted by the Conference.[8]

In the final half hour with half the members gone, it was moved that "a Children's Bureau should be established by the Federal Government." Opposed by several speakers on the grounds of the lateness of the hour and the absence of many members and "because it was felt that the Federal Bureau of Health already asked for should cover a large part, at least, of the work of a Child Welfare Bureau," the motion was defeated on a standing vote.[9] Nevertheless, renewed interest was sparked in a federal Child Welfare Bureau.

Child Welfare and The Department of Health
Although a Children's Bureau was never central to the federal government's public health plans, it would appear as part of the recommendations for the establishment of a Dominion Department of Health. First broached in a Report of 25 October 1918 to the Vice-Chairman of the War Committee of Cabinet, child welfare or more particulary infant mortality was identified as an area that would benefit from the enfranchisement of women, who were seen as a potentially powerful force behind demands for improved social welfare. Moreover, the Report recognized that organizations supporting a Department of Health expected a Bureau of Child Welfare or Hygiene to be part of it.[10] Consequently when Bill 37 was introduced in the House of Commons on 26 March 1919, the proposed Department of Health was authorized among other things to "deal with questions relating to the consideration of child life and child welfare generally."

The debate occasioned by the introduction of the Department of Health Act is instructive on a number of matters.[11] First, Newton W. Rowell, president of the Privy Council and Vice-Chairman of the War Committee of Cabinet, intended that the Department would have responsibilities beyond a narrow medical definition of health. During second reading, Rowell argued that since war losses represented "a great drain upon the best life" in Canada, it was fitting that Parliament should consider "better measures for conserving the health of our people." In particular, he contrasted unfavourably the infant mortality rates in Canada with those of other nations. He then rang the alarm on venereal disease by citing the report of Mr. Justice Hodgins in Ontario and on physical and mental defects by citing the rejection rate of men called up under the Military Service Act. Rowell then summarized the sources of public support for a Federal Department of Health: women's organizations and meetings, labour organizations, and medical associations and conferences. He added that the Department would "deal not only with matters relating to public health, but also with the social welfare of the people of Canada." With reference to the latter he observed "that after all the most important thing is not to cure disease but to prevent it." It is obvious that although Rowell sensed that the scope of the Department should be broad he still saw it as a Canada Public Health Service.

If Rowell had a limited understanding of "social welfare," other members reduced everything to medicine and hygiene. Dr. Charles Sheard argued that the proposed Department "must be ancillary to the Provincial Health Departments ... and not conflict with the operations of municipal and provincial health boards." Sheard then went on to urge that the reference to the conservation of child life and child welfare be struck out because there would be "no possibility of doing any work along that line without encroaching upon the authority and rights and operations of the provincial health departments." Finally, Sheard defined his idea of child welfare by asserting that

> Whenever the benefits of child welfare work have been observed, the benefits have always been achieved through hospital effort...Where the women are housed in hospitals and the children have the benefit of hospital care for the first two or three weeks of their lives, infant mortality is materially reduced.[12]

During debate in the House in Committee, Rowell was forced to give ground on the "social welfare" clause and eventually the reference to "social welfare" was struck from the bill.

Subsection (b) of clause 4, which referred to "the conservation of child life and child welfare," also came under strong criticism. Sheard again called for its deletion on the grounds that "child welfare...embraces the establishment, the operation, and the management of *eleemosynary* institution," which under the BNA Act were under provincial jurisdiction. Moreover, Sheard raised the spectre that federal legislation would encourage the provinces and municipalities not to act.

Rowell finally agreed to delete subsection (b) and to include "the conservation of child life and the promotion of child welfare" in subsection (a). He subsequently attempted to amend (b), which provides for the "collection, publication and distribution of information to promote good health, and improved sanitation" by adding the words "and social welfare." Forced to withdraw the amendment, Rowell returned the next day with a new wording suggested by Tom Moore of the Trades and Labour Council. Accepted by the House, the information was described as "relating to the public health, improved sanitation and social and industrial condition affecting the health and lives of the people."[13]

As finally passed, the Department of Health Act defined the duties and powers of the Minister as extending to and including "all matters and questions relating to the promotion or preservation of the health of the people of Canada over which the Parliament of Canada has jurisdiction." In particular, under 4 (a) the Minister was empowered to

> cooperate with the provincial, territorial, and other health authorities with a view to co-ordination of the efforts proposed or made for preserving and improving public health, the conservation of child life and the promotion of child welfare.

The debate and the amendments demonstrated that child welfare within the Department of Health would be limited in both concept (to maternal and child welfare in the English style) and influence. Although Rowell was eager for an expanded federal role, his remarks in the House did not demonstrate a particularly strong social vision. The medical and public health organizations supporting the establishment of a Department of Health had a public health service in mind. As Rowell indicated, organized labour, notably TLC President Tom Moore, argued in favour of a more inclusive definition of health; but to no avail.

The operative words concerning child welfare in section 4(a) which specifically identified the duties and powers of the Minister administering the Department of Health were "cooperate" and "coordination." How they were understood, within the context of federal-provincial relations, would determine the exact role of the Federal government in child welfare for the next two decades. Even if a narrow view of maternal and child welfare were accepted and even if the federal role were limited to "the collection, publication and distribution of material relating to" the conservation of child life and the promotion of child welfare, there still remained considerable scope for direct federal action.[14]

A Child Welfare Branch was featured in the early organizational plans for the Department of Health. A staff memorandum of 12 January 1920 to Rowell stated that a "branch to cooperate with the Provinces in Child Welfare and with associations doing approved work in this direction is being established at the present moment." Indeed, the advertisement for a chief of the "branch" was already out and by May 1920 Dr. Helen MacMurchy had taken up her position as chief.[15]

Continued Pressure for a Children's Bureau for Canada
Although the expression "the conservation of child life and the promotion of child welfare" in Bill 37 suggested a wide scope for the Department of Health and its child welfare division, the bill displeased many Canadian child welfare advocates. The establishment of the United States Children's

Bureau had provided a model regarding philosophy, organization and staffing.

In January 1919, before Bill 37 had been introduced in the Commons, *Social Welfare*, the official journal of the SSCC, welcomed the idea of "A Children's Bureau for Canada" with a proposal for an organization very similar to the United States Children's Bureau. As with the U.S. model, the recommended home for Canada's Bureau was the Department of Labour. Arguing that the loss of 55,000 Canadians in the war had ironically "added to the dignity, worth and national value of the individual life," the article stressed the importance of conserving infant life. The 1918-1919 Children's Year in the United States had as its goal the saving of 100,000 lives, nearly twice the number of Americans killed during the war. The campaign promised to succeed because it had been "conceived *nationally*...planned *nationally*...[and was] being carried out as a concentrated *national* effort." Because it lacked a central Children's Bureau, Canada could not have mounted a similar campaign.[16]

The article bemoaned the inability to study and report on areas of high infant mortality, to collect and disseminate data on the "problem" of feeble-mindedness, to publicize successful mothers' pensions schemes in Manitoba and Saskatchewan, or to investigate and report on the care of dependent and neglected children. By collecting data and issuing reports, a central bureau "would make possible immediate and concerted national action in...child welfare work." The Bureau would be limited to investigating and reporting on matters of hygiene, education, delinquency, and industrial relations through its five divisions of child hygiene, education, delinquency and dependency, industrial relations, and extension and information.

The agitation for a federal Child Welfare Bureau continued throughout 1919 in *Social Welfare* with articles by D.B. Harkness, and Mary Power, chief of the Ontario Child Welfare Bureau.[17] The SSCC executive voiced its concern that placing the Bureau within the Department of Health would "limit its activities to the medical side of Child Welfare." The SSCC strongly opposed such a development on the grounds that a "narrowly conceived agency would fail to secure the large place which it should have in contributing to the well-being of the Nation's children."[18]

The worse fears of the child welfare progressives were confirmed by the civil service commission announcement in January 1920 inviting applications for the post of chief. While preference was given to women candidates, the advertisement called for a specialist in child welfare who was a physician with at least seven years' experience and with a thorough knowledge of social hygiene. Added to the medical qualifications were such skills as "organizing, administrative and recognized literacy ability; tact and good judgement; ability in public speaking." Preference was to be given to applicants who had teaching experience and were experienced as a propagandist and investigator on the whole range of social welfare problems.[19]

Emily Murphy complained to Sir George Foster, Acting Prime Minister, that "the keenest disappointment [would] be felt throughout Canada and co-operation [would] be neither wholehearted nor general" if a medical specialist were appointed. The March issue of *Social Welfare* argued that the child welfare effort must "see the child as a whole in the natural and normal life." It noted that the insistence on medical qualifications and experience demonstrated the health side of child welfare was to be the central focus of the new agency.

The philosophy underlying the United States Children's Bureau and expressed by eminent Canadian child welfare advocates was part of the larger Northern American progressive movement with its insistence on the organic nature of human life and its environment and on scientific inquiry as a base for solving human problems. As with progressive education, the "whole child" was the focus of progressive child welfare. Moreover, the recognition that child welfare was peculiarly a women's cause meant that women's organizations were significant in the constituency supporting the movement and that "competent women" were the natural pool of talent from which the chiefs of the bureau were to be selected. Although the Child Welfare Division was to be headed by a woman, the requirements were such that no outstanding woman child welfare reformer could have qualified. Indeed, the post seems to have been advertised with Dr. Helen MacMurchy in mind.[20]

Shifting Gears: The Move to Establish
a National Voluntary Council
The early promise of federal leadership in child welfare faded quickly. The Dominion Council of Health (DCH), consisting of the deputy minister (chair), the chief public health officer of each province, and up to five other members named by the Governor-in-Council, had been created by the Department of Health Act. At its first meeting in October 1919, the DCH served as a forum for the expression of national interest in child welfare as well as public health generally. The expectation that the Department would pursue a vigorous program in child welfare was evident in a motion by Helen Reid and Tom Moore requesting it to undertake investigations in child welfare ranging from prenatal care to factory life and its effects on maternity. Reid, who in 1884 had been one of the first women admitted to McGill University, had established a notable reputation as a feminist and a social welfare advocate with the Canadian Patriotic Fund during the war. Tom Moore, TLC president, was a consistent champion of a more active federal role in social welfare. Although the confused nature of the first meeting allowed the progressive members of the Council to push for a general attack on social problems, Dr. John Amyot, Deputy Minister of Health, had indicated a more restricted role for the Health Department by asserting that it was to be modelled along the lines of the U.S. Bureau of Public Health.[21]

By January 1920, the SSCC was agitating for a child welfare week in May to coincide with the British national baby week and urging the Department of Health to hold a child welfare conference in Ottawa. Citing the disorganized condition of his department, Amyot declined to issue the call. The SSCC then organized an informal conference in Toronto on March 23. The meeting was attended by forty representatives including Amyot, who promised that in a few months the Deparment would be able to call the desired meeting. The meeting accepted Dr. Amyot's proposal.[22]

At the second DCH meeting, 17-19 May 1920, Amyot finally spelled out the role in child welfare that the federal government would play:

> The limitation of the Department of Health makes it clear that we have no administration outside the Department. We are reduced in this Department to gather any information that can be got to further any legislation that might be devised and which we can get the Government to carry through.[23]

Reid then suggested the establishment of a national child welfare organization, similar to those for tuberculosis, mental hygiene, and venereal diseases, that would coordinate "the numerous societies already existing and filled with enthusiasm." As the first step in its creation, Reid called upon the Department of Health to sponsor a child welfare conference. In answer to Amyot's concern that the child welfare interests might resist the establishment of a national society, Mrs. H.E. Todd, Women's Institutes of Ontario, and Dr. Roberts, New Brunswick, testified that there was popular support for reducing the number of organizations.[24]

At this point, Professor J.G. Fitzgerald, representing the Canadian Public Health Association, outlined CPHA's child welfare activities, which included establishing a Child Welfare Section in 1919. In April 1920, the CPHA had approved "a definite plan to make the section of Child Welfare of the Canadian Public Health Association a real national Child Welfare Organization," with the assistance of the Canadian Red Cross.[25] With the hiring of a public health nurse as a full-time national organizing secretary, Fitzgerald claimed that the section was now in a position to launch "a scheme looking after child welfare work and working with the officially constituted Public Health Departments." Amyot for his part encouraged the CPHA to "enlist the sympathy of every organization and combine them and, once that is done, there will be no difficulty in co-operating, and the provinces will have no difficulty in leaning on the National Association and getting them to carry on."[26]

Thus, by May 1920, governmental policy in public health included the principle of cooperation with and use of existing national voluntary associations, which would circumvent the issue of dominion-provincial jurisdiction while limiting federal financial responsibility for health and welfare programs. A 1920 memorandum to Rowell stated that Department of Health policy was "to cooperate with approved associations...in so far as the public health is concerned." Although some national associations had an interest in child welfare, none had it as their primary concern. Moreover, provincial child welfare officials, judges and officers of family and juvenile courts, and superintendents of institutions saw themselves as a special sector of child welfare with its own unique needs. Amyot's support for the CPHA initiation was as much based on the urgent need for such a voluntary agency as on a natural predilection for a medical approach to child welfare.[27]

Despite his initial enthusiasm for the CPHA's proposal, Amyot was finally compelled to call the promised meeting of all those interested in child welfare for 19-20 October 1920 in Ottawa. The conference brought together one hundred and eight delegates representing one hundred and fourteen societies and institutions. If child welfare advocates had not welcomed CPHA efforts, the Dominion Conference on Child Welfare disappointed public health interests in the DCH members who wished to organize provincial associations in co-operation with the CPHA. Amyot supported this proposal on the grounds that provincial associations would then be in place to join the national council and thus create a national child welfare system. Moreover, to allay provincial fears, Amyot added that "the National Council is not going to go out at any tangent and spoil the whole thing" and that it would "work through and under the Department of Health." Responding to Amyot's remarks, Reid, quoting Amyot's address to the Conference, asserted that the national organization would work not "under" but "in cooperation with" the Department of Health.[28]

To Roberts, of New Brunswick, who insisted that the national organization must "submit what they are going to do to the Department of Health...[which] like a parent, will endorse it if it is possible and if it is in accordance with Public Health Legislation ideas," Reid forthrightly pointed out that the new organization included people interested in child welfare from a variety of perspectives and would not accept "dictation from a Public Health official," and since many voluntary organizations had never received the least assistance from public health officials, they would not be driven.[29]

Social service advocates represented by the SSCC were also unhappy with the conduct and results of "Canada's First Child Welfare Conference." *Social Welfare* offered a not too subtle criticism of the Department of Health by noting that Dr. Amyot "in response to an oft repeated request [had] agreed at a meeting in the SSCC offices in March, to summon a Dominion Child Conference at Ottawa this autumn" and that other than "that of general preparation," the Government had not undertaken any expense for the Conference. Dr. MacMurchy was faulted because she

doubtless in the usual unhappy director's absence of time, and somewhat modest in the high importance of the office she graces, refrained from giving the address many of us desired, but supplied all the delegates with copies of the full and careful details of the aims of her department.[30]

The general aims of the child welfare division were broad indeed: to assist the home, to help find a true home for every homeless child, to save and preserve maternal and child life, to promote and secure maternal and child welfare, and to maintain and improve the health, strength and well-being of mothers and children. These aims were to be achieved through cooperation with provincial and local medical officers of health and directors and officers of departments and bureaus of child welfare, with provincial departments of education, and with voluntary societies.

Social Welfare described the emphasis on organization over methods, standards and legislation as "unfortunate" and expressed hope that the creation of a National Council on Child Welfare would ultimately justify the expenditure of so much time and effort. Indeed, the establishment of the Canadian Council on Child Welfare to cooperate with the Child Welfare Division (CWD) seemed to be the only outcome of the conference. The proposed Council would be composed of one representative from each national organization interested in child welfare work and four representatives each from provincial organizations that served as the unifying bodies for child welfare within their provinces.

In establishing the CCCW, the conference had rejected as "logically undemocratic and unsatisfactory" a proposal that the Council become the governing body for the recently established Child Welfare Section of the Canadian Public Health Association. The decision to reject the CPHA offer is amply explained by Helen Reid's comment at the Dominion Council of Health that the non-public health interests in child welfare would not be driven by those with a medical orientation. Moreover, American child welfare progressives had successfully kept its national centrepiece, the Children's Bureau, out of the U.S. Public Health Service and in the Department of Labor. Thus, while the failure of Canadian child welfare advocates to convince Federal Government to establish a child welfare agency based on a whole child philosophy was galling, turning the national voluntary council over to medical interest would have represented the ultimate in impotence.

The decision not to establish a national child welfare association is perhaps best explained by the need to create a national voluntary organization that could be a non-governmental counterpart of a "Children's Bureau for Canada." It will be recalled that the 1909 Conference on the Care of Dependent Children, which had set the stage for the successful campaign for the U.S. Children's Bureau, had also supported a minority position that called for "the establishment of a permanent organization to undertake, in this field, work comparable to that carried on by...other similar organizations in their respective fields."[31]

The development of a permanent voluntary association in the United

States was slow, with its beginnings in 1915 when a Bureau for Exchange of Information was organized. Despite assistance from the Russell Sage Foundation, the Bureau was unable to secure independent funding. It was not until June 1920, when the Commonwealth Fund provided an annual grant of $25,000 for four years that a full-time director was appointed and the name changed to the Child Welfare League of America (CWLA).

Although voluntary organizational initiatives in child welfare in Canada were running nearly parallel with those of the United States, the decision to reject a national association similar to the emerging CWLA grew out of an effort to secure the advantages of a Children's Bureau on a voluntary basis. Indeed, the criticisms levelled by the progressives at the emphasis on organization rather than methods, standards and legislation were disingenuous. The provisional executive composed of Mrs. William Todd, Federation of Ontario Women's Institutes, president; Mrs. Arthur Rogers, Social Welfare Commission, Winnipeg, vice-president; Dr. W.J. Tillman, professor of pediatrics, University of Western Ontario, secretary; and Dr. Walker, Saskatoon, treasurer, demonstrated the failure to organize the Council on a scientific and professional basis. The progressives fared better in the provincial representation with Helen Reid, J. Arthur McBride of the Montreal Family Welfare Association, and Charlotte Whitton being available to consult and possibly take over the Council if the provisional executive faltered.[32]

The Canadian Council on Child Welfare
When the CCCW provisional executive met in Ottawa on 15 April 1921, only Mrs. Todd, president, Ontario Women's Institutes and Madame Tessier, along with Dr. MacMurchy were present. Rev. J.G. Shearer, SSCC General Secretary, joined the executive as a substitute for Whitton. Although the constitution did not permit proxies, Shearer was invited to stay as a visitor. His presence reaffirmed SSCC interest in child welfare reform and continued the pressure for action. The first meeting of the Canadian Council on Child Welfare (CCCW) took place on 30 May 1921 in Ottawa, under the auspices of the Department of Health. Although Charlotte Whitton was later to claim that the CCCW had survived due to the good offices of the SSCC, the correspondence in the Department of Health records indicates that Dr. MacMurchy provided the official support that kept the CCCW alive between the Dominion Conference in October 1920 and the first annual meeting in May 1921. The SSCC and the child welfare progressives were crucial to the survival of the Council in quite a different way. The failure to secure a proper federal child welfare agency meant that if the progressives were to have their "Children's Bureau for Canada" they would have to create a national voluntary one. This commitment was markedly different from the interest expressed by philanthropic women and men who had flooded the founding conference.

At the May meeting, Dr. Amyot finally put an end to any hopes for substantial voluntary federal cooperation by emphasizing that the

Department's Child Welfare Division "was to be forgotten" in the Council's deliberations, and that if the Council hoped for federal aid, it would have to demonstrate that it represented "voluntary bodies and all people of Canada non-officially." Thus, while the CCCW would have to coordinate voluntary activity nationally and cooperate with provincial authorities if it was to receive federal grants, at the same time the Department would distance itself from direct cooperation with organized national voluntary effort. Such a stance doomed any chance for CCCW and the Child Welfare Division together to emulate the work of the United States Children's Bureau.[33] Despite Amyot's message, the progressives, who were in full control, pushed ahead with the business of giving the CCCW a working executive and permanent constitution. The key figures included a solid Montreal contingent of Reid, J. Arthur McBride, and J. Howard T. Falk, and Charlotte Whitton. The new president was McBride, of the Montreal Family Welfare Association; vice presidents were Mrs. Todd and Elizabeth Breeze, a public health nurse from Vancouver; Charlotte Whitton and Madame Jules Tessier were named secretary and treasurer respectively. The new officers reflected a shift from voluntarism to professional social service.[34]

The constitution, which owed much to J. Howard Falk of McGill University, provided for six sections dealing with various aspects of child welfare: (1) children in need of special care; (2) defective, neglected, dependent and delinquent children; (3) ethical development of children; (4) child hygiene; (5) children in industry; and (6) education and recreation. Such an organization closely matched that of the USCB. The Council would sponsor annual conferences in connection with its work, serve as a link between the Child Welfare Division and the constituent units of the CCCW, and coordinate the child welfare programs of its constituent bodies.[35]

In addition to the disappointing prospects for federal action, the progressives found the unity of the child welfare movement threatened by the disaffection of child protection officers, i.e., juvenile court magistrates, officers of children's aid societies, and provincial superintendents of dependent and neglected children. Led by K.C.McLeod, Alberta superintendent, F.J. Reynolds, Saskatchewan superintendent, and Ernest Blois, Nova Scotia superintendent, these officials had expressed their unhappiness with the 1920 Dominion Conference. Immediately after the conference, W.L. Scott, who had drafted the federal Juvenile Delinquents Act (1908) wrote to MacMurchy in support of a national meeting of "members of Children's Aid Societies, Juvenile Court Judges and Officers and others directly interested in Child Welfare Work and Juvenile Court Work, with a view to forming a Dominion Association of Children's Aid Societies and Juvenile Court Workers." With Amyot's concurrence, MacMurchy issued the call for the requested conference, which was finally held in Winnipeg in October 1921.[36]

On 5 September 1921, McBride excitedly wrote MacMurchy that the

Winnipeg conference would have serious effects on a CCCW conference scheduled for late September. McBride's letter had been precipitated by a telegram from Charlotte Whitton. Both McBride and Whitton were unhappy about what they saw as a rival in child welfare. In both her correspondence with McBride and her report to Amyot, MacMurchy vigorously denied the charges that the Department had undercut the Council. She produced documents that detailed both the Department's financial support for the CCCW and the separation of the CCCW from the official program of the Child Welfare Division. In the first matter, shortly after the May 1921 council meeting, McBride had requested two thousand dollars from Amyot "to secure an executive secretary - with working office equipment." Although D.A. Clark, assistant Deputy Minister, pointed out that grants were ordinarily given to organizations that had demonstrated sufficient public support to ensure their operation, he noted that Amyot had secured the Minister of Health's consent to a preliminary grant of one thousand dollars "to hasten the work of organization and to enable active work to be begun." With regard to the second, the correspondence with McBride as well as the deliberations in the DCH illustrated the voluntary nature of the CCCW.[37]

The Winnipeg meeting saw the creation of the Canadian Association of Child Protection Officers (CACPO), which overlapped the CCCW's fourth section that dealt with "neglect, dependency, delinquency and defect." The agitation against CACPO started by McBride and Whitton continued through the 1920s. Although public officials were never comfortable within the CCCW, they represented too small a group to exist separately. Whitton made several attempts to affiliate the organization with the CCCW. Their meetings, usually held in conjunction with the CCCW, were poorly attended and by the end of the decade CACPO was a paper organization.[38]

The dispute with MacMurchy over the Department's relationship with CACPO was more than a matter of territoriality. The progressives understood that a link with the Department of Health was crucial if federal funds were to be secured and that federal grants went to national voluntary associations that coordinated national efforts and attracted national support. Although prominent child welfare advocates were willing to commit themselves to building a national organization, ultimately only a permanent office and full-time paid professional staff would make the CCCW a significant fact in Canadian child welfare. CACPO represented a continuation of the old child saving tradition dominated by public-spirited clergymen and laity. The progressives, whether older workers such as Falk and Reid or newcomers such as Whitton were pioneering full-time professional careers based on expertise and scientific training. If a federal children's bureau was unattainable, a voluntary equivalent required governmental sponsorship and grants that would legitimate a claim of national leadership. In turn, these would enhance the Council's and its officers' international standing as a quasi-governmental agency. In brief, if the federal government could not establish a Canadian children's bureau, then it had to promote unity within the voluntary sector.

Conclusion

By late 1921, the future direction of child welfare in Canada was beginning to take shape. The ground work laid by nearly seventy years of child saving associated with orphan asylums, children's aid societies, and provincial acts had merged with women's organizations and the social gospel in the early twentieth century to create a belief that child welfare was uniquely a women's domain — either as a vocation or a career. The campaign to establish a Canadian children's bureau was in large part a women's cause. The major national women's associations supported the cause, its most eloquent advocates were women, and the resulting organization, the Canadian Council on Child Welfare, was controlled by women. Although the failure to prod the federal government to establish a genuine children's bureau was a serious setback, women such as Helen Reid and Charlotte Whitton, along with their male colleagues, were determined to achieve on a voluntary basis what eluded them governmentally.

Any assumption that the Child Welfare Division and the CCCW represented a children's bureau for Canada was erroneous. The essence of the children's bureau concept was a national, governmentally supported effort based on a whole child philosophy of child welfare. In contrast, the child welfare division was a narrow understaffed child and maternal hygiene unit. It was the utter failure of the progressives to secure an appropriate federal agency that drove them to voluntary action. The co-existence of the federal division and the CCCW was not an example of the genius of institutions but rather the consequence of a failed campaign.

NOTES
My indebtedness to Patricia Rooke, who has shared in the research and discussions upon which this study is based, is amply demonstrated by three books and a score of articles that we have produced together. The Social Sciences and Humanities Research Council, the University of Calgary Research Services Office, and The Association for Canadian Studies have in their inimitable ways provided the funds that made the research possible.

1. The old studies by James A. Tobey, *The Children's Bureau: Its History, Activities and Organization*, Baltimore, 1925, and Dorothy E. Bradbury, *Five Decades of Action for Children: A History of the Children's Bureau*, Washington, D.C., 1962, have been superseded by Nancy P. Weiss, "Save the Children: A History of the United States Children's Bureau, 1912-1918," Ph.D., UCLA, 1974; Louis Covotous, "Child Welfare and Social Progress: A History of the United States Children's Bureau, 1912-1935," Ph.D., University of Chicago, 1976; Susan Tiffin, *In Whose Best Interest?*

Child Welfare Reform in the Progressive Era, Westport, CT., 1982; and Lela B. Costin, *Two Sisters for Social Justice: A Biography of Grace and Edith Abbott*, Urbana, 1983.

2. Tiffin, 232-33; and U.S. President, *Proceedings of the Conference on the Care of Dependent Children*, Washington, 1909, 6 and 13-14.

3. E.L. Newcombe, Deputy Minister of Justice, Circular Letter, 10 October 1913, Minnie Julia Beatrice Campbell Papers, MG14, C4 file: Child welfare, Provincial Archives of Manitoba (PAM).

4. R.H.Murray and Ernest H. Blois, *Report and Recommendation Regarding the Establishment of a Children's Department or Bureau, at Ottawa*, Halifax, 1913.

5. Richard Allen, *The Social Passion: Religion and Social Reform in Canada, 1914-1928*, Toronto, 1973, chs. 2 and 15.

6. *Social Service Congress, Ottawa-1914: Report of Addresses and Proceedings*, Toronto, SSCC, 1914. See pages 89-115 for the Child Welfare addresses and page 358 for the resolutions passed by the Congress.

7. Veronica Strong-Boag, *The Parliament of Women: The National Council of Women of Canada, 1893-1929*, Ottawa, 1976, 296 and 432-33; and IODE, *1918-1919 Yearbook*, 464.

8. *Report of the Women's War Conference Held at the Invitation of the War Committee of the Cabinet, February 28 - March 2, 1918*, Ottawa, 1918, 3, 13, and 19.

9. Ibid, 43-44; F.J. Billiarde, *A Brief in Favour of the Establishment of a Canadian Child Welfare Bureau*, Winnipeg, March 1918.

10. *Report to the Vice-Chairman of the War Committee of the Cabinet on the Establishment of a Federal Department of Public Health*, 25 October 1918, RG29, vol. 19, file 10-3-1, 2, PAC.

11. *House of Commons Debates*, 4 April 1919.

12. Ibid, 1178.

13. Ibid, 1205; and April 7, 1919, 1366.

14. Department of Health Act, 88.

15. Department of Health, List of Activities and Duties of Each Branch and Division, 8 November 1920, RG29, vol. 19, file 10-3-1 (vol. 2), PAC.

16. "A Children's Bureau for Canada," *Social Welfare*, 1 January 1919, 84-86.

17. "A Child Welfare Bureau," *Social Welfare* 1 March 1919, 134-135; "Child Welfare," *Social Welfare* 1 June 1919, 207-208.

18. "The Chief of the Children's Bureau of Canada," *Social Welfare*, March 1920, 150.

19. Ibid, 149-150; and Emily Murphy to Sir George Foster, acting Prime Minister, 17 February 1920, Robert L. Borden Papers, MG26, H1(C), microfilm C-4385, 101834A, PAC.

20. Department of Health, List of Activities and Duties of Each Branch and Division, November 8, 1920. The Organization Chart, prepared by the Civil Service Commission, had been approved by Amyot on 15 March 1920. RG29, vol. 19, file 10-3-1 (vol. 2), PAC. MacMurchy's accomplishments are listed in MG28, I10, vol. 3, file: Child Hygiene Section (vol.3), pt. 1, 1933, PAC.

21. Margaret Gillett, *We Walked Very Warily: A History of Women at McGill*, Montreal, 1981, 260-261; and *House of Commons Debates*, 7 April 1919, 1366; and Meeting of the Dominion Council of Health, 7 October 1919, RG29, vol. 2119, PAC.

22. "Executive Report," *Social Welfare*, 1 February 1920, 121; and "Child Welfare Week for Canada," *Social Welfare*, 1 May 1920, 208.

23. Report of Second Meeting of the Dominion Council of Health, 17-19 May 1920, 5, MG28, I63, PAC (Reel C-9814).

24. Ibid, 6-7.

25. Ibid, 7-8.

26. Ibid, 8-9; May 19, 1920, 33-34, and "Resolution #2," 2.

27. Department of Health, List of Activities and Duties... November 8, 1920.

28. Report of the Third Meeting of the Dominion Council of Health, 25-26 October 1920, 10-11. Dr. Fitzgerald assured Dr. MacMurchy and Mrs. Todd that the CPHA would cooperate with the CCCW. The CPHA section would be renamed child hygiene. Minutes, CPHA Conference, 26 October 1920, RG29, file 499-3-7, pt. 1, PAC.

29. Ibid, 11-12.

30. "Governmental Activities in the Field of Social Work -Canada's First Child Welfare Conference," *Social Welfare*, 1 January 1921, 111.

31. *Proceedings of the Conference on the Care of Dependent Children*, 13-14.

32. Report of Committee on Organization and Programme [n.d.], RG29, vol. 992, file 499-3-7, pt. 1, PAC.

33. Minutes of First Meeting of the Canadian Council on Child Welfare, 30 May 1921, 4. MacMurchy expressed the same point to J. Arthur McBride, President, CCCW: "There are many things the Council can do which would not be suitable for a Government Department or any division of it, to do, and our functions, with the exception of the great function of the co-operation already mentioned, must remain entirely apart." 22 June 1921.

34. Minutes of First Meeting of the Canadian Council on Child Welfare, RG29, vol. 992, file 499-3-7, pt. 1, PAC.

35. Ibid, 6.

36. W.L. Scott to MacMurchy, 22 October 1920, RG29, 992, file 499-3-7, pt. 1, PAC.

37. J. Arthur McBride to MacMurchy, 5 September 1921; and MacMurchy to Dr. J.A. Amyot, Deputy Minister, 24 September 1921, the correspondence collected by MacMurchy, RG29, vol. 992, file 499-3-7, pt. 2, PAC.

38. Whitton to A.G. Cameron, CACPO President, 3 February 1925; Ethel MacLachlan to Whitton, 24 June 1927; and MacLachlan to Whitton, 27 June 1932, MG28, I10, vol. 1, file CACPO, 1922-1932, PAC.

A Profession in Crisis:
Charlotte Whitton and
Canadian Social Work in the 1930s

James Struthers

The 1930s produced an explosion of public welfare in Canada as governments at the federal, provincial, and municipal level spent more than a billion dollars on the care of the unemployed and their families.[1] The suddenness and sheer magnitude of this expenditure forced major changes in Canada's social welfare structure. Before the Depression, private charities played a dominant role in caring for the victims of joblessness. By 1940, however, the federal government had created a national system of unemployment insurance and employment offices and most of the provinces along with the larger municipalities had developed permanent welfare bureaucracies with at least the rudiments of professional administration. Out of the "dirty thirties" then, came a belated acknowledgement that social welfare was a major responsibility of the state.

Perhaps no group benefitted as much from this transition as the social work profession, one of the few occupations to experience "practically one hundred percent employment" during the Depression.[2] Yet we know little about the role social workers played during the decade in shaping government policy. It is usually assumed that the lack of an experienced welfare bureaucracy was largely responsible for the abysmal conditions endured by those on the dole. In this view, public welfare became "professionalized," during the thirties, in order to improve living standards for the unemployed and their families.[3]

However, an examination of the role of Charlotte Whitton, executive director of the Canadian Council on Child and Family Welfare (CCCFW), in shaping the relief policies of the Bennett and King governments casts serious doubts on this assumption. In the mind of Canada's "best known social worker,"[4] at least, the interests of the unemployed and of the professionals entrusted with their care were by no means identical.

Like the rest of Canadian society, social workers were unprepared for the Depression. Although the 1920s had been formative years for the profession,[5] for the most part, what little expertise the country possessed in welfare matters still existed within its private charities and this did not amount to much. There were only two schools of social work in the entire country and even Ontario, Canada's wealthiest and most industrialized province, had "practically no such thing" as a "corps of trained social workers," according to a 1930 Royal Commission report. The profession itself had only organized its first national associations during the 1920s and possessed but a fledgling status on the eve of the 30s.

The public welfare field had expanded significantly during the preceding decade, but this generally occurred within patronage-ridden provincial bureaucracies with the result that complaints about partisanship, inefficiency, and corruption in the administration of mothers' allowances and old age pensions were widespread throughout the country.[7] Consequently, many Canadian social workers shared their American colleagues "long tradition of disdain" for state relief. Its bureaucratic emphasis upon "classification, determination of eligibility, and routine surveillance" seemed scarcely related to their own more "scientific" skills of investigative casework and professional counselling.[8] Canada thus entered into the greatest crisis of dependency in its history armed with only a few well-organized charities in its larger cities, a municipal relief structure built upon the nineteenth-century poor law, and an underdeveloped social work profession that viewed the whole field of public welfare with some skepticism.

As long as government officials viewed the Depression as a temporary "emergency," this lack of expertise and organization in the welfare field was not considered alarming. R.B.Bennett, after all, had been elected in 1930 on a promise that he would "abolish the dole" through stiff hikes in the tariff.[9] As a result, he had little interest in perfecting public welfare administration. Out of the $20,000,000 provided in his first relief act, $16,000,000 went for public works and only $4,000,000 was slated for direct relief. Not a cent of this was spent on developing competent local welfare bureaucracies. The same pattern prevailed the following year despite the fact that Ottawa's expenditure on direct relief almost doubled.[10] Adamant that the care of the jobless was primarily a municipal obligation, Bennett washed his hands of any responsibility for ensuring that federal money was expended in an equitable and decent fashion.[11]

The consequences of this policy were horrendous. By the winter of 1932, Canada's few well-organized charities were overwhelmed as unemployment rose above 20 per cent of the workforce. Their plight was effectively described by one harassed official in Toronto's Neighbourhood Workers Association:

> In 1930 we thought...that we were pressed to the uttermost and that we could not possibly drive the staff any harder. Never in our experience have we faced anything to equal this winter. The staff is working literally day and night to deal with the situation...The District Offices are interviewing anywhere form 50-90 clients daily. The toll on the physical and nervous energy of ones workers, who day in and day out, are interviewing 20-30 clients each is appalling... Just how we can go on facing it I do not know. We are trying to secure additional workers, but even that does not solve the problem. One reaches the saturation point when further supervision and guidance are difficult, if not impossible.[12]

The problems of the private charities, however, paled in comparison to those of the municipal relief offices. The charities, at least, were experienced in the welfare field. The cities were not. Only four had bothered to establish permanent welfare departments to distribute public relief before 1930.[13] More importantly, the sheer cost of financing their one-third share of direct relief upon a rapidly declining property-tax base did not incline most communities towards developing elaborate or overly-generous structures for relieving human need.

This fact was made abundantly clear by a devastating indictment of Ontario's relief system published by Harry Cassidy, of the University of Toronto's School of Social Work, in the spring of 1932. After surveying the relief practices of the province's twelve largest municipalities, Cassidy discovered that, depending on where they lived, an Ontario family of five could receive anywhere from $3.50 to $8.50 a week in direct relief food orders. In two-thirds of the cities he studied, relief officers themselves admitted that their food allowances were inadequate to maintain health. Most municipalities, moreover, did not even attempt to determine what a minimum food budget should be and in no city did Cassidy discover a budget which came even close to existing nutritional guidelines. Since neither the province nor the dominion provided any assistance towards the cost of relief administration, trained social workers were in charge of dispensing aid in only four of the cities he studied. Residence and eligibility requirements for relief varied from town to town; few cities provided any facilities for relieving unemployed single men and none aided single women.[14]

Cassidy held the provincial and federal governments directly to blame for this situation. By assuming that the unemployment crisis was an emergency "likely to be of brief duration," they had taken no steps to replace the present haphazard organization of relief with "adequate governmental machinery of a permanent nature." Most importantly, their policy of holding the municipalities primarily responsible for the care of the jobless guaranteed "neither uniformity of treatment nor even distribution of justice for the unemployed."

As a solution, Cassidy recommended permanent provincial and federal "leadership" in the welfare field to ensure well-planned public works; food allowances that provided the "minima requisite for the maintenance of health"; adequate rent and clothing allowances; uniform eligibility requirements that guaranteed a right to relief, regardless of where one lived; and the placing of trained social workers in charge of social aid. These recommendations might require a "large increase in relief expenditure," Cassidy realized, but to skimp on the care of the unemployed now would only lead to the "deterioration in the quality of our working-class population" and "huge social service expenditures later on."[15]

When it became clear, in the spring of 1932, that the Bennett government was about to abandon relief works entirely and rely solely upon direct relief in order to conserve funds, other members of the profession began to echo Cassidy's concerns. At a social work conference in April, some welfare administrators, disgusted at the spectacle of "families who had become sick on the miserable relief minima that had been paid," urged their colleagues to "take (a) stand for adequate relief" and "express their conviction that people could be kept idle, dragged on the most miserable rations, from day to day."[16]

Their most influential colleague, however, disagreed. Although better known today for her tempestuous career as mayor of Ottawa, Charlotte Whitton, by 1932, was already acknowledged as "one of the outstanding women of her generation"[17] through her prodigious work in the area of child welfare. Born in Renfrew, Ontario, in 1896, Whitton attended Queen's University and graduated with a brilliant academic record and an MA in history in 1918. That same year, she entered the burgeoning field of social work by becoming assistant secretary to Dr. John Shearer of the Social Service Council of Canada.

A diminuitive woman with a sharp wit, a fiery temper, and enormous energy, Whitton lost no time in moving to the top of her profession. In 1920, she was appointed honorary secetary of the newly-formed Canadian Council on Child Welfare, a national federation of social agencies established to promote the development of child welfare programmes across Canada. Starting with "no office and no money," Whitton six years later (with the help of federal government funding) was the full-time director of Canada's most influential social work organization. For the remainder of the decade she worked tirelessly, arranging conferences, conducting research surveys, and publishing reports in order to bring professional standards and prestige to the rapidly expanding sphere of family welfare.[18]

Even before the Depression struck, Whitton had been convinced that the growth of social aid programmes was far outstripping the supply of people who could capably run them.[19] As a result, she was hardly surprised when Bennett's first unemployment relief effort collapsed in disarray in the spring of 1932. The problem, she wrote the prime minister that April, was not a lack of money, but rather the way it was being spent. At the present, she noted, the provinces and municipalities were packing relief rolls with thousands of indigents, who, under normal circumstances, would not be considered unemployed, simply to get a federal subsidy. In Quebec, relief funds were being distributed according to the "racial or religious proportions of the population," not actual need. Finally, Whitton pointed to the wide variation in relief expenditure among Canada's six largest cities (from 84 cents per person in Montreal to $6.80 in Winnipeg) as evidence of the need for imposing "more rigid schedule of conditions" upon the way federal money was spent. And here her profession could help. Social workers had a "wealth of knowledge in the annual administration of hundreds of thousands of dollars" for social aid, she argued, that was "open and ready" for Ottawa's benefit if it seriously wanted to bring relief costs under control.[20]

More than generosity lay behind Whitton's offer. Her outrage over the waste and inefficiency surrounding relief reflected a strong sense of professional alarm at the rapid changes overtaking Canada's welfare structure. Thousands of untrained and frequently patronage-appointed personnel now staffed municipal and provincial relief offices across the country. Unless her profession could somehow gain control of this swelling bureaucracy, Whitton was convinced that social workers would soon be by-passed within their own field by a new class of government employees, particulary now that investigative casework, the skill upon which they rested their professional identity, was being undermined by the sheer volume of applicants for aid.[21]

The abandonment of public works as Bennett's chief form of unemployment aid in the spring of 1932 seemed to offer just such an opportunity for "professionalizing" the dole. The "whole aspect" of relief, Whitton argued, had now changed "from one of...registration and unemployment to one primarily of social welfare." Such a "changed situation" demanded "different procedure...knowledge and experience" and presumably different administrators as well. "Social work has its own technique as have engineering and construction," she pointed out to Bennett a few months later, "and the processes and personnel of the one cannot be automatically interchanged with the other without serious mismanagment and loss."[22]

Coming at a time when Bennett was gravely worried that the ballooning cost of relief might bankrupt the country, Whitton's arguments could not have been more apropos. While Cassidy's study, with its recommendations for a "large increase in relief expenditure," evoked a negative response from the Prime Minister's Office, Whitton was called to a meeting with Bennett in early April in order to "talk over" the contents of her memo. A month later she was hired by the federal government to "work as quietly as possible" on a study of unemployment relief in western Canada, the area of the country hardest hit by the Depression.[23]

After four months of extensive travelling throughout the prairies, Whitton submitted a two-hundred-page report that autumn. Since it was the only detailed unemployment relief study that Bennett ever commissioned during his five years in office, it had enormous influence in conditioning his subsequent response to the Depression, although in ways Whitton hardly suspected at the time.

Her most startling conclusion was that almost 40 percent of those presently receiving relief in the West did not really need it. In fact, over the past two years Bennett's relief work programme had succeeded in actually "raising...the standard of employment and living of the great volume of the underemployed."[24] Farmers and their sons, for example, had been employed on relief projects in large numbers "when there was no actual question of the need of food, fuel, clothing or shelter for themselves and...when ordinarily the winter was a period of idleness." In southern Alberta the widespread availability of direct relief had "arrested...any natural disintegration" of dying mining communities and "served to 'suspend' them on direct relief." The same was true of "dead communities" in the northern fringes of all provinces that had been "swept back or left behind as settlement moved elsewhere." The plight of their people was pitiful but it was "not one deriving from the present emergency" and therefore should not be supported by federal relief.

Jobless women fell into the same category. Their problems arose primarily from desertion, death and illegitimacy, not from unemployment; therefore, they did "not form a justifiable charge on...(relief) legislation." Direct relief was also raising the living standards of unemployed single men and immigrant families. Too many of the former, who could have stayed on farms during the winter, were "going to the cities where 'they could get two good meals and a bed a day on relief' and 'have a real rest for the winter.'" Immigrant families were receiving "supplies on a scale neither attained nor desired by these people from their own resources or efforts."[25] In short, lax standards of administration were allowing thousands of casual workers, who were *normally* unemployed six to eight months of the year to "swarm...into relief..on a 'year round basis'" and thus raise their standard of living "beyond anything that they have ever known."[26]

The problem, Whitton concluded, was that western municipalities had neither the incentive nor the expertise to restrict relief to only the genuinely unemployed. Fear of bankruptcy had acted as a deterrent to generosity in the past, but now many cities were so hopelessly in debt there was a real danger they might "cut loose" from all fiscal restraint in order to avoid social unrest,[27] particularly now that Ottawa was paying such a large share of their costs. More importantly, municipal administration of relief had subjected it to "the most contemptible type of local...politics." Relief offices were being staffed "on the...basis of party preferment," and as a result, most of the people Whitton found in charge of the dole "would never be considered by even a small business for any responsible position."[28]

Not surprisingly, her principal recommendation was that trained professionals be placed in charge of relief administration throughout the entire country. This had to be made the "*sine qua non* of any continuance of federal aid." By attaching rigorous conditions to its relief grants, demanding "minimum standards of education, experience and similar qualifications for all appointments in provincial or municipal relief offices," Ottawa could, in effect, "professionalize" the dole, improve its efficiency, and thus reduce its cost. Unlike Cassidy, however, Whitton counselled against any national minimum standard of relief itself. This would make the dole too attractive in too many communities. Her object, in contrast, was to tighten up relief administration before the casually unemployed became "permanently dependent at a scale of living which they never had and never will be able to provide for themselves."[29]

Whitton's October report with its confused distinctions between "casual" and "genuine" unemployment confirmed Bennett's worst fears that widespread abuse of the dole lay behind its rapidly increasing costs. This was certainly no coincidence. Exaggerating the extravagance of the present system was her most effective means of stressing the importance of her profession's administrative skills to the government. However, although Whitton's analysis made an impact upon Bennett, it was not in the way she had hoped. Although his suspicions of waste were now confirmed by "the most capable woman engaged in social welfare in the Dominion,"[30] Bennett did not believe that forcing the provinces to hire trained social workers was the answer. Instead, he opted for a quicker remedy. If the provinces and municipalities were wasting federal money, the solution was simply to give them less money to waste. Rather than spurring Bennett on to exert bold new leadership in the relief field, Whitton's report merely increased his desire to get out of the whole business as soon as possible. By emphasizing the extravagance rather than the suffering surrounding the dole, Whitton thus destroyed whatever chance there was that it might be reformed.

Over the next two years those without jobs paid the price. Although unemployment rose to 30 percent of the workforce during 1933 and the number dependent upon the dole climbed to over a million and a half,[31] Bennett and his labour minister W.A. Gordon turned a deaf ear to the growing demand from across the country that Ottawa assume a larger reponsibility for relief. People were flocking to the dole, Gordon told the premiers in 1933, because "sufficient emphasis was not being placed upon the responsibility of the individual to maintain himself." If Ottawa assumed a larger portion of the relief burden, "administration will be without restraint."[32]

As a result, the federal share of direct relief costs was held at one-third and an arbitrary $1,000,000 ceiling was placed on the budgetary deficits of the western provinces as a condition for further federal loans.[33] Apart from establishing relief camps for single men, Bennett's government refused to take any responsibility for the way relief was administered. Faced with absorbing the largest share of the dole's soaring cost, the provinces and municipalities thus had little incentive to insure equitable and decent treatment for the unemployed.

By the beginning of 1934, this continued federal indifference towards the chaotic state of relief had produced a growing "sense of futility and frustration" among Canadian social workers who, as Whitton pointed out, were the ones "closest to actual evidence of...(its)...course and effects."[34] But while calls for "more centralized leadership" were widespread throughout the profession, there was less agreement over where exactly Ottawa should lead.[35] On the left, critics such as Leonard Marsh and Harry Cassidy demanded a "much greater degree of dominion participation and control" in the care of the unemployed simply to insure that the dole was made "as adequate and as fair as possible."[36]

Whitton, however, continued to undercut their arguments by insisting that the real victim of Ottawa's *laissez-faire* policy was not the unemployed but the taxpayer. In a memo sent to Bennett's office early in 1934, she argued that by leaving responsibility for relief in the hands of the "unit of government most susceptible to direct political control and manoeuvre" Bennett had created a "wide open" system of relief administration that encouraged "loose organization and lavish expenditure."[37] As one relief administrator complained to Whitton, cities such as Calgary, where labour exerted a strong political influence on city hall, were "giving us all a lead which the unemployed cannot be blamed for urging we should follow and which fifty percent of the members of our City of Winnipeg council are trying hard to catch up and pass."[38] Small wonder, Whitton concluded, that there was a "growing tendency to seek relief and to stay on it over an increasing period of time. The system has bonussed such developments."[39]

The director of the Council on Child and Family Welfare undoubtedly hoped these sweeping accusations would finally convince Bennett to rationalize relief administration through enacting stiff conditional grants that would place trained social workers in charge of the dole. Instead, the prime minister once again moved in the opposite direction. Frustrated by the failure of the numbers on relief to decline in response to his economic policies, Bennett seized upon Whitton's arguments during the summer of 1934 to justify a severe reduction in Ottawa's support for the unemployed. At first threatening to terminate all contributions to relief, he ultimately settled for a 22 percent cut in federal spending, achieved through replacing Ottawa's one-third percentage contribution to the dole with a system of fixed monthly grants-in-aid.[40]

Relief had become a "racket", he told the premiers in justifying his move. Twenty percent of its cost was going not to the genuinely unemployed, but to "partially employed" workers whose wages were as high as before the Depression. "Relief conscious" municipalities had thus accustomed many of the jobless to a "hitherto unknown" standard of living. Moreover, nearly every province was attempting to "scrap the constitution" by packing the dole with indigent unemployables who normally were an exclusively local responsibility.[41]

Although his arguments were borrowed almost entirely from Whitton's 1932 report on relief in western Canada, Bennett drew a different conclusion. For Whitton, the logical remedy to these abuses was closer federal supervision of relief through more stringent conditional grants. The prime minister rejected this approach on the grounds that "divided authority was not efficient."[42] Instead, the "proper method" he argued, was simply "to make the grant-in-aid and to place the whole responsibility upon the Provinces and Municipalities." Up to now, local governments had "not taken any steps to prevent abuses."[43] Limited to a fixed federal grant, they might.

In effect, Whitton was hoist upon her own petard. Using her arguments, Bennett opted for a change in relief policy which, as she ruefully admitted, was "almost directly contrary" to her suggestions.[44] Instead of increasing federal supervison of the dole, he simply cut back Ottawa's support. The ledger, not the social work profession, the prime minister obviously concluded, would provide the most efficient check upon "waste" and "lavish expenditure" in relief.

Bennett adhered to this policy for the remainder of his administration. Even the introduction of unemployment insurance as part of his famous "New Deal" in 1935 contained no provision for the reform of relief.[45] In frustration, Whitton turned to the business community for support in her attempt to change government policy.[46] This time she found a receptive audience. By the beginning of 1935, businessmen across the country were becoming increasingly alarmed at both the growing leftward trend in municipal politics and the threat to government solvency posed by soaring relief costs, developments which many felt were not unrelated.[47] Thus, when Whitton's annual "Relief Outlook," at the end of 1934, pointed to the "increasing core of permanent dependency developing from the tendency to exploit the vote of the dependent unemployed and to offer more and easier relief," business organizations quickly began to echo her call for the "removal of relief standards, practices and administration from the realm of political influence and manoeuvre."[48]

Early in 1935, the Canadian Chamber of Commerce noted, in a letter forwarded to all members of Parliament, that although the dole was now the "heaviest burden on...government treasuries," it was "loosely integrated" and "subject in many cases... to political influence." As a result, the chamber demanded that Ottawa "should immediately take such action as will result in lifting control of relief administration and financing directly out of the field of the local political influence" in order to "conserve public funds."[49]

With the victory of Mackenzie King's Liberal party at the end of the year, the time for such a step seemed to have come. Although King had never insisted that Ottawa should administer relief itself, he had called, while in opposition, for a national commission that would investigate the real conditions surrounding relief administration and keep a close eye upon the way federal money was spent. True to his word, in April 1936 King established the National Employment Commission to "find ways and means of providing remunerative employment," to register and classify those on relief, and to supervise and audit provincial and municipal relief expenditures.[50] By bringing to light the "obvious abuses, rackets, overlapping and like" surrounding the dole, he was convinced, the NEC would soon "save the Treasury &...the taxpayers many millions of dollars."[51]

For help in discovering how to do this the NEC hired Canada's foremost authority on the subject, Charlotte Whitton. Now she had the chance to put into effect all the recommendations which she had so fruitlessly urged upon Bennett over the past five years. Whitton wasted no time in returning to her familiar theme. "(T)he most important phase of the whole problem," she warned the commission upon taking the job, was the "continuous interference and exploitation of the situation" by the municipalities. Consequently, the first step in reforming relief was to guarantee the social work profession "administrative freedom (and) adequacy of personnel" by attaching strict conditions to the new relief agreements with the provinces.[52]

Within a year, the NEC's interim report made public her ideas of what should be done. They had changed little since her first report to Bennett in 1932. The dole, Whitton told NEC commissioner Tom Moore when the interim report was released, was providing many people with the a "regularity of income" they had "not known in their usual occupation."[53] Not suprisingly, then, the thrust of her recommendations was to tighten up control over those on relief.

Whitton suggested three principal ways this could be accomplished. First, those now receiving unemployment aid should be divided into two categories: those who could work and those who could not. Ottawa would be financially responsible only for the first group. In this way, the federal government could both limit its expenditure and concentrate all its efforts upon devising efficient policies for getting the employable unemployed off relief.[54]

Second, the actual administration of unemployment aid should remain with the provinces and municipalities. Although this recommendation would fly in the face of the NEC's final report which argued that the federal government should assume total responsibility for the jobless, it nonetheless reflected Whitton's belief (shared, as it turned out, by King as well) that a nationally-adminstered relief system could not effectively keep payments to the unemployed below regional and local wage rates.[55] In other words, a national dole would erode the work ethic.

While these two proposals would have limited Ottawa's responsibilities, Whitton's third recommendation involved an important extension of federal authority. The present unconditional block grants for relief, introduced by Bennett in 1934, should be replaced by new agreements which attached strict and comprehensive conditions to all federal aid. The goal Whitton argued, was to "make it certain that those unemployed...will move into employment as rapidly as employment opportunities offer."

To insure this would take place, she recommended surrounding local administration of relief with close federal supervision to guarantee that work was kept more attractive than the dole. The new relief agreements, Whitton argued, should contain provincial "standards of eligibility"; a "limitation of shelter allowanes to a definite relationship with assessments"; and procedures for maintaining a "running record of earnings" of those on relief in order to "facilitate the acceptance of casual employment" through quick "cancellation of aid." In addition, there should be reports on "schedules of allowances, costs of living and average earnings of unskilled workers" as well as on those "in receipt of Aid continuously for twelve months"; and above all, constant "investigation into the circumstances of individual relief recipients."

But while all these recommendations called for increased standardization of unemployment aid across the country, in one crucial area flexibility would remain. The new relief agreements, Whitton stressed, should enforce "the principle of maintenance of incentive to accept employment by relating the *maximum* Aid to actual earnings of unskilled labour in each centre or regional division."[56] There was to be no "national minimum." The goal of reforming relief was not to abolish the poor law doctrine of "less eligibility," but to make it work more effectively by removing control over relief rates from the unit of government "most susceptible to every wind of popular demand."[57]

Six months after she submitted her report, Whitton's recommendations began to take effect. In January 1938, as part of a series of cost-cutting measures designed to reduce Ottawa's expenditure on the dole, Norman Rogers, King's minister of labour, inserted into relief agreements with the provinces the new stipulation that "material aid given to any family head or individual...must be less than the normal earnings of an unskilled labourer in the district as averaged over the preceding year."[58] When CCF spokesmen denounced this change as an attempt to reduce the living standards of the unemployed, Rogers denied that the government had "in any way brought pressure to bear upon provincial governments with respect to any change in relief scales."[59] This was simply untrue. While not interested in insuring a *minimum* standard of support, the federal government was now actively enforcing a *maximum* on the level of relief provided by any community. Whitton's advice had finally triumphed at the expense of those on the dole.

Her contribution in pushing Ottawa towards a reform of relief thus sheds significant light upon some of the motivations behind the professionalization of public welfare in the 1930s. Although other social workers (such as Leonard Marsh and Harry Cassidy) were equally vigorous in their condemnation of Canada's obsolete municipal relief structure,[60] none was as successful as Whitton in seeing their suggestion translated into federal policy during the Depression.

Whitton's influence stemmed not simply from her reputation, her expertise, or her position as head of Canada's most important social work federation, but also from the fact that she told businessmen and federal leaders what they wanted to hear. By claiming that municipal politicians were "exploit(ing) the vote of the dependent unemployed and...offer(ing) more and easier relief," she implied that Ottawa should be spending less, not more, on the dole. By arguing that 40 percent of those on relief in the West did not really need it, she hinted that efficient social administration could succeed, where economic policies had failed, in reducing the volume of the unemployed. Finally, by stressing that relief scales had to be kept below the "actual earnings of unskilled labour," Whitton, unlike some of her colleagues, never lost sight of the fact that the primary goal of public welfare in any market society is not simply to relieve human need, but to maintain the work ethic.[61]

Her reward, by the end of the Depression, was national recognition as Canada's leading social work advisor to the state on welfare policy. For her colleagues, however, this was a dubious achievement. Ultimately, the skills

Whitton made most attractive to the government were those of a profession that could limit the costs of social welfare and keep a close surveillance over the unemployed. In return for such services, social workers could expect increasing employment within a burgeoning state sector. In effect, they, not the jobless, would become the chief beneficiaries of Canada's "reformed" relief system.

NOTES

This paper has been published previously in *The Canadian Historical Review*, LXII, 2, June, 1981.

I would like to thank Veronica Strong-Boag for her helpful comments on this paper.

1. Canada, *Report of the Royal Commission on Dominion- Provincial Relations*, Book II, Ottawa, 1940, 18.
2. Dorothy King, "Unemployment Aid (Direct Relief)," in L. Richter, ed., *Canada's Unemployment Problem*, Toronto, 1939, 94-5.
3. Ibid. For recent versions of this argument see Linda Grayson and Michael Bliss, eds., *The Wretched of Canada: Letters to R.B.Bennett 1930-35*, Toronto, 1971, x, xii, xvi, xxi; or H. Blair Neatby, *The Politics of Chaos: Canada in the Thirties*, Toronto, 1972, 25-7.
4. The phrase is from an article on Whitton in *Canadian Welfare*, XVIII, 7, Jan. 1942.
5. Particularly through the development of mothers' allowance and minimum wage commissions and systematic child welfare surveys in the 1920s. On these developments see Veronica Strong-Boag, "Wages for Housework: Mothers' Allowances and the Beginnings of Social Security in Canada," *Journal of Canadian Studies*, XIV, 1, Spring 1979, and by the same author, "The Girl of the New Day: Canadian Working Women in the 1920s," *Labour/Le Travailleur*, IV, 4, 1979.
6. Ontario, *Report of the Ontario Royal Commission on Public Welfare*, Toronto, 1939, 6. In 1929 there were 100 openings for every 30 graduates from Canada's two schools of social work. James Pitsula, "The Emergence of Social Work in Toronto," *Journal of Canadian Studies*, XIV, 1 spring 1979, 41.
7. Canadian Council on Social Development Papers, Public Archives of Canada (CCSD), 25, "Retrospects and Prospects: Canadian Council on Child and Family Welfare, 1922-1935," 5-7. See also Kenneth Bryden, *Old Age Pensions and Policy-Making in Canada*, Montreal, 1974, 84; Veronica Strong-Boag, "Wages for Housework," 27-8; and Peter Oliver, *G. Howard Ferguson: Ontario Tory*, Toronto, 1977, chaps. 11 and 15.
8. Roy Lubove, *The Professional Altruist: The Emergence of Social Work as a Career*, 1880-1930, Cambridge, 1965, 53-4.
9. Canada, House of Commons, Debates, 11 Sept. 1930, 174.
10. Harry Cassidy, *Unemployment and Relief in Ontario, 1929-1932*, Toronto, 1932, 91-2. Canada, *Report of the Dominion Commissioner of Unemployment Relief*, 30 March

1935, 33. It should be noted that the federal government itself spent only $43,000 of its first relief grant on administrative expenses. Ibid, 47.

11. Canada, House of Commons, *Debate*, 11 Sept. 1930, 91; 12 Sept. 1930, 174.

12. CCSD Papers, vol. 14, file 68, J.S. Driscoll to Charlotte Whitton, 8 Jan. 1932.

13. King, "Unemployment Aid (Direct Relief)", 89.

14. Cassidy, *Unemployment and Relief in Ontario*, 202-11, 256.

15. Ibid, 276-89.

16. Bennett Papers, PAC, vol. 706, "Summary of the Proceedings of the Second Bilingual Conference on Family and Child Welfare," Montreal, April 1932.

17. *Canadian Welfare*, XVII, 7, Jan. 1942, 1. Whitton's pre-eminence was revealed when she became one of seven Canadian women to receive a CBE upon the resumption of the Crown's Honour List in Canada in 1934. See *Child and Family Welfare*, IX, 5, Jan. 1934.

18. Phyllis Harrison, "In the Beginning Was Charlotte..." *Canadian Welfare*, LI, 2, 1975, 14-15; *Canadian Welfare*, XVII, 7, Jan. 1942, 1-3.

19. See her comments in "Retrospects and Prospects: Canadian Council on Child and Family Welfare, 1922-1935," 5-7, CCSD Papers, vol. 25, and Pitsula, "The Emergence of Social Work in Toronto," 41.

20. Bennett Papers, vol. 798, memo from Whitton to Bennett on the "Distribution of Unemployment Relief," 9 April 1932. See also vol. 706, Whitton to Bennett, 18 April 1932.

21. See for example, the complaint of Whitton's colleague Dorothy King that "Few of those employed have had training in social welfare administration...In the administration of unemployment aid, in, for example, Northern Alberta, the Royal Canadian Mounted Police are the agents; in other provinces, Provincial and City Police, Public Health Nurses and officers of the Children's Aid Society have been pressed into investigation services. 'White collared' and other unemployed, have been used freely, the general supervision being usually assigned to officers of the municipal or provincial government, whose previous experience has been in other fields." King, "Unemployment Aid (Direct Relief)," 94-5. On Whitton's fears for her profession see CCSD Papers, vol. 25, "Retrospects and Prospects; Canadian Council on Child and Family Welfare, 1922-1935" (nd (c April 1931); vol. 21, file 85, Whitton to CCC & FW Board of Governors, 6 May 1931; and memorandum by Whitton to Canadian Chamber of Commerce, 31 Aug. 1932, on "Public Welfare in Canada."

22. Bennett Papers, vols. 779-780, "Report re Unemployment and Relief in Western Canada, Summer 1932," 478107-9.

23. Ibid, vol. 789, Bennett to W.F. Nickle, 26 April 1932; Nickel to Bennett, 3 May 1932; ibid, vol 706, Bennett to Charlotte Whitton, 26 April 1932; Whitton to Bennett, 31 May 1932.

24. Ibid, vols. 779-80, "Report re Unemployment and Relief in Western Canada," 478800-1, 478928-30.

25. Ibid, 478093-9, 478105, 478823, 478858-9.

26. Ibid, 478946-7, 4788812.

27. Ibid, vol. 706, Whitton to Bennett, 16 June 1932.

28. Ibid, vols. 779-80, "Report re Unemployment and Relief in Western Canada," 478125-8, 478848.

29. Ibid, 478848-55, 478812.

30. Ibid, vol. 706, Bennett to J.T.M. Anderson, 4 June 1932.

31. *Census of Canada*, 1931, vol. XIII, "Monograph on Unemployment," 374;

Canada, Department of Labour, *Report of the Dominion Commissioner of Unemployment Relief*, 30 March 1935, 52.

32. Bennett Papers, vol. 561, "Minutes of the Dominion-Provincial Conference, 17-19 January 1933," 346894-955.

33. Ibid, vol. 566, Bennett to the four western premiers, 9 March 1933.

34. CCSD Papers, vol. 15, file 68, Whitton to A.A. Mackenzie, 4 Jan. 1934; Bennett Papers, vol. 798, Charlotte Whitton, "The Essential of a Relief Programme for Canada, 1934-35," 19 Jan. 1934.

35. See, for example, "Problems in the Social Administration of General and Unemployment Relief," the discussion and findings of a conference on this subject, called at Ottawa from May 1-4th 1933, under the auspices of the Canadian Council on Child and Family Welfare, reprinted in *Child and Family Welfare*, IX, 1, May 1933. Disagreement was particularly sharp over the issue of unemployment insurance. Harry Cassidy and Leonard Marsh insisted it could relieve "the major part of distress occasioned by unemployment," while Whitton maintained that any "actuarially sound" scheme would only absorb the "smaller part" of any future relief load. See Whitton, "The Essential of a Relief Programme for Canada, 1934-35," and the criticisms of it by Cassidy and Marsh in CCSD Papers, col. 16, Leonard Marsh to Whitton, 13 Feb. 1934.

36. Harry Cassidy, "Is Unemployment Relief Enough?" *Canadian Forum*, Jan. 1934; CCSD Papers, vol. 16, Leonard Marsh to Whitton, 13 Feb. 1934.

37. Bennett Papers, vol. 804, Charlotte Whitton, "The Challenge for Relief Control," March 1934.

38. CCSD Papers, vol. 16, file 68, A. MacNamara to Whitton, 5 Feb. 1934.

39. Whitton, "The Challenge for Relief Control."

40. The first suggestion that Ottawa would withdraw from relief was a warning by W.A. Gordon to the premiers at the January 1934 dominion-provincial conference. Subsequently, Gordon was forced to back away from his proposed June 15th cut-off date because of severe pressure from the premiers and from within his own party. For further details on this episode see my "No Fault of Their Own: Unemployment and the Canadian Welfare State, 1914-1941" (unpublished Phd thesis, University of Toronto, 1979), chap. 6 The percentage cut in Ottawa's relief spending is calculated from the *Report of the Dominion Commissioner of Unemployment Relief*, 30 March 1935, 5-6, 34; and ibid, 31 March 1936, 36.

41. Bennett Papers, vol. 182, "Minutes of the Dominion-Provincial Conference," 31 July 1934.

42. Ibid.

43. Ibid, vol. 182, Bennett to Jimmy Stitt, 30 July 1934.

44. CCSD Papers, vol. 15, file 68, Whitton to W.H. Lovering, 1 Aug. 1934.

45. Much to the chagrin of one of the consulting actuaries who worked on the bill. See Department of Insurance Records, PSC, vol. 1, "Actuarial Report" by H.H. Wolfenden, 1 Feb. 1935.

46. In this endeavour, Whitton had a well-placed ally. Wendall Clarke, secretary of the Canadian Chamber of Commerce, was also a member of the CCC & FW governing board. As early as 1932 Clarke had suggested to Whitton the "need for a more intimate tie-up with the business interests in this very important work of yours" since "the importance of Social Service (was) growing increasingly in Canada." CCSD Papers, vol 21, file 85, W. Clarke to Whitton, 14 March 1932.

47. See for example, John Taylor, "Urban Social Organization and Urban Discontent: the 1930s," in David Bercuson, ed., *Western Perspectives I*, Toronto, 1974, 33.

48. CCSD Papers, vol. 15, Charlotte Whitton, "The Relief Outlook in Canada," Dec. 1934.

49. Bennett Papers, vol. 812, letter and memo from Wendall Clarke, secretary to the Canadian Chamber of Commerce, to all members of Parliament, 13 April 1935. See also vol. 790, resolution forwarded to Bennett by the Ontario Associated Boards of Trade and Chambers of Commerce, 14 Jan. 1935, urging the same policy in almost identical language.

50. Department of Labour Records, PAC, acc 70/382, vol 60, copy of the National Employment Commission Act, 1 Ed. VIII, C 7, 47-50, 8 April 1936.

51. King Diary, PAC, 8 April 1936.

52. Department of Labour Records, NEC files, vol. 66, Charlotte Whitton to Harry Baldwin, 22 July 1936.

53. Ibid, NEC files, vol. 66, Charlotte Whitton to Tom Moore, 24 July, 1937, See also her article, "The Relief of Unemployment," in *Child and Family Welfare*, May 1936.

54. National Employment Commission, *Interim Report*, Ottawa, 1937, 15-16.

55. Ibid. A position Whitton made quite explicit in her criticisms of the Rowell-Sirois Report's recommendation that Ottawa should administer unemployment aid itself. "I am...appalled," she wrote to Harry Cassidy, "to find that plans apparently contemplate the actual setting up of staff and budgets and the actual administration of aid in cash or in kind - I presume the former - right across Canada in city, rural, mining and widely differing areas. Mr. MacNamara and I have both been telling them that a Dominion power will not be able to pay $27.00 in Saint John, $13.00 in a nearby town, $40.00 in Calgary, and $45.00 in Winnipeg; that these differentials must be left to local authority." CCSD Papers, vol.99. file 179, Whitton to Cassidy, 16 Dec. 1940.

56. NEC *Interim Report*, 16-17 (my emphasis).

57. Department of Labour, NEC files, vol. 75, memo by Whitton on "The Organization of Aid to Persons in Distress," March 1937. See also her article on "The Relief of Unemployment."

58. Norman Rogers Papers, Queen's University Archives, 28 April 1938, 2379.

59. Canada, House of Commons, *Debates*, 28 April 1938, 2379.

60. See for example, Harry Cassidy, *Unemployment and Relief in Ontario, 1929-1932*, Toronto, 1932; Leonard Marsh, *Health and Unemployment*, Montreal, 1938; or the collection of essays in L. Richter, ed., *Canada's Unemployment Problem*, Toronto, 1939.

61. A theme elaborated eloquently in Frances Fox Piven and Richard A. Cloward, *Regulating the Poor: the Functions of Public Welfare*, New York, 1971.

"Lord Give Us Men": Women and Social Work in English Canada, 1918 to 1953

James Struthers

Over the past decade, Canadian social workers have been confronted with an embarrassing paradox. Although women pioneered the profession's development in this country, as elsewhere, and today comprise almost 60 percent of those working in the field, men disproportionately occupy its key teaching and administrative positions and earn substantially higher salaries for similar work. As a recent study of seventeen hundred social service positions in the Atlantic region pointed out, two-thirds of those earning less than $15,000 per year in social work were women; an almost identical proportion of those earning more than this figure were men. In the two highest income quintiles in social work (over $20,000 per year), men outnumbered women by a proportion of more than three to one. When education, experience and type of work are held constant, men still earned higher salaries in 91 percent of all job categories it was possible to compare. Nor is this sexual disparity confined to the Atlantic region. Similar studies of men and women in social work in Ontario specifically, Canada generally, and the United States conducted during the 1970s reveal an identical pattern.[1] Although the profession has prided itself, historically, on its role as a vehicle for social change, the sexual division of labour within social work mirrors rather than challenges the job ghettoization and power and income disparities which surround women's work in the larger society.

This paper examines the historical origins of sexual inequality within Canadian social work. Why, in the crucial years between 1918 and the early 1950's, when social work first evolved as a paid career, did women, although numerically dominant within the profession, fail to capture its key administrative positions? How did women in the profession view the place of women within Canadian society as a whole? Finally, to what extent are these two questions related? In other words, to what extent was women's role within social work constrained by their view of women outside of it?

In 1947, Charlotte Whitton, six years into retirement from her pioneering career as head of the Canadian Welfare Council between 1920 and 1941, set out to expose the issue of sexual discrimination in Canada in an article for *Macleans* magazine entitled "The Exploited Sex". After systematically documenting gross salary and administrative inequalities for women in nursing and teaching, Whitton turned her wrath to social work, the other key female-dominated helping profession to which, up to that point, she had devoted the bulk of her working life. Social work, Whitton claimed, although one of the newest professions, was perhaps the "most...discriminatory" of them all:

> In the early twenties and on into the thirties, as it struggled along, it was overwhelmingly a woman's field, still is largely so, but the boys have discovered it now, especially its enlarging administrative and executive opportunities, and they have come, some transferring from Arts or theology courses, more from other occupations, especially the "good mixers" and "good contact men". The few real male topnotchers in the profession will volunteer chivalrously and truthfully, that there are ten excellent, competent women to every one qualified male worker in the field...But... notorious preferment to executive posts is going weekly to young, inexperienced men...over experienced competent women. Some of the older and mature male executives have fought valiantly for the advancement of women with whom they have worked, but with little success, and all across Canada, and particularly in government service, men with little or immature training or experience in the field are being put into major welfare posts.[2]

Whitton's revelations, although perhaps startling to the general public, were no surprise to the hundreds of unmarried career women like herself who had dedicated their lives to developing social work as a professional occupation in Canada in the years following World War I. Complaints about abysmally low pay for women and preferential treatment for males, although by no means frequent, existed as an undercurrent of anger and frustation throughout the profession's formative years in the 1920s. Because social workers did not "strike for shorter hours and higher salaries for themselves," Kate MacPherson, a Toronto caseworker for the Neighbourhood Workers Association pointed out in a 1920 article, the "business world hears and knows comparatively little about them." As a result, the "stigma of overwork and underpay" was "especially odious" in the profession. Church deaconesses, she argued, were sacrificing the "flower of their youth...[for]...$15 monthly with board and room provided." A trained, experienced, caseworker was "offered $60 a month for a position which would claim her whole time for seven days a week." To MacPherson, the lesson was obvious. "The time is ripe," she concluded, "for dispossessing our minds of the old pharisaical, hypocritical notion that such work should be undertaken for the love of it, and not for the remuneration, that a pittance just sufficient to keep soul and body together, to be received with humble gratitude, is the correct financial treatment of those engaged in it."[3]

Nine years later, although salaries for trained caseworkers had improved somewhat, women's relative position in the profession had not.

"Equal pay for equal work," a special Ottawa conference on social work pointed out in 1929 "is a principle which is recognized but not practiced." According to conference delegates, the reason was that "often the same salary which will attract superior women will interest only mediocre men."[4]

Mediocrity did not stop men's rise to the key administrative positions within the profession, however. Even the "most cursory survey of field of social work," Lyra Taylor, a district secretary of Montreal's Family Welfare Association pointed out in 1930, revealed that "the really trained and experienced women workers greatly outnumber the men." Despite the fact, Taylor argued that there was a "strong prejudice against allowing women to occupy the highest executive positions in the family social work field...[M]any women in family case-work...who are adequately equipped, well-trained, and sufficiently experienced, work under the direction of men executives whose experience equipment hardly makes up for their obvious lacks in education...vocation, and personality." It was a situation which called for "much forbearance on the part of the family case-worker," Taylor concluded. "She must, day by day, work to improve the casework standards of her organization and be content to see the man executive get all the credit, and, in addition, to see him draw a salary two or three times as large as her own."[5]

As these articles reveal, women in Canadian social work were aware of and angry about their low salaries and unequal authority compared to men, long before Whitton's revelations of the 1940s, let alone the more recent upsurge of concern in the 1970s. What is less clear is why a pattern of male dominance emerged so early within the profession when women constituted over two-thirds of all social welfare workers in Canada before 1941 and over 84 percent of the professionally trained membership.[6]

Two of the most important sources of low pay for women social workers were external to the profession itself. Excluded in large part from the male-dominated fields of business, government, and the liberal professions, a new generation of college-educated, middle class women, after the turn of the century, provided a large pool of available labour for emerging fields such as nursing, teaching, and library and social work. In the years following World War I, moreover, the supply problem was complicated by the death of so many Canadian men in that conflict. Countless of her colleagues, Charlotte Whitton pointed out in 1937, "who in the normal life of their generation would have been the heads of families and occupied in their home life" instead found themselves forced to "live their lives on a permanent basis of self-support...because...the husbands with whom they would have built homes were many years dead on the...fields of battle."[7] The availability of this pool of low cost labour was undoubtedly one incentive for governments and private charities to expand low-paying employment in the social sector in the years before World War II. As the 1929 Ottawa conference on social work observed, low salaries in the field could still, after all, attract "superior women."

Additionally, although trained women caseworkers were in short supply throughout the entire interwar era, governments and charitable organizations were by no means easily convinced that the most costly skills they had to offer were either desirable or necessary. In this sense, women in social work faced even a greater disadvantage than their counterparts in nursing and teaching, where skills were older, more easily identifiable, and practiced on a far wider scale.[8] As a result, by far the greatest amount of energy expended by women in social work to expand their own status and income between the wars took the form of attempting to demonstrate to skeptical male authorities that the profession did, in fact, possess a body of recognizable, scientific skills that took years of education, training, and experience to acquire. Lyra Taylor accurately pinpointed this problem in 1930:

> We still have with us the occasional board member who feels that a family case-worker need not be highly educated and specially trained for the job. He thinks there is nothing the family case-worker does which could not be equally well done, say, by one of his smartest stenographers. We still also have with us, in the ranks of the professional social workers themselves, the man who, in his in-most heart (although he is fast becoming afraid to voice the opinion) really thinks that the job of the family case-worker could best of all be done by some nice, sensible, motherly woman. Such a man views only with apprehension the fast-growing number of trained, intelligent, highly-equipped women who are definitely choosing social work as a profession, and who feel that no sacrifice which they make in order to add to their professional equipment is too great for the demands that their work makes.[9]

Throughout most of the 1920s and 30s, professional mobility for these women that Taylor described primarily took the form of displacing, not men, but rather other unpaid, volunteer married women working in the nation's private charities and welfare institutions. It was to this end that Charlotte Whitton, from her posiiton as executive secretary of the Canadian Council on Child and Family Welfare, dedicated with such zeal her famous social surveys of the 1920's and 30's. By ruthlessly exposing and holding up to ridicule the "amateurish" and "overly sentimental" activities of a previous generation of unpaid women volunteers, Whitton and her colleagues were able to justify the creation of paid casework positions for a newly emerging cadre of professional women social workers, in many cases hand-picked by Whitton herself.[10]

Apart from these external problems of supply and skill recognition, women's advancement in social work was also handicapped by what Dr. Helen Reid, director of the federal government's Division of Child Welfare, referred to as a "tremendous turnover" of "constantly disappearing staff."[11] Part of this problem of rapid turnover within social work, which later surveys between 1948 and 1953 put at 16 percent of all positions per year, was a result of low salaries, as workers drifted quickly into other jobs within and outside of the profession in search of better pay or more responsibility. A large part, however, was also due to marriage. Social work was, above all, a career for single women. Employment for married women within the profession, as within most other lines of women's work in Canada before World War II, was extremely rare, so rare in fact, that a 1930 article in *Social Welfare* on "Married Women in the Profession" simply assumed that "bereavement" was the only reason for married women to work in the field. A survey of 478 women graduates of the University of Toronto's School of Social Science between 1914 and 1938, confirmed this point. One hundred and twenty-one or 25.3 percent of the graduates, the survey revealed, had since married and only six of those women remained in social work. A later, more comprehensive survey of almost four thousand positions in Canadian social welfare in 1953 discovered that 22 percent of all women in the field resigned their positions each year. The reason in 41 percent of these cases was marriage.[12] This pattern of career disruption due to marriage clearly played some role in preventing women's advancement into greater executive responsiblity within the ranks of Canadian social work.

By far the most significant constraint shaping women's career patterns within social work, however, was the sex-typing or sexual division of labour that was built into the profession from its origins. Eli Zaretsky, in a seminal article on "The Place of the Family in the Origins of the Welfare State", has explained the roots of this dilemma. "The central problem that all tendencies of the [first] women's movement faced," Zaretsky points out, "was that of reconciling the spread of the marketplace, with its emphasis on individualism and competition, with the traditional values of 'women's sphere' - benevolence and selfless nurturance." One way in which the first generation of college-educated women tried to do this was by "search[ing] for a politics that could combine wage labour and economic independence, especially for middle class women, with state protection of the family, especially among the poor."[13]

Through asserting a need for the protection of the working class family, and particularly of mothers and children within it, middle-class, college-educated single women could define a professional field for themselves, linked closely to women's traditional nurturing identity. To the extent, then, that the rise of social work in the early twentieth century was linked to the protection of the family, and particularly women's traditional role within it, the sex-typing of women by profession, and the sex-typing of women in the profession, was assured.

The result was a paradox. Although composed primarily of career-oriented single women, social work as a profession, in the years following World War I, could not view the role of women in Canadian society outside of the constricting framework of motherhood. From the 1920s until the 1940s, keeping women in the home, as part of its crusade to reduce infant mortality and to enhance family life, became a principal objective of the profession. "The fundamental need...of every family," professional spokes-persons argued in the 1920s, was "a mother who can be with her children until they reach maturity."[14] Twenty years later, even as tens of thousands of married women began entering the workforce under the impetus of World War II, the essential message of social work remained unchanged. The working mother was a "threat to the stability of the home." Instead, her true "patriotic duty", women in the profession argued, was to "see to the security and safety of her young before embarking on any enterprise which takes her from the home." Women who had worked during the war, and thus learned to "make all the decisions while the husband was away," were advised during the reconstruction period, to "learn to share responsibility, to make a place for him and to help him recover his role as head of the family."[15]

Within the family, women's role was viewed by the profession in equally traditional terms. The mother was the "constant companion of her children and the central figure in every family group," Dr. Janet Long of the Canadian Welfare Council remarked in 1940, "who cares for every need of her infant, growing children, and husband."[16] If the family was in trouble, chances were high that the mother was at fault. Often, sheer "ignorance and apathy on the part of the mothers themselves" was a principal cause of infant death. At the other extreme, a "mother's love, if...not controlled by insight," women in the profession warned, could "become a cloak for the most intense selfishness" that could destroy a child's happiness in adult life.[17] More typically, a mother's inability to manage her household properly was a continual source of family breakdown, as Malca Friedman, a Montreal social worker related in one case study of "Behaviour Problems" within the family.

> Sammy's father works hard in an iron foundry at some distance from his home. After the heat, the noise, the physical strain and mental tension, he craves at the day's end a restful home atmosphere which Sammy's mother has not been able to create. She also lacks the ability to buy or prepare food economically, or to make her husband's hard-earned wages meet the needs of the family, It is not difficult, then, to know why Sammy's father sometimes abuses his wife, and has at times deserted his family, even if his actions are not entirely justified.

Here was a woman who needed to be "taught to buy and prepare food carefully and [to] keep her home clean and inviting," Friedman concluded.[18] "If a housekeeper cannot be thrifty with $18.00 a week, why give her $25.00 a week to mismanage," Jean Walker of Toronto's Big Sister Association pointed out in putting forward the social work case against family allowances in the 1920s. "Why not give her instead a home economist... who will take the drudgery out of her life?"[19]

Anxious to bolster the family and women's traditional role within it as a means of defining a field for their own casework intervention, women in social work, ironically, themselves became vulnerable to a similar form of sex-typing which ghettoized their sphere of influence within the profession. "The natural born social worker," leading American social work educator Frank Bruno pointed out in a 1930 article in Social Welfare, "[is] usually...a young woman who shows from the first day of her work...an almost uncanny intuition in choice of method of approach to a client or community problem."[20] Ethel Dodds Parker, one of the most prominent women in the Canadian profession agreed. "Social work with families is more successfully carried out by a woman," she wrote in her 1939 survey of welfare services in Moncton:

> The essential element in the budget of a [social] Service Bureau is not material aid, but qualified, understanding staff....A woman, with the discerning mind and understanding heart, which good personal service demands, must possess the natural gift of arousing and encouraging the confidence of men and women.[21]

Why were women more likely than men to possess this "natural gift" of encouraging confidence in their clients? Insofar as casework within family agencies focused primarily on the mother, women social workers were assumed to possess a more likely bond of rapport with this key element of the family. The successful caseworker, according to Vera Moberly, a Toronto Children's Aid Society supervisor, had to be "well-trained in child care;" she had to "have a knowledge of health needs" as well as the ability to "help the...mother with housekeeping problems and budgeting to be sure that the family are getting...well balanced meals." Women, it was assumed, were more likely than men to possess such knowledge. As a consequence, they would be able, on their first visits, to "engage the interest of...[the] mother," and "gradually...as the mother talks about her own family, her children, her husband, her difficulties [and] her neighbours," Moberly continued, "...her habits, housekeeping ability and personality will be evident and so the worker will learn the heart of the home."[22]

Beyond their "uncanny intuition," "understanding hearts," and natural bond of rapport with working-class mothers, women were deemed particularly suited for social work for one other reason. As single career women without a family, they more than men, it was widely assumed, were willing to work primarily for love, not money. Today's professional social worker, Stuart Jaffray, director of the University of Toronto's School of Social Work, told the readers of Saturday Night in 1942,

> increasingly is a young woman who has prepared for her profession and loves it, who works long hours for too low a salary, but who reaps deep satisfaction from an intensely human job well-done.... Her interest in humankind is fundamental.[23]

Women social workers in the interwar years agreed that a spirit of self-sacrifice was essential equipment for the profession. "One who selects a profession like social casework must live a large part of her life through the lives of others," Bertha Reynolds, the great American social work educator told the readers of *Child and Family Welfare* in the 1930s.[24] "Life is under no bond whatever to give her happiness," Lyra Taylor pointed out in the same decade. "Indeed as she looks at her clients' problems, life must sometimes seem a clever invention for causing pain. But these same clients are the only reason she knows of for her existence and certainly the only reason for her work."[25] Alluding to the impact of World War I in thwarting many in her generation's hopes for family life, Charlotte Whitton made a similar point in 1944: "many a woman preferred to go proudly unwedded, dedicated to throwing into her life's work, the strength, affection, and inspiration laid away with shattered dreams."[26] Although insisting that university education and extensive training in casework skills were essential prerequisites for the practice of social work, leading spokespersons for the profession in the interwar years were still convinced that women, as in the nineteenth century, by reason of natural aptitude, personality and a sense of vocation, were best fitted for social work.

What about men? Here too sex-typing was equally prevalent. If women were suited by temperament and experience for family casework, then the proper sphere for men in the profession, apart from working with delinquent boys in juvenile and probation work, was administration. This was held to be the case for a variety of reasons. First, precisely because many people both within and outside of social work agreed with Charlotte Whitton's 1944 observation that women were "on the whole more sensitive souls, naturally more finely attuned to the sharp twinge of conscience...than men,"[27] they could not be trusted to administer efficiently and economically the large sums of money granted to private charities and government relief agencies. Margaret Gould, director of Toronto's Child Welfare Council in the 1930s, and one of the leading radicals in the profession, illustrated this point well in relating a 1934 conversation she had with one government official as to why more social workers were not appointed to administer public relief:

> He looked at me quizzically and said, 'I wouldn't trust social workers with the big job of administering large sums of money. After all, who are social workers but the old set of "uplifters" in modern dress? They are theoretical, impractical, sentimental, with expensive ideas.'

Gould recounted that she "tried hard to explain that the modern social worker is a different species from the old-time 'uplifter'...[with]...knowledge and training which makes her different."[28] The official remained unconvinced, however.

His skepticism was hardly surprising since even within the profession it was widely assumed that women lacked essential administrative skills.

"Business administration is foreign to the tasks of the average social worker," one anonymous contributor to Social Welfare pointed out in 1928,

> and therefore in a vast number of cases is done very badly by executives and department heads in social agencies...This feeling of inadequacy in business administration is shared by most women's boards and leads then to appoint a male "Advisory Board" and then to refuse recognition to their paid executive at their meetings.[29]

Where women did form a majority on an advisory board, their advice was often distrusted precisely because of their sex. In the spring of 1936 Harry Cassidy, Director of Social Welfare for British Columbia, successfully pushed through an amendment to the province's Mothers' Allowance Act stipulating that a majority of its five person advisory board should be women. Cassidy claimed he was acting in order to "satisfy women's organizations,"[30] but his reward for this experiment in positive discrimination was a sharp blast from none other than Charlotte Whitton. "I tell you, you will be a sorry boy if an advisory board composed chiefly of women — and I think I know who some of them will be — set out to exercise as much power as they really have under...[this]...statute," she warned the British Columbia director. If the administration of Mothers' Allowance was shaped primarily by women's organizations rather than trained professionals, the act would soon be "wide-open to...abuse and deterioration" as a result of emotional decision-making. "I would be willing to take a bet that within a year the majority of the women on your Board will force the inclusion of certain cases," Whitton argued. Instead, such a board should be composed of the "five best people you can get in British Columbia in this field" and Whitton confessed she did "not think they would [be women]."[31] It was perhaps in part to counter her own fears as well as the widespread stereotype that women were "overly sentimental" and therefore "poor administrators", which led the CWC director to drive home so ruthlessly the need for economy and efficiency in relief administration to both the Bennett and King governments during the 1930's.[32]

By far the most flagrant example of women within social work being sex-typed as untrustworthy administrators, occurred within Ottawa's Public Welfare Board in 1936. From 1933 onwards, Ottawa had been one of the few Canadian cities to employ professionally trained social workers in the distribution of public relief and, in consequence, the city dispensed a scale of aid that was relatively generous by provincial standards. Complaints had been growing within the local press and on city council against the steadily rising cost of the dole and a federal relief cutback in the spring of 1936 brought the whole issue to a head. In order to make up the difference, the city was forced to hike property taxes stiffly. The result was an immediate backlash against the city's new Welfare Board. Social service was an "evil", one city controller charged, that was "creeping into the

Public Welfare Board which had been appointed to administer relief, not to build up a body of social workers." The local press agreed. Social workers in the Welfare Board, the *Ottawa Citizen* pointed out, had tended "to treat those on relief as chronic help-receivers, as public charges and as a class apart [which] leads on the one hand to a recognition of a class of professional relief beneficiaries and on the other, to a class of professional social workers whose career is to treat the unfortunate according to well-defined principles."[33]

Forty women social workers, employed by the Public Welfare Board, became the scapegoats of this attack. Over the course of the summer, in response to these criticisms, they were fired by the Ottawa city council and eleven male "detectives" were installed in their place to reinvestigate the Board's caseloads and to root out chisellers. "Women were good for social service," Ottawa's mayor pointed out in justifying this move, but it was the city's intention to "divorce direct relief from social service...The men investigators did better work than women; they were not interested in social service but in seeing that those on relief gave the city the right information and reported their earnings."[34]

This purge sent shock waves throughout the ranks of Canadian social work. Bessie Touzel, staff supervisor of the Welfare Board and the person most responsible for building up its professional staff, resigned in protest against the arbitrary dismissal of her female colleagues and the destruction of relief policies she had worked so hard to establish. Her resignation and the dismissals became, briefly, a *cause célèbre* within Canadian social work.

What is significant about the profession's response to these firings is that the sex-typing issue — that is, the assumption that women were too "service-oriented" and therefore poor administrators — was ignored almost entirely. Touzel herself, commenting on the events in *The Social Worker*, simply claimed that the whole question of "whether male or female investigation is preferable" had been "misunderstood". The fundamental issue, she argued, was that "employees who had given service of good quality were being dismissed without any adequate examination of...their work."[35] Other commentary within the profession took a similar position of ignoring the sex-typing issue entirely. Instead, letters to the editor of *The Social Worker* either focussed on the question of wrongful dismissal, claimed that Ottawa's relief expenditures were not that high, or argued that the stress on relief chiselling was false economy.

To those within Canadian social work, the fundamental principle at stake in the firings of Ottawa's forty women social workers was not sexism, but professionalism. What angered Touzel and her colleagues was not that women were being replaced by men, but rather that trained caseworkers were being replaced by untrained detectives. To Ottawa's press and city council, however, it was precisely the "feminine" nature of social work that made it suspect in the first place, particularly where public money was concerned.

Once the entire public welfare field began to expand enormously in the 1930s and 40s, one fact became clear. Unless trained men could somehow be attracted into social work, its future prospects for professional recognition and acceptance within the emerging public welfare sector remained bleak. As a result, luring men into social work became one of the profession's key priorities during the 1930s and 40s in order to enhance its prestige and general salary level. "Qualified men are even more urgently needed than women," a University of Toronto School of Social Service recruiting pamphlet pointed out in 1930, and those who showed competence could "anticipate rapid advancement to executive posts carrying salaries... rang[ing] from $2400 to $5000 per annum or more". Although the field had been "looked upon as peculiarly a woman's preserve," the pamphlet conceded, social work nevertheless contained many positions that "offer[ed] scope for activity quite sufficient to satisfy masculine ideas of dignity and difficulty in work."[36]

To drive home this point, others in the profession urged that the period of social work training be lengthened. "In order to bring in enough young men...of the right type," Ethel Parker argued in 1928,

> we may have to batter at the doors of our universities and insist upon a graduate course in social work. There is no lack of fine young men starting long courses in medicine, engineering and law. The very length and thoroughness of these courses is a challenge to them. Our shorter courses...will probably always exist, but for executive, administrative, and research work, we need a higher type of education and special training than is available.[37]

Once the Depression struck, Charlotte Whitton hit upon an even quicker strategy. Why not simply recruit unemployed male professionals and businessmen directly from other fields? With the Depression now in its fourth year, she told the Toronto branch of the Canadian Association of Social Workers in 1934.

> the task becomes one of a businesslike organization of relief.... Excellent staff officers are emerging from the ranks of businessmen; engineers, and other professions are giving fine leadership and will soon take their place with us as social work leaders....I say: "Lord give us men." Speaking absolutely professionally, there are administrative problems which are by their weight beyond the nervous capacity of the average woman to carry for a long time.[38]

Ironically, five years later Whitton herself, on the verge of a nervous breakdown, would be asked to step down as executive secretary of the Canadian Welfare Council by its president, Southam publishing magnate, Philip Fisher, in favour of a man. "The question of finance and routine administration must drive you to distraction," George Davidson, her eventual successor, wrote to her in conveying Fisher's suggestion:

You are not by any means the easiest person in the world to work with and I think that that may be influencing Fisher in his suggestions in regard to a man rather than a woman [as your replacement]... as he seemed to have in the back of his mind...that he could not think of any woman...who could maintain, in such a delicate position, a satisfactory working relationship with you.[39]

Throughout the 1930s and 40s, recruiting pamphlets published by the University of Toronto School of Social Work, and the CASW, continued to stress the need for males within the administrative hierarchy of the profession. As one 1938 CASW pamphlet pointed out,

the opportunities for men who take up social work as a profession are particularly good. They are most likely to be in demand in connection with boys' work, juvenile delinquency, hostels, prisons, relief administration...and executive positions in all parts of the social work field. Women will occupy the greater number of positions in child welfare, medical social work, and family welfare.[40]

The same recruiting pamphlets also routinely noted in passing that while women in the profession could make a maximum of $3000 a year, "men may receive more, especially in...a few executive positions where their salaries will range up to... $5000 and $6000 annually."[41]

This strategy of upgrading the profession by attracting more trained males into its administrative ranks was only marginally successful. Until the late 1940s, women overwhelmingly comprised the bulk of graduates of Canada's schools of social work, 93 percent of the total between 1931 and 1935, 83 percent between 1940 and 1945.[42] Men did increasingly move into the field during the 1930s and 40s, and they did move into its administrative positions, particularly in the burgeoning public welfare sector. For the most part, however, they remained untrained and those men who were trained in social work did not receive any particular advantage because of it in the newly-emerging welfare state bureaucracy. "The men who openly joined our ranks and took the necessary training plus a good deal of banter from their friends," Amy Leigh, one of British Columbia's leading women social workers, observed bitterly in 1942,

are earning salaries of from $85.00 to $100.00 per month. Men who are going into the new jobs have not, generally speaking, had social work training, nor are they known as 'social workers', with the excellent result that they get quite decent salaries.[43]

A growing number of articles in social work periodicals during the 1940s on the issue of salary and job disparities within the field of social welfare bore Leigh's point out. There was a "great disparity in the salaries of men and women executives in comparable positions," the Hamilton branch of the CASW noted in 1942. In that city men in the profession were making as much as $700 per year more than women.[44] A 1946 CASW survey of personnel practices in the profession reached similar conclusions on a national scale. Although men represented only 13 percent of the CASW membership, they occupied 32 percent of the executive positions surveyed and were often receiving twice as much as women for comparable work. As the 1946 study concluded, "numerically the field continues to have more women than men but there is evidence of an unfair disadvantage to qualified women who are paid less for equal work or are sometimes excluded from administrative posts because of their sex."[45]

Even Canada's leading social welfare organizations were serious offenders. In 1944, when the position of director of family allowances within the newly formed Department of National Health and Welfare was advertised, only men were invited to apply.[46] Within the Canadian Welfare Council, sexual discrimination was openly practiced well into the 1950s, albeit in the face of growing resistance. When Bessie Touzel rejoined the Council in 1947 as assistant executive director she was informed that her position as second in command in no way implied the second highest salary in the organization. "In order to secure the services of a particular man for the staff...it might be necessary to pay [him] a larger salary than you are receiving," CWC director R.E.G. Davis told Touzel in offering her the job. However, he was sure this was a "practical problem which...you and I can work out if and when the necessity arises."[47]

Six years later, Elizabeth Govan, one of the first women in Canada to hold a Ph.D. in social service administration, proved to be less agreeable. Offered a research position within the CWC, Govan first demanded to know the salaries of men working within the Council. Arguing that she knew there was a "considerable discrepancy...between the salaries given the men on the staff and those given the women...which is not related to training, experience, or ability," Govan told Davis that it was a "matter of principle" for her to be paid on the basis of her competence, not her sex.[48]

Such forthright protests as Govan's remained the exception rather than the rule during this period, however. More typical, perhaps, was the experience of one Calgary social worker as described by CWC recreation division secretary John Farina:

> She is charming, bright, live-wire girl, full of energy...just a shade under 30 years old...She joined the staff of the Calgary Recreation Department...about 1950 and quickly moved up to the second in command position. I would say she is presently one of the most competent municipal programme directors in the country. Like so many girls, however, she will never get to be the director of recreation for the city simply because she is a girl. She has a lot more on the ball than many of the present directors and is beginning to feel a bit frustrated.[49]

The massive Department of National Health and Welfare survey of four thousand social welfare positions within Canada, conducted between 1948 and 1953, confirmed this pattern of male dominance and sexual inequality beyond a doubt. Fifty two percent of all those working in social welfare, the department discovered, had no training whatsoever. Of this total, 63 percent were men, although they represented less than half of those working in the field. On the other hand, 71 percent of all those with completed social work degrees were women. Men, nevertheless, occupied 60 percent of all administrative positions surveyed by the department.[50] As of the 1951 census, men in social work averaged $2657 annually compared to $1824 annually for women, an $800 or 30 percent differential, although there was almost no appreciable difference in average age.[51]

Within the social welfare field as a whole, the Health and Welfare survey noted, "family and child welfare paid the lowest salaries...because these two areas are largely voluntary agencies and employ the largest number of women."[52] From a slightly different perspective Albert Rose, of the University of Toronto's School of Social Work, pinpointed in 1948 why men within the profession were more likely to be found in its executive and administrative positions:

> They are very often married and have children. They cannot, literally, afford to become social work practitioners at the professional level and meet postwar costs of maintaining a family. They seek, demand, and obtain supervisory and executive or administrative posts carrying much higher salaries.[53]

By the end of the 1940s, three decades after social work first emerged as a paid career in this country, a pattern of male dominance within the profession and a sexual division of labour was firmly in place. Women, although comprising a majority within the profession and over 70 percent of all those with social work degrees, were concentrated in the low-paying practitioner sector. Men, with much less training, occupied the better-paying adminstrative positions throughout the field. In this regard, and for much the same reasons, social work merely duplicated a pattern of sexual inequality which also emerged in its sister helping professions, teaching and nursing, a pattern, indeed, which was reflected in the double ghetto of women's work within Canadian society as a whole.

The position of women within social work also contained a special irony, however. Although from the profession's earliest years as a form of paid employment in the post-World War I era, women had protested against the injustice of men, with less training, dominating the administrative hierarchy, they were, in some ways, protesting against the results of an image of women they had themselves helped to foster. Much of the drive for the professionalization of social work first emerged out of an assertion that women's special capacity for nurturing within the family had a larger role to play within society itself. Well into the 1940s, women leaders within the profession continued to insist that just as women's natural role was within the family, so too within social work were the unique characteristics of the female psyche especially suited for work with families.

At the same time, in order to attract men into social work as part of a campaign to enhance its prestige within society as a whole throughout the 1930s and 40s, women and men in the profession stressed that males were particularly needed to fill its enlarging administrative dimensions. As a consequence, employment patterns within social work simply mirrored the images of appropriate male and female spheres of work which the profession itself disseminated.

Confronted with structural barriers to equality which perhaps provided few alternative strategies for mobility, women within Canadian social work nevertheless paid a heavy price for their professionalism. By concentrating so exclusively on the advancement of their occupation in the three decades after World War I, they also remained wedded to a social work vision of women's role in society which made their own eclipse by men within the social service sector difficult to challenge.

NOTES

This paper has been published previously in *Historical Papers, Vancouver, 1983*. I would like to thank Art Kilgour for his help in researching this paper and Veronica Strong-Boag for her comments on an earlier draft.

1. Joan E. Cummings, "Sexism in Social Work: The Experience of Atlantic Social Work Women," *Atlantis*, VI, Spring, 1981, 64-5; Michael Landauer, *Social Work in Ontario: A Study for the Committee on the Healing Arts*, Toronto, 1970, 62-3; James Gripton, "Sexism in Social Work; Male Takeover of a Female Profession," *The Social Worker*, XXI, June, 1974, 80; James Grimm and Robert Stern, "Sex Roles and Internal Labor Market Structures: the 'Female' Semi-Professions," *Social Problems*, XXI, June, 1974, 701-2.

2. Public Archives of Canada (hereafter PAC), Charlotte Whitton Papers, MG 30 E256, vol. 88, copy of "But He's a Man", 1947, later retitled "The Exploited Sex."

3. Kate McPherson, "Service at Sacrifice," *Social Welfare*, June, 1920.

4. "Reports of Committees on Findings of the Special Conference on Social Work Held in Ottawa, 25-26 June 1929," *Social Welfare*, October, 1929.

5. Lyra Taylor, "Essentials in the Equipment of a Family Case-Worker," *Social Welfare*, December, 1930. For similar complaints about salary discrimination against women in the profession see University of Calgary Library, Canadian Association of Social Workers Records, vol. 18, file 18.25, Minutes of the Toronto Branch, 21 January 1931, which noted a "wide divergence...between the salary standards of men and women executives in social work". The problem, according to one woman case-worker at the meeting, was the prevalence of too many "sheltered women" on family agency governing boards who did "not know the needs of nor recognize the claims of decent salary requirements."

6. "The Employment of Social Workers in Canada," *The Social Worker*, July-August, 1953.

7. On the restricted access of women to the liberal professions see Veronica Strong-Boag, "Canada's Women Doctors: Feminism Constrained," in Linda Kealey, ed., *A Not Unreasonable Claim: Women and Reform in Canada, 1880's-1920's*, Toronto, 1979, 110; Charlotte Whitton, "In Home and Office, In Factory and Shop," *Child and Family Welfare*, XIII, November, 1937.

8. Ronald Walton, *Women in Social Work*, London, 1975, 14.

9. Taylor, "Essentials in the Equipment of a Family Case-Worker."

10. Patricia Rooke and R.L. Schnell, "Child Welfare in English Canada, 1920-1948," *Social Service Review*, September, 1981.

11. Dr. Helen Reid, "Volunteer Values", *Social Welfare*, October, 1927.

12. B.H. McKinnon, "The Married Worker in the Family Welfare Field," *Social Welfare*, June 1929; Agnes McGregor, *Training for Social Work in the Department of Social Science, University of Toronto, 1914-40*, Toronto, 1940, p. 30; PAC, Canadian Council on Social Development Records, MG 28 110, vol. 148, file 528, "Committee on Personnel in Social Work, Survey of Welfare Positions: Discussion of Implications", 15 November 1954, chapter 7.

13. Eli Zaretsky, "The Place of the Family in the Origins of the Welfare State," in Bonnie Thorne and Marilyn Yalom, eds., *Rethinking the Family: Some Feminist Questions*, New York, 1982, 211-2; Jill Conway identified the same dilemma in an earlier article. "Middle-class American women of Jane Addams' generation...had to work within the tradition which saw women as civilizing and moralizing forces in society...Yet within American society there was no naturally occurring social milieu in which these assumptions about the exclusive attributes of women could be seen for what they were. Women had to create the very institutions which were their vehicle for departure from middle-class feminine life, and in doing so they naturally duplicated existing assumptions about the sexes and their roles," See "Women Reformers and American Culture, 1870-1930," *Journal of Social History*, V, Winter, 1971-72, 174.

14. "The Canadian Mother," *Social Welfare*, May, 1923. For an excellent discussion of maternal inadequacy and the professionalism of child care in the 1920s see Veronica Strong-Boag, "Intruders in the Nursery: Childcare Professionals Reshape the Years One to Five, 1920-1940," in Joy Parr, ed., *Childhood and Family in Canadian History*, Toronto, 1982.

15. Jean Henshaw, "Child Welfare and the War," Canadian Conference on Social Work *Proceedings* (hereafter CCSW *Proceedings*), VIII, 1942. Charlotte Whitton was even more vociferous in her opposition to married women entering the labour force. In her view, the "gravest attacks upon the family" had come from the "disinclination of [middle-class] women who married to take up their traditional place and task within their homes". In Whitton's view, the "full-time gainful occupation of married women" was inevitably associated with "a decreasing birth-rate...more legal separations, looser divorce provisions...and such attempted rationalization of sexual indulgence as companionate marriage". PAC, Whitton Papers, vol. 82, "Towards a New Era in Family Life", n.d. but *circa* 1942. Concerns over married women working were not limited to conservatives in the profession. Radicals such as Bessie Touzel were also disturbed at the trend. For Touzel, equal pay for equal work was to be supported as a means of *reducing* the demand for married women workers. See Touzel, "Women in Industry," CCSW *Proceedings*, VIII, 1942.

16. Dr. Janet Long, "Maternal Health is Family Welfare," CCSW *Proceedings*, VII, 940.

17. Ibid, Helen Bott, "Child Study and Parent Education," *Social Welfare*, July, 1927.

18. Malca Friedman, "Behaviour Problems as Related to Family Rehabilitation," *Social Welfare*, April, 1927.

19. Jean Walker, "Gaps in Social Resources and Their Relation to Caseworker," *Social Welfare*, June-July, 1926.

20. Frank Bruno, "Why Have Schools of Social Work?", *Social Welfare*, November, 1930.

21. PAC, Canadian Council on Social Development Records, vol. 132, file 600, A.E. Parker, "Welfare Services in Moncton — Report 1939."

22. Vera Moberly, "Supervision," *Social Welfare*, September, 1931.

23. Stuart Jaffray, "Social Work: The Newest Profession," *Saturday Night*, July, 1942.

24. Bertha Reynolds, "Social Casework: What is It? What is its Place in the World of Today?", *Child and Family Welfare*, XI, June, 1935.

25. Lyra Taylor, "Essentials in the Equipment of a Family Case-Worker."

26. PAC, Whitton Papers, vol. 88, "Canada Looks Forward: The Place of Women," 1944.

27. Ibid, "Where Do We Go From Here", n.d. but *circa* 1944.

28. Margaret Gould, "For Whom Do Social Workers Work?", *The Social Worker*; III, November, 1934.

29. "What Should Be the Relationship Between the Board and the Staff of a Social Agency?", *Social Welfare*, July, 1928. A similar attitude was expressed by Ethel Parker in her survey of welfare services in Moncton. "A danger to be avoided is the tendency to select the directors [of the proposed Moncton Welfare Council] to 'represent' other agencies...The financial stability and good administration of the whole Council depends on drawing into this Board the best of Moncton's many socially minded business men. It is not intended to imply that it should have been no women, but they too should be selected for their business capacity..." Parker, "Welfare Services in Moncton - Report 1939".

30. PAC, Canadian Council on Social Development Records, accession 1983, box 60, file "B.C. Provincial Secretary's Department," Harry Cassidy to Charlotte Whitton, 28 December 1937.

31. Ibid, Whitton to Cassidy, 13 December 1937. Whitton's fears proved to be misplaced. As Cassidy pointed out, "the [three women] members of the Board are willing to back up the Department in what we consider to be sound policies. There has been some small agitation for an increase in the age of dependent children under the act from 16 to 18 years, but the members of the Board backed [the Department] recently in opposing any such change....As it happens the Board does not...contain any women who were troublesome on the question of mother's pensions when you did your survey in British Columbia." Cassidy to Whitton, 28 December 1937.

32. For Whitton's attitude to relief administration and social work professionalization during the 1930s, see James Struthers, "A Profession in Crisis: Charlotte Whitton and Canadian Social Work in the 1930s," *Canadian Historical Review*, LXII, June, 1981.

33. PAC, Canadian Council on Social Development Records, vol. 155, memo from Jean Walker, 22 October 1936 containing extracts from the *Ottawa Citizen*, 18 August and 12 September 1936.

34. Bessie Touzel, "What Happened in Ottawa," *The Social Worker*, V, November, 1936.

35. Ibid.

36. PAC, John Joseph Kelso Papers, MG 30 C97, vol. 6, copy of pamphlet published by the University of Toronto School of Social Service entitled "Social Work as a Profession," n.d. but *circa* 1930.

37. A. Ethel Parker, "The Art of Helping," *Social Welfare*, July, 1928.

38. Canadian Association of Social Workers Records, vol. 18, file 28, minutes of the Toronto Branch meeting, 30 January 1934, containing speech by Charlotte Whitton on "Some Forward Glimpses in Canadian Social Work."

39. PAC, Whitton Papers, vol. 18, George Davidson to Whitton, 19 April 1939. Whitton replied, somewhat testily, that she had on her desk "three letters and...two personal assurances and a long distance call, coming in all from six different women," who were willing to work with her if she stayed on in some capacity at the Council; Whitton to George Davidson, 26 April 1939. She eventually resigned, under similar pressure, in 1941.

40. PAC, Canadian Council on Social Development Records, vol. 155, copy of CASW pamphlet, "Social Work: A Vocation," 1938. The 1944 CASW recruiting pamphlet made an identical statement.

41. Ibid.

42. Svanhuit Josie, "Canada's Professional Social Workers," *The Social Worker*, XVI, February, 1948.

43. Amy Leigh, "Recruiting," *The Social Worker*, XI, April, 1942.

44. "Report of Hamilton Branch Committee on Salary Standards and Employment Practices," *The Social Worker*, XI, December, 1942.

45. "Report of a Study on Salaries and Other Employment and Personnel Practices in Canadian Social Work," *The Social Worker*, XIV, April, 1946. All seventeen members of the committee which wrote the report were women.

46. Ibid. Due to stiff protests from the CASW and several women's organizations throughout the country, the competition was finally opened to women, although as the report noted, "the few days allowed for filing...remained a handicap in obtaining a nation-wide recruitment."

47. PAC, Canadian Council on Social Development Records, accession 1983, box 295, file "T1-TZ", R.E.G. Davis to Bessie Touzel, 3 May 1947. Touzel was described as "one of Canada's most capable social workers," in the CWC press release announcing her appointment. Her starting salary was $5200.

48. Ibid, box 290, file "Govan", Elizabeth Govan to R.E.G. Davis, 12 May 1953; 24 January 1953.

49. Ibid, box 295, file "WO-WZ", John Farina to Kenrick Marshall, 23 July 1957.

50. Ibid, vol. 148, file 528, "Committee on Personnel in Social Work, Survey of Welfare Positions," 15 November 1954.

51. "Employment of Social Welfare Workers in Canada," *The Social Worker*, XXI, July-August, 1953. Women comprised 63 percent of the 3995 people listed as social welfare workers in the 1951 census. Their average age was thirty eight years compared to forty one years for men. Significantly, the proportion of married women in the field rose from 7 percent to 24 percent of the female total between 1941 and 1951.

52. "Committee on Personnel in Social Work, Survey of Welfare Positions."

53. Albert Rose, "Personnel Practices in Canadian Social Work," *Canadian Welfare*, September, 1948.

Sources of Political Conflict
in the Thirties:
Welfare Policy and a Geography of Need

John H. Taylor

Many elements combined in the development of welfare policy in the 1930s, especially with respect to the unemployed. Many of these elements are now being identified.[1] One was what might be called a geography of need. It was shaped by the forces of urban-industrial change, and, in turn, it was central to the political and jurisdictional tensions that surrounded policy evolution.

A geography of need can be described as the pattern made by the indigent, the needy, the unemployed, or other type of impoverished person.[2] It asks where are the poor? Rather than who are the poor? How many? What kind? Or who is helping them? It is a simple question, and hard to answer.[3] But where the poor are and the sort of pattern they present, admits some understanding of why and how they act and the sort of response that is made to them. The question also leads to a crucial link between the broad — or secular — forces of change and the politics of welfare policy.

It is important to note that patterns of poverty change in much the same way as patterns of affluence change. It is also highly probable that patterns of poverty are in large measure residual. In geography, as in economics, the poor get what is left over. As the tastes of the rich change, they move, and if their former places of residence are not filled by commercial uses they are often filled by the poor: the phenomenon of invasion and succession.[4] However, some social areas, as they have been called, can be very sticky. Particularly desirable areas of wealth, especially where much capital has been invested, can be very persistent. Equally, pockets of poverty persist over generations for reasons that are not entirely clear.[5]

A second important point to make is that within a particular area of poverty, ideas and attitudes can change, just as they do in wealthy areas. Poverty areas are often quite coherent communities that have a common understanding of how the world works from their perspective. At times that perspective changes.[6]

A third point worth making is that policy for poverty seems to lag reality. The policy that emerged in the "thirties", for example was one designed to deal with the consequences of urban-industrial change, but it came at a time when the cities, at any rate, seemed to be moving to a post-industrial or what has been called a corporate configuration.[7] Likewise, the policy abandoned in the "thirties" was one that had been designed for the era of the commercial city. It is the change from the commercial to the industrial city that is of most interest to this discussion of a policy for the "thirties".

The Urban Pattern

Though much work remains to be done in this area of urban history, some broad shifts can be identified. In the classic form, the change is from a small commercial city with elites and trades mixed heterogeneously near the core and transient labour isolated on the periphery. Social segregation did exist in the commercial city, but where it did, it was often on cultural rather than class lines. In Ottawa, for example, the Catholic populations, French and Irish, of all classes, were concentrated in the Lower Town; the Protestant English — the "lousy Scotch" — in the Upper Town.[8] Ownership of culture rather than capital was the critical criterion of division. As an aside, one might hypothesize that is why denominational and national charities through religious and ethnic benevolent associations were so well adapted to this phase of welfare policy. It needs to be investigated.

In the industrial phase, much of this pattern changed. The elite shifted out of the core areas, which were penetrated by industrial and transportation facilities, notably the train. And accompanying the factories and the rail yards, were a labouring force, hitherto, it would appear, confined to the periphery of urban areas, or, if of the artisan class of the commercial city, dethroned and homogenized in the emerging factory system.[9] Middle classes, especially with the development of the horse car and later the trolley car, could also shift into their suburbs.[10] That is to say, classes rather than cultures had their respective social areas. In the commercial city a cultural ghetto might contain all cultures: in an industrial city a class ghetto might contain all cultures, like the North End of Winnipeg. This shift in geography was also paralleled, it seems, by a shift in thought, perspective, or mentalité. The inhabitants of these industrial social areas seem increasingly to have perceived themselves less in terms of their ethnicity or religion and more in terms of their common social class.

Political Patterns

By the beginning of the twentieth century, changes in social patterns intersected with the liberalization of the franchise.[11] Liberalization is perhaps the most apt word for the period up to and including the Second Great War. While by the twentieth century, there was more or less complete male suffrage at the federal and provincial level, the property franchise and plural voting still limited even male participation at the local level. For example, while most urban dwellers were able to vote for candidates, they generally had to own property to run for office — the qualification — and to vote for money bylaws. As well, ownership of property generally conferred a vote in each ward or other division in which property was owned: the plural vote. A poll or head tax was also used in some jurisdictions. Its major purpose was to discourage short-term residents — that is drifters and those who lacked a commitment to the place — from voting. Local franchise and qualification was thus designed to concentrate power in the hands of those who had both substance and a commitment to place. It represented a political dimension of the "Booster Ethic," an ethic that identified individual fortune and growth with the fortune and growth of a place. By boosting one's place, one boosted one's fortune. It was in many respects the corrollary at the local level of the state-capital nexus.

Being a growth-oriented and materialist philosophy — though it doubtless has (a still unstudied) philosophical dimension, probably through religion — it focussed primarily on those aspects of urban development that would represent a material investment in place. It was not much interested in social or human capital, and therefore not much interested in the development of a social welfare policy as a "state" matter. Individual responsibility, supported when needed by the private sector charities, was the preferred solution, even in the so-called urban reform phase of the turn of the century. Not much of the property tax was to be spent to build the social side of "Tomorrow's Metropolis."[12]

The vote, even at the local level, was nonetheless liberalized, probably most effectively by a general inflation in property values that made the property franchise and qualification less restrictive, especially for rentors. Liberalization of the vote had a number of consequences. In most areas west of the Ottawa River, it seems to have enhanced political activity in labouring areas of cities, and the emergence of minority representation on city councils. There seems to have been little change in the Maritimes cities. Meanwhile, in Montreal, where male suffrage was introduced in 1912, there were dramatic changes.[13] In that metropolis, the controlling elite was largely shut out of power by a series of populist movements and mayors from Médéric Martin to Jean Drapeau. But because their supporters were the poor, and other "consumers" of social goods and services, frightened property owners successfully appealled to Quebec City for controls over the populist mayors.[14]

As a general rule, however, conventional forces[15] ruled the roost in the nation's cities. There were many reasons. Generally high levels of prosperity and the prospect of material improvement kept discontent at a low level, and the organizations that might have mobilized it did not have the sort of consistent success that made them a threat. As radical organization was weak and inconsistent, so too was its constituency unreliable. Immigration was large in the decades before and after the Great War and appears to have contributed to a reserve labour pool that favoured the rich. The opening of the west provided a safety valve, and the (sometimes realized) land of opportunity, that could sap long-term grievance. As well, the more general movement of peoples in the early twentieth century — transiency — perhaps provided the most effective control of all. Long distances (in the day of the railway) and a fluid potential constituency made organization extraordinarily difficult. Moreover, the development of vernacular radical thought was in its infancy, and derivative ideas and their attendant structures may well have done more damage to radical organization than good. And there was, at the last, the strength and the political momentum of the established elites with all their capacity to resist, to co-opt, and to control.[16]

Fiscal Crisis

Relief funding of the depression was only the final straw in a fiscal crisis evident at the municipal level from the time of the First Great War, and one that had its roots in the nineteenth century. In that century, urban-industrial growth had led to explosive city growth, and, in turn, to the demand and, indeed, the necessity for collective provision of certain critical services, what might be called infrastructure. They included transportation services to admit the daily movement of people over an expanded urban landscape; prevention services, like fire-fighting, to protect property and people; and health services to protect city peoples from drowning and dying in their own pollution. Of critical importance, a switch was made from labour-intensive provision of such services (for example, water carriers) to capital-intensive ones (for example, piped systems). They were costly services: tram cars, water and sewage systems, purification plants, police and fire departments, public health units, hospitals, and good roads, sidewalks and drainage systems.

Fortunately for the major cities of the nation, it was also a time when they were the engines of economic growth, and, as a result, the foundation of the tax system, property, was steadily expanding in value. There was a much-increased flow of tax monies. The growth of the tax *base* meant that civic improvements could be funded without much increasing the tax or mill *rate*, a course of action pregnant with political hazard.

About 1919, however, the expansion of the property tax *base* seemed in many centres to stop growing, and for reasons that are not clear. Money for new urban services, including the emerging social services like welfare and pensions, could only be generated by increases in the tax *rate*. In addition, the federal government in 1917 levied income and corporation taxes. That is, it began competing in a tax field that hitherto had been exploited, if only in a small way, by mainly local governments, and they were soon to be retired from the scene.[17]

At the time of the depression, then, most cities were in a fiscal squeeze in terms of sources of revenue. Relief of the large numbers of unemployed created by the depression imposed an expenditure crisis on top of the revenue one. More money was needed at exactly a time when relatively less was available.

In more general terms, there was by 1930 a dislocation between revenue and responsibilities as set out in the British North America Act.

But underlying this one dislocation, was one of a more subtle kind. The assignation of certain tax fields to specific levels of government gave them, willy nilly, a vested interest in promoting or developing policy that would enhance the revenue-generating capacity of those fields. The federal authority, with the bulk of its revenues from tariffs, evidenced almost an obsession with tariff policy to at least 1935. Provincial governments, with a major source of revenue in resource royalties had a major vested interest in exploiting resources and thus in resource policy.[18] And local governments, of course, had a vested interest in policy that would enhance the development and value of property. There was, as is evident, no obvious link between social policy and revenue sources at any level. Social policy could only be framed in a negative way: to reduce demands on the expenditure side of the ledger by getting people off relief and welfare rolls. And this was the central thrust and motivator of social policy at all levels. For the two senior levels of government it was expressed by unloading responsibility onto the local levels. Insofar as local levels were unable to pass the burden on to private charity, social services were linked to the property tax, and in this way tied to both the political and social geography of the city.

Impact of Depression

With the onset of depression, transiency was minimal. Immigration stopped. Internal migration slowed. And though a persistent image of the depression is the roving, drifting men on boxcars, their numbers were insignificant compared to the vast numbers who had ridden inside the trains in the decades before, or who languished in the cities in the "thirties." People in the "twenties" could take their discontent and move. In the "thirties" they and their discontents moved little. Moreover, that discontent was much broader and deeper in the "thirties." More people saw the future that prosperity promised foreshorten and then disappear altogether. At best there was stasis. Also by the "thirties," organization to exploit that distress was more mature. It had also had some success at all levels of government. And it had increasing legitimacy, while the conventional order was increasingly being questioned, especially the more so as it failed to deal with the persistence of depression. The depression closed down the traditional outlets. But it did more.

Of great significance, especially with relative stasis in movement of peoples, the depression focussed poverty. It put it in a place. And the association of poverty and class was not too blurred, by the "thirties," with the over-burden of denomination and culture. Poverty, in a sense had been secularized. What was also new was that poverty in the cities was segregated, and even the poor had the vote. Poverty by class, and geography by class could be turned, via the franchise, into a mainstream political threat. And it could not be bought off. Prosperity had vanished and there was little prospect of its renewal. And charity — whether voluntary or out of the taxes of the owners of city property — was by mid-depression exhausted.

The scale of the problem, in addition to its persistence, had led most cities by 1934 into serious financial difficulties. Almost every device to reduce controllable expenses was tried: cut back work, wages and establishment; reduce or eliminate services; or dodge debt charges, among others. But the demands of relief overwhelmed every expedient and by 1934 nearly every major city in Canada was funding its relief, either directly through borrowing, or indirectly by suspending sinking fund payments.

Voluntary donations were insufficient for the scale of the problem of the unemployed and the property tax was close to reaching the limit of its exploitation. It was also a political red flag. Those who were of the middle and upper classes not only formed the bulk of the taxpayers, they also lived apart in their own segregated parts of the cities, parts different from those of the poor. Two hostile, class-differentiated groups, looked at each other across the social and political geographies of their cities. In a curious sense, the poor had for the first time an opportunity to exploit the booster ethic. It had meant the identification of power and place for the wealthy; in the "thirties" it could be seen as the identification of power and place for the poor.

The poor could win. They had the vote, they had propinquity, that is, at least one requisite of organization; they had a common grievance or threat; and they had organizations in place. They formed not only a human problem. They were not only the potential objective of good works. They had the potential of political control.

In some places, they took control. These were mainly the cities where segregation was most explicit, that is where social and political areas were congruent and the unemployment problem the worst. Most cities also held annual elections where political successes could be measured and confidence could grow. By 1934, left and labour organizations had won in Edmonton, and were threatening in Winnipeg, Regina and Vancouver. In Ontario, they had shown strength in Hamilton, London and Toronto. East of the Ottawa River, the old verities tended to prevail.

By the mid-thirties, then, the poor — the bulk of them consisting of the persistently unemployed — posed a double threat. The first was to pocket-books of the employed and the coffers of the municipal government through the demand and the need for relief payments; and the second was to the political control of the cities, or even the more senior levels of government, through a franchise that was focussed by class and by geographical area and therefore by political constituency. The unemployed in the "thirties" were from the lower levels of the social pyramid. The lower levels of the social pyramid were geographically segregated. Poverty and geography coincided.

Search For Policy
In the development of a welfare policy to deal with the poor —largely the unemployed — of the depression, a social problem, and a fiscal problem,

had to be solved. But it had to be done in such a way that the political consequences were minimized. Any welfare policy, in that sense, had to provide social relief to the have nots, political relief to the haves,[19] and financial relief to both.

There was the further complication of the federal system. This complication was introduced at the point that voluntary charity as a means of providing relief collapsed. The local governments, by tradition though rarely by law, were the designated agencies to pick up the pieces of the voluntary or private sector, which for so long, through the era of the commercial city, had largely insulated governments from poverty, and therefore from policy-making.

Had the local governments — particularly the cities where unemployment was concentrated — been able to cope with relief of the poor, which was also threatening the local political system, a jurisdictional problem might not have emerged. But they were not able to cope. Perhaps more to the point, relief monies generated by a city were generated from one social group — the unemployed property owner — in one part of the city, and given to another social group — the unemployed poor — in another part.

In this way, too, social policy and fiscal policy became both entangled and polarized. By 1935, the poor had the political potential to frame both kinds of policy to their advantage. In the circumstances, their social and political opposites were not only calling on the senior governments for financial relief, they were calling upon them to exorcise a political threat that might well extend itself to the senior levels. The geography of need, as it had emerged in the cities of the thirties, could also translate into a political threat at the senior levels. Federal and provincial constituencies, like municipal wards, were a geographical phenomenon. So was unemployment and need. Grasping the nettle of relief was a dangerous business for any government. It meant not only financial responsibility, but political hazard. The cost as well as the hazard needed to be isolated, or when that became impossible, spread around.

The first of these policies was the traditional one of private sector relief (or in the Maritimes, Parish relief), a policy that kept the public sector neutral and avoided questions of politics or jurisdiction. But it didn't work. Indeed, even before the depression it was being supplanted. Local governments were getting formally, if minimally involved with ministering to the poor and this was especially true in western Canada, where, it seems, the voluntary sector was less mature and weaker than in longer established areas of the country.[20] Even with government assistance, the voluntary sector proved even by 1930 to be helpless in the face of unemployment, and local government agencies rapidly emerged, supported by ad hoc, temporary and emergency funding from the senior levels. Social and financial need of the poor — the sheer magnitude of the problem — broke the back of the original policy, one favoured by all levels of government, especially the senior ones. Governments were engaged, however much an effort was made to confine their activities to the local level.

Use of local government as a surrogate for private sector charity was a good idea. It worked. For a while. It relieved the poor, though perhaps not adequately or in a manner entirely satisfactory to the poor. But it also took relief and welfare policy squarely into the political arena, where, in the cities especially, because of the geography of need, traditional political control was threatened.

The answer to these difficulties from the local point of view was fairly straight-forward. In their great conference of 1935, the mayors of the nation's cities put a three-element solution to the federal government, one that in somewhat varied forms had been put to the provincial governments earlier and was rejected by them.[21] The mayors asked first for "Relief from Relief." They argued that the burden should be shifted completely from their shoulders and assumed by the federal government. That would obviously solve their political and social problems. And by asking the senior governments for debt-refunding to rid them of the costs of past relief, the city governments would be relieved of their financial problems. Finally they asked for constitutional amendments to make the two proposals possible. The proposals were rejected and the cities were told to talk to provincial governments that had already turned a deaf ear to their pleas. The local governments were failing and by 1935 their solutions for a new policy were rejected.

The third noxious element — that of jurisdiction —nonetheless had been introduced by the local governments. The jurisdictional question, itself, was enough to give the federal authorities reason to reject the local governments.[22] But, in addition, the senior government, under both Bennett and King in 1935, had other plans. They had a policy proposal of their own, one that might be called relief by administrative oversight. Administration of emergency unemployment relief funds between 1930 and 1935 had given the federal authorities some sense of the control that could be exerted through such conditional grants.[23] This sense of control had been underscored by the advice of Charlotte Whitton to the effect that much welfare cheating was going on at both the provincial and local levels, and that in effect, the junior governments were using federal relief money to relieve more than the deserving unemployed.[24] But again, it seems, it was just another neutral mechanism that would avoid the problem of jurisdictional conflict, and really only an effort in policy making that would isolate, like some kind of a disease, relief and other kinds of welfare at the local level.

This effort didn't work either. It could not solve the problem of the poor. Nor did it solve the political and financial problems of local government. Nor did it solve the jurisdictional problem. If anything it exacerbated it through funding restrictions and control. Certainly local and provincial governments continued to protest.[25]

A Solution

The final solution — not elaborated until the 'forties' —did, with the distraction of war and a boost from prosperity, work. The central element was to fragment responsibility and control, and to shift funding from sources that were less place-sensitive. This was perhaps inevitable in the history of Canada, in the evolution of its welfare policy, and perhaps inevitable in a federation. And more to the point, it was politically and jurisdictionally safe.

For the unemployed, financial responsibility was divided among the federal government, employers, and a large portion of the work force, in the form of an insurance plan that was class neutral. It could not become a focus for class politics, since theoretically most everyone was both a contributor and a potential beneficiary. It removed the question of relief from the local level, where it had created the most political difficulties. And, with some resistance from the provinces at the outset, confined management of the entire program to the federal level.

Other social welfare programs worked differently, but on the same principle of fragmentation. Most of these followed a similar pattern that is, delivery at the local level, policy-making at the federal or provincial levels or both, and funding from all three levels, and a diversity of tax fields, especially the growing one of income.

The important overall effect was to demote place as a priority. Need that can be identified with a social and therefore a political area breeds dangerous politics and hazardous policies in a representative democracy.

All policies in time, however, produce their own internal contradictions or become victims of change. Since the "forties" and the establishment of a welfare state based on an urban-industrial pattern, at least two major changes of importance seem to have occurred. Urban-industrial society, itself, and particularly the cities have moved into a corporate phase. Boosterism — the identification of personal fortune with place — has been supplanted by the identification of personal fortune with corporation. The landscape of the cities has changed to more of a core and ring configuration, and recently, transportation trade-offs and other factors have made the core once again attractive to wealth. The poor may once again be condemned to the periphery, as in the commercial city. The cities, as a result of conditional grants, including welfare grants, have been largely made impotent as autonomous institutions. And in the country as a whole, need is increasingly being identified with the province as place, and a political hazard, as well as the jurisdictional one, is emerging from that quarter.

The more general notion remains valid: that when need develops a sense of place — or identity with place — it can generate political hazards in jurisdiction where social and political geography coincide. Such is the case in Canada in many local jurisdictions and both senior ones. In such situations, any social policy, as well as the means of funding it, is bound to have as its first priority, political security.

NOTES

1. The process has been incredibly slow and is best seen recently in Dennis Guest, *The Emergence of Social Security in Canada*, Vancouver, 1980, James Struthers, "Prelude to Depression: The Federal Government and Unemployment, 1918-29," *Canadian Historical Review*, LVIII, 3, Sept. 1977, 277-293, and the work of Bernie Vigod, "Ideology and Institutions in Quebec," *Social History*, XI (21), May 1978, 167-182.

2. This is really an aspect of the study of social segregation on which there is a large and distinguished literature, most notably associated with the Chicago School of Sociology and its notions of human ecology. Most of it, however, uses standard social categories of class, ethnicity, religion and the like, and rarely focusses on poverty by type — eg. the unemployed — or by dependence, whether on state or private charity. I know of no formal, historical study of this nature in Canada.

3. The reason it is hard to answer for the period is in large part due to lack of good data. Records of the indigent, including their location, are not easily located, and where available, have not much been used. There are some, for example, in Vancouver.

4. The term used by the Chicago School, ibid.

5. An excellent discussion of this problem can be found in several articles and a review essay in the *Journal of Urban History*, 7:4, August 1981.

6. Again a new field — the culture or mentality of poverty. The best work seems to be in works on the third world and people like Paulo Friere, *Pedagogy of the Oppressed*, Harmondsworth, 1972, use the notion. The concept has been most widely used in Canadian history by the "culturalists" in labour history, such as Greg Kealey and Bryan Palmer; or those of the annales school, like Fernand Ouellet.

7. See W.K. Tabb and M. Sawer, *Marxism and the Metropolis*, New York, 1978.

8. See National Capital Commission, *Lower Town Ottawa*, Vols. I and II, M.S. Cross, "Stoney Monday", *Ontario History*, LXIII, 3, 1971, 177-190.

9. 9. See esp. Greg Kealey, "The Honest Workingman" and "Workers' Control: The Experience of Toronto Skilled Workers, 1860-92," *Labour* 1, 1976, 32-68, and *Toronto Workers Respond to Industrial Capitalism, 1867-1892*, Toronto, 1980.

10. For Canada, see Peter Goheen, *Victorian Toronto*, University of Chicago, Geography Research Paper no. 127, 1970.

11. Its importance for the senior levels of government can be seen in Martin Robin, *Radical Politics and Canadian Labour*, Kingston, 1968, or in his "The Working Class and the Transition to Capitalist Democracy in Canada," *Dalhousie Review*, XLVII, 3, Autumn, 1967.

12. See especially A.F.J. Artibise, *Winnipeg: A Social History of Urban Growth*, Kingston, 1975.

13. See Guy Bourassa, "The Political Elite of Montreal", in *Politics and Government of Urban Canada*, L.D. Feldman and M.D. Goldrick, eds., Toronto, 1969.

14. The most recent interpretation of this phenomenon is in Annick Germain, "Les mouvements de reforme urbaine à Montréal au tourant du siecle" Les Cahiers du CIDAR, Sociologie, Université de Montréal, Montreal, 1984.

15. For use of "Convention" and "conventional politics", see John H. Taylor, "Mayors a la Mancha", *Urban History Review*, IX, 3 Feb. 1981.

16. See Robin, *Radical Politics*.

17. See J. Harvey Perry, *Taxes, Tariffs and Subsidies*, Vol. I, Toronto, 1955.

18. See H.V. Nelles, *The Politics of Development*, Toronto, 1974.

19. And that was the sense of the mayors' meeting: Dominion Conference of

Mayors, Montreal and Ottawa, 25-28 March 1935, *Report of Deliberations*.

20. For some indication, see John H. Taylor, "The Urban West", A.R. McCormack and Ian MacPherson, eds., *Cities in the West*, Canada, Museum of Man, Mercury Series, History Paper #10, Ottawa, 1975.

21. See John H. Taylor, "Relief from Relief": The Cities Answer to Depression Dependency, *Journal of Canadian Studies*, 14, 1, Spring 1979.

22. See, ibid.

23. The best history for Canada is Luella Gettys, *The Administration of Conditional Grants*, Chicago, 1938.

24. See Struthers, "Prelude to Depression...," on Whitton.

25. The mayors' conference, (fn. 19), evolved into a continuing conference and ultimately the Canadian Federation of Mayors and Municipalities, to do just that.

The Development of a Provincial Welfare State:
British Columbia 1900-1939

Allan Irving

"British Columbians are inclined to boast about their social services."[1] So wrote Harry Cassidy in 1945. As the province's first director of social welfare, from 1934 to 1938, he had been instrumental in significantly advancing the provinces's social services. By the end of the 1930s, British Columbia could be considered a provincial welfare state; in fact, a case could be made that British Columbia had a more progressive system of social services by the end of the Depression than any other province. This chapter discusses the evolution of the welfare state in B.C. from 1900-1939 within the context of the province's historical development.

Even though the provincial welfare state in B.C. was relatively well advanced by 1939, there were, nevertheless, some serious shortcomings. For example, during this entire period there was at best a great deal of ambivalence about the treatment of the unemployed, particularly the single, able-bodied transient; and the attempt to establish North America's first plan of state health insurance in the mid 1930s foundered when the province's medical profession mounted sustained opposition. Providing explanations for the rise of social welfare in a capitalist culture always poses problems.[2] Here, a multi-cause interpretation is offered.

First, more generally, social welfare is seen as functional to the needs of B.C.'s burgeoning capitalist economy.[3] During the early years of the twentieth century, the primary function of the state in British Columbia, comments historian Martin Robin, was to protect private property and to provide a stable environment that would encourage investment. During this century the British Columbia economy has been almost entirely dependent on the extraction of natural resources, especially forest and mineral products. Historically, as in Ontario, there was a close alliance between industry and government, "and the state was used to create and consolidate company empires which flourished in the frenetic business environment of the mountain province."[4]

Ian Gough's *The Political Economy of the Welfare State* (1979) adds another dimension: he envisages the welfare state "*both* as functional to the needs of capitalist development *and* as the result of the political struggles of the organized working class."[5] Working class and labour agitation is thus seen as a second contextual element in the creation of the welfare state in British Columbia. From the late nineteenth century on, polarization developed quickly between capitalists and workers; the B.C. labour movement has been "the most militant and politically conscious in the country."[6] Martin Robin has noted that "the question of labour's political action, together with a host of issues arising from working-class participation, form enduring themes of the British Columbia political culture."[7]

There are three other factors that constitute the five part explanatory framework being considered here. Third, the influence of women's organizations on social policy development was a critical factor in B.C.[8] Fourth, the CCF after 1933 and other, more radical, socialist movements in the province pushed parties in power — particularly the Liberal Party — towards including social welfare measures as part of their platforms.[9] It was in British Columbia, that "Canadian socialism came of age."[10] Harry Cassidy observed that "the influence of the labour and radical groups did something to bring questions of social reform to the fore even in periods of the most rapid growth, so that for many years there...(was) an undercurrent of social politics to which the older parties...had to give some attention in spite of their preoccupation with the development of natural resources and the central political business of being 'in' rather than 'out'."[11] Fifth, and finally, the contribution of enlightenend politicians and civil servants, such as Mary Ellen Smith, T. Dufferin Pattullo, George Weir, Ernest Winch and Harry Cassidy, to the making of social policy in B.C. ought to be included; they genuinely believed that progressive social welfare legislation could enlarge the area of human need that was served by the state.[12]

Some Early Developments

By the early years of the twentieth century, there had already been some significant social welfare developments in British Columbia. In the field of mental health, there was the Insane Asylums Act of 1873, and in 1913 the opening of a new mental hospital at Essondale on the Fraser River. In 1893, a public health act, concerned with sanitary conditions and the control of communicable diseases, was passed; the act established a provincial board of health. The public health code soon was extended by amendments, and new legislation was enacted to include the control of tuberculosis (1901), increased sanitary inspection and regulation (1904), inspection of foods (1906), and the medical examination of school children (1910). Administrative responsibility for the provincial board of health was transferred from the Department of Agriculture to the Department of the Provincial Secretary in 1907. From 1908 to 1920 the Tranquille Sanatorium for tuberculosis patients in the province's interior was supported largely by provincial funds; in 1921 the province purchased the sanatorium. Dr. Henry Esson Young, a physician from the province's northern mining districts, who was minister of education and provincial secretary from 1907 to 1916, can be credited with laying many of these foundations for the province's public health services. In 1919 Young, now the provincial health officer, established a public health nursing course at the University of British Columbia; it was the first of its kind in the British Empire.[13]

Kamloops was chosen in 1893 as the location for a provincial home to care for the old and infirm. An Infants Act (1901), modelled on Ontario's 1893 and 1897 Children's Protection Acts, provided for the appointment of a provincial superintendent of neglected children and for the setting up of children's aid societies, which were organized in Victoria and Vancouver in 1901. The detention and training of juvenile delinquents was taken care of by the Provincial Industrial School and Boys' Home, established in Point Grey, a Vancouver suburb, in 1905; in 1914 an industrial school for girls was constructed. British Columbia was the third province to pass workmen's compensation legislation (1916); again, as in the case of social legislation for the care of children, the act was patterned after Ontario's statute of two years earlier.[14]

The most intractable social welfare problem of all in capitalist society has been unemployment, and in this B.C. was no exception. Early on, Vancouver became a "mecca for the unemployed" attracting, because of its mild climate, seasonally unemployed workers (fishing, logging, mining) from the vast B.C. hinterland and prairie farm workers from the previous fall's harvest. During any given winter, large numbers of transient, able-bodied single men swelled the ranks of the unemployed in the city; in economically buoyant times the seasonally unemployed, if they managed their resources carefully, could survive the winter by living in one of Vancouver's many flophouses. During bad times such as the recession of 1907 it was a different story, as hundreds of unemployed flooded to Vancouver seeking whatever relief they could find.

While some private relief was available through various missions in the city, public relief was not granted, in the best poor law tradition, to single transients who had not established residence. In December 1907, several hundred desperate unemployed men threatened to resort to stealing unless the city considered their plight. Vancouver city council, fearful of riots and social disorder, reacted by granting three thousand dollars for temporary work relief, set up a labour bureau, provided meal tickets, made the old city jail available for a dormitory and asked the province to provide work for wages. Historian Patricia Roy observed that during the winter of 1907-08, Vancouver's response to transient unemployed workers became firmly established: "they would not be allowed to starve; they were expected to prove their worthiness working for relief; and preferably, a senior government rather than city rate payers would pay for that work."[15] This whole episode is a good illustration of Gough's thesis that social welfare concessions, albeit usually limited ones, are often wrung from the state by working class agitation.

Public assistance generally was taken care of by an amalgam of voluntary benefit societies and charitable institutions, such as the Friendly Help Association in Victoria. Vancouver organized a city relief department in 1914 at the height of the 1912-1915 economic depression. However, its attitude towards those in need was highly restrictive; in April of 1915, for example, the department curtailed all outdoor relief to nonresident single men. (An unruly demonstration by 1,500 unemployed men soon developed, and a number of store windows were broken.) Unemployed single women in Vancouver tacitily were expected by male aldermen to support themselves by prostitution. This problem was remedied to some extent in 1915, when the City of Vancouver assumed responsibility for operating the Women's Employment Bureau; several years earlier, the city had established a municipal child care service for working mothers. To assist families whose breadwinner was in the armed forces, the Vancouver War Fund, a branch of the Canadian Patriotic Fund, was established during World War I; this was a strictly voluntary effort.[16]

War to Depression: 1916-1929

In the 1916 provincial election, the B.C. Liberal Party took office after thirteen years of Tory rule; it would remain in power until 1928. The leader and premier for most of this time (1918-1927) was John Oliver. Known as "Honest John," he was a farmer and an expert on railways and agriculture who "worshipped thrift, prudence and the wholesome rural life." He had a reputation as "a hard-nosed debater, a skillful parliamentarian...and a politician of great energy and endurance." Because of his agrarian background, Oliver was not very sympathetic to the labour movement and the plight of the unemployed. His secretary once commented: "He confessed that his sympathy was rather with the hard working and producing taxpayer than with those who claim much and gave nothing in return." Oliver felt that many were unemployed simply "as a result of their lack of shift and thrift."[17]

However, by the end of World War I, the Liberal Party had introduced some progressive legislation: workers in major industries were guaranteed regular payment of wages every two weeks; a revised workmen's compensation act was passed; a separate department of labour was created; the eight-hour day was extended to cover more workers and government employment agencies were created. The first woman to enter a provincial legislature and the first woman cabinet minister in the British Empire, Mary Ellen Smith, a feminist, was elected in 1918; she had run as an independent and campaigned "on a reform program advocating women's rights." She was the moving force behind other important social legislation: an act relating to the guardianship and custody of infants was passed and "was intended to give equal rights to husband and wife under conditions of cohabitation and separation;" there was a minimum wage bill for women and, in 1920, a mothers' pension act was passed.[18] As one of the province's earliest forms of income security, the pension scheme is worth describing in more detail.

Discussion on the merits of mothers' pensions — payments to women with dependent children to enable them to remain out of the workforce — had been carried on throughout North America for the previous decade.[19] Unions generally favoured such legislation, since they saw the increasing number of women in the labour force as contributing generally to depressed wages. The British Columbia Mothers' Pension Act had its origin in 1918, when a delegation of women's groups, supported by the mayors of Vancouver, New Westminster and Chilliwack, petitioned Oliver's government for such legislation. Since April 5, 1917 when women had been granted the right both to sit in the provincial legislature and to vote in provincial elections, women's organizations in B.C. had become a powerful lobby for social welfare reform. A clear indication of the increasing influence of women in social welfare in the province was the appointment in July 1917 of Helen Gregory MacGill, one of the key leaders in the suffrage campaign, as judge of the juvenile court of Vancouver. Shortly afterwards, a new progressive Juvenile Court Act was passed largely at MacGill's insistence.[20] Late in 1919, the government, about to be tested at the polls on its social policies, established a Royal Commission to examine the questions of health insurance, mothers' pensions, maternity benefits and public health nursing. It became obvious through public meetings held by the Commission that there was wide-ranging public support for mothers' pension legislation, particularly for war widows.

A contributing factor to the act's rapid passage in 1920 was the upcoming provincial election in which women could vote for the first time in the province and it was women's organizations such as the New Era League that had been pressing the government for action. The act covered indigent mothers with one or more children under sixteen, who were either widowed or deserted, or whose husbands were disabled or detained in a prison or mental institution. Monthly allowances were $42.50 for a woman with one child, and $7.50 for each additional child under sixteen. All costs were met by the province; this relieved the municipalities of a large financial burden of poor relief for which they had been responsible.

The Workmen's Compensation Board administered the scheme; this enabled recipients of mothers' pensions to benefit from the board's medical and legal services. As well, it was thought that the stigma attached to receiving public assistance would be lessened by having the scheme administered by a board that already issued another kind of pension. By the end of November 1920, 636 pensions had been granted, three times what was expected; by the end of the 1920s, mothers' pensions covered 1,370 families at a cost of $778,000. There were, however, rather restrictive eligibility requirements; therefore, the number of women needing such financial help was undoubtedly much higher. Eligibility requirements included a three-year residency period, the woman had to be a British subject, native Canadian mothers were excluded, applicants had to be "of good character" and were required to provide two letters of reference, and a means test required an applicant to have less than $500 in cash and property valued at less than $500.[21]

The same 1919 Royal Commission that found in favour of mothers' pensions submitted a report in March 1921 recommending that the province establish a broad plan of state health insurance. Again women's organizations as well as labour groups had presented evidence before the

Commission strongly supporting such a plan. Another factor creating a favourable climate for public health insurance was the devastating world-wide Spanish flu epidemic of 1918-19 that hit Vancouver particularly hard. In its report (which was never published), the Commission argued that health insurance would, in the interests of reducing costs, encourage both employers and governments to improve services; for example, better ventilation, lighting and sanitation in the workplace and better public water supplies, sewage systems and public health in cities. Behind these arguments, though, lay a more critical consideration. In the report's words: "The Bolsheviks of today are mainly the neglected children of yesterday. The big majority of them spring from the homes of the poor, the handicapped, the sick and the scantily educated."[22] Health insurance in conjunction with other social policies would undercut revolutionary sentiments and help to maintain public order in a capitalist society threatened by waves of social unrest following the end of the War.

Despite the proposed and new social legislation, there was considerable labour unrest in B.C. in the years following the end of the War. Contributing to this instability were a number of factors: fear of unemployment because of the large number of returned soldiers, the example of the Russian revolution, the use of soldiers as strike breakers, the fear of increased Oriental immigration, and certain repressive actions by the federal government which restricted civil liberties in the spring of 1918 by limiting the rights of free speech, publication and organization. In 1918, British Columbia accounted for 35 per cent of all work time lost in Canada as a result of strikes. The coal fields in the Eastern Kootenays and on Vancouver Island experienced a great deal of labour unrest; Vancouver described as "a hot bed of the more violent socialistic thought," was disrupted by many strikes. Some radical union members advocated the idea of the general strike as a way of promoting revolutionary change. A general strike did take place in Vancouver in August 1918; it was intended to honour the memory of "Ginger" Goodwin, a radical union leader who had been shot and killed by the police. Shortly after, socialist rallies often included the question of affiliation with the Third International, the recently founded international organization of communist parties.[23]

In June 1919 the One Big Union (OBU) was organized at the Western Labour Conference in Calgary, to "unify all workers in a single union which could achieve its purposes, economic or political, through general strikes. The OBU was to be the embodiment of proletarian solidarity."[24] Its greatest strength was in B.C., with 29 locals and over 19,000 members.[25] For over a year there was a rising tide of militant industrial unionism in British Columbia and Premier Oliver was convinced that Bolshevists were behind the turmoil.[26] During 1920, however, the OBU began to collapse, three of its prominent leaders were imprisoned, and more stable social conditions led to a reduction in postwar militancy.

During the 1920 provincial election campaign, the Liberal Party attempted to win as many labour votes as possible. One party advertisement read: "The Liberal is the apostle of orderly reform, and there can be no reform which leaves out labour." Liberal candidates throughout the province put themselves forward as special friends of the working class, and suggested that workers avoid supporting more extreme positions. The Liberals won a slight majority, electing twenty-four members to the Tories' fifteen; four labour candidates were also elected.[27]

In the 1920s the Liberal government, which was re-elected again in 1924, faced increasing criticism of its welfare program, which was described by labour representatives as "piece meal and inadequate": a proposed amendment to the Workmen's Compensation Act, which would have given workers 100 per cent instead of 55 per cent of their wages, was defeated; the Mothers' Pensions Act was dismissed by Tom Uphill, the Labour member from Fernie, as a "mere skeleton" that had been passed simply to gain women's votes; and the Oliver government offered little in the way of relief to the unemployed. The Liberal Party supported employers in destroying unions such as the one at the Powell River Pulp and Paper Company in 1923. Labour member Samuel Guthrie from New Castle riding criticized the government's failure to enforce coal mines regulation legislation, and remarked that coal miners viewed the Liberal government "as nothing more than an executive committee of the Capitalist class."[28]

There were, however, some important social welfare developments during the 1920s. An adoption act was passed in 1920. In 1927, the Canadian Council of Child and Family Welfare was invited by the City of Vancouver to survey child welfare problems including the work of the Vancouver Children's Aid Society. As a result, later that year Laura Holland, "an able and experienced professional social worker from Toronto," was appointed as director of the Vancouver CAS. She introduced modern methods of child welfare work and encouraged the employment of trained social work personnel. Several years later, Holland was appointed by the province as deputy superintendent of neglected children. Her "appointment marked the beginning of a professional approach in the welfare programme of the province, in place of the amateur (if useful and well intentioned) efforts which had been made previously by untrained personnel."[29]

Just before and during the 1920s, too, there was an explosion of private health and welfare agencies in Vancouver and Victoria: a provincial tuberculosis society and tuberculosis clinics in Vancouver and Victoria; visiting nursing societies; missions and hostels for homeless men, homes for the aged and infirm, orphanages, relief societies, YMCA's and YWCA's; the Canadian National Institute for the Blind and veterans' organizations. Vancouver established the Vancouver Welfare Federation in 1930, which fulfilled the role of a community chest and council of social agencies; the Family Welfare Bureau was founded in Vancouver in 1928; and, The University of British Columbia established "a modest graduate curriculum in social work" in 1929.[30]

British Columbia's provision for public assistance was augmented in 1927 by the passage of the Dominion government's Old Age Pensions Act. The West Coast province was the first to take advantage of the fifty-fifty cost-sharing arrangement with the central government which provided means-tested pensions of $20 per month to those over seventy. Administrative responsibility for the new program was assigned, as in the case of mothers' pensions, to the Workmen's Compensation Board, "on the theory that this agency, successful in its own field and trusted by the public, could do a better job of distributing large sums of money to individuals than any department of the government under direct ministerial control."[31]

During the provincial election campaign of 1928, "the Liberal campaign literature was filled...with protestations of sympathy for the labour interest and government candidates in labour constituencies proudly recounted the government's achievements in the areas of reform legislation." The campaign pamphlet used by the Liberal party, British Columbia's Progress, proclaimed that B.C. led Canada "in the matter of legislation beneficial to the workers." The same pamphlet revealed the government's functional approach to social welfare: "progressive legislation reasonably assures contented labour and operates as an insurance policy for Capital." There were, however, no specific statements of proposed new labour and social welfare reforms. In fact, during the years 1925-28 Labour members in the provincial legislature had been active in attempting (unsuccessfully) to strengthen Liberal social legislation: to raise the compensation offered under the Workmen's Compensation Act; to improve the Mothers' Pensions Act and to extend its application; to change municipal laws to allow labourers to participate in municipal politics without restrictive property qualifications; to abolish child labour in the fishing and packing industries and to extend the minimum wage to include all industries.[32]

The Depression and Social Welfare
In July 1928, the Conservative Party was returned to power with Simon Fraser Tolmie as premier. Like his Liberal predecessors, Tolmie did not develop a general approach to provincial social policy. His response to the mounting unemployment of the early Depression years was to increase public works spending; however, only limited aid was offered to municipalities to help with their relief costs. By August of 1931, it was clear that more had to be done to help the unemployed; Tolmie's major response was to construct work relief camps where the single unemployed could be housed while working on highways and other public projects.[33]

British Columbia, more than any other province, and particularly the City of Vancouver, was the centre of agitation and of the organization of the unemployed during the 1930s. Three reasons for this have been advanced: B.C. simply had a long tradition of radicalism and agitation; the B.C. economy was particulary unstable because of its dependence on the extraction of natural resources; and many unemployed were attracted to B.C.'s moderate climate in the winter months. In December 1929, the

Vancouver Unemployed Workers' Association was formed; it organized raids on city relief offices, which resulted in the arrest of two leaders as communist agitators.

Many mass meetings and protest marches of the Vancouver unemployed were broken up by attacks from the RCMP, the provincial police and a specially-trained group of police armed with long, leadweighted clubs. During these demonstrations many hundreds of unemployed were injured. Hence, the Tolmie government's move to set up work relief camps in 1931 was, in part, an attempt to put an end to the protests, or to at least reduce the number of protesters. Those in the camps were at first paid $2.00 a day; this was soon reduced to $7.50 a month. By May 1932 there were 8,000 men in the B.C. work relief camps, and another 64,000 on relief throughout the rest of the province. The relief camps had a reputation for being inefficiently run by corrupt officials. In 1933 the administration of the camps was transferred to the Dominion government under the Department of National Defence, which had set up its own camps in 1932; the pay was now twenty cents a day. It was from the B.C. work relief camps that the "On-to-Ottawa Trek" began, which culminated in the bloody Dominion Day riot in Regina in 1935.[34]

Martin Robin has noted that, "true to the principles enunciated before the 1928 election, the Tory welfare and labour programs were severely limited in scope." Tolmie, described as "British Columbia's Calvin Coolidge, a bluff genial buffalo," was utterly unprepared for the Depression, and ideologically and politically unsuited to understand a society in social ferment. The Conservative Party was a business party, and in 1928, Tolmie had promoted the idea of a government by and for businessmen. Social reform was not a priority; initially it was not even a consideration.[35]

By 1931, British Columbia had the highest percentage of male wage-earners unemployed (27.5 percent) of any province; in attempting to meet the mounting demands for relief payments, the province incurred a substantial deficit. A government-appointed committee — the Kidd Committee, named after George Kidd, a prominent chartered accountant — was set up in 1932 to examine and report on the province's financial state. Typically, the committee blamed the financial crisis on negligent administration and past financial mismanagement, and commented that "the public purse had been regarded as an inexhaustible booty upon which all may prey." Immediate and drastic retrenchment was, not suprisingly, proposed as the remedy. This included cutting budgets for various social services: mothers' pensions were reduced from a basic $42.40 monthly for a mother and one child to $35.00; and grants to hospitals went from seventy cents per patient per day to forty-five cents. In 1931 Charlotte Whitton had submitted a critical report on mothers' pensions in British Columbia, which had recommended, among other things, that munici-palities share in the costs. The Kidd Committee heartily endorsed this suggestion, and the Tolmie government introduced legislation in 1932 which required municipalities to pay 50 per cent of the costs of these pensions, as well as the costs of other social services. "The policy of provincial economizing at their expense was naturally resented bitterly by the municipalities," wrote Harry Cassidy, "and it set the stage perfectly for years of controversy, ill-will; and lack of cooperation between the two levels of government." One assessment describes the 1932 Kidd Report as "a confused and dreamy retreat from the theory and practice of liberal democracy and the welfare state."[36]

The Reform of Welfare Under Pattullo and Cassidy

By 1933, Simon Fraser Tolmie's Conservative Party was a spent force, unable to deal with the province's overwhelming financial problems which had arisen out of the Depression. On the other hand, the Liberal Party, reinvigorated under the aggressive leadership of T. Dufferin Pattullo, offered what it termed a "New Deal" to the voters of the West Coast. Pattullo claimed that he had not borrowed the phrase from Franklin Roosevelt; he remarked that Roosevelt's inaugural address, "in respect to proposals to meet the present situation, would lead one to think that he had been reading our Liberal platform, and some of our speeches." The Liberals' 1933 election campaign slogan was "Work and Wages" and election promises included economic development, health insurance, educational reform, the expansion of the social services, and the stabilization of provincial and municipal finances. As a "new Liberal," Pattullo supported the idea of an economic council of experts and technocrats who could direct state economic and social planning. Further, Pattullo argued, what was urgently needed was a "socialized capitalism" which, while maintaining individual initiative and ownership, would use capital to benefit everyone in the society. According to Martin Robin, "Pattullo was convinced that British Columbia...was entering on a new period in which the state was destined to play a fresh creative role in lightening the burden of others 'unable to carry the load.'"[37]

The November 1933 election resulted in a significant realignment of the British Columbia political system. The Liberals won thirty-five seats and the new democratic socialist party, the CCF, contesting its first major election in Canada, formed the official opposition with seven seats, having gained a surprising one-third of the popular vote. The B.C. wing of the party was probably the most radical in Canada; its campaign slogan was "Humanity First." The CCF campaign advocated a radical transformation of society, "including the socialization of the financial machinery" of the province, the basic resource industries and the health services; the immediate expansion of the social services; and a major redistribution of income. The party was subjected to a bitter attack from both the Conservative and Liberal Parties during the campaign, as well as from the media. The Victoria *Daily Colonist* became almost hysterical: "The program for provincial purposes which the CCF had prepared...is not Fascism. It is not Bolshevism, Socialism or even Syndicalism. It is merely a collection of phrases — a phantasmagoria of platitudinous generalities out of the maze of which creeps the ever-sinister specter of intolerance through dictatorship of a junta of self-appointed socialists." W.B. Farris, a well-known Liberal lawyer and a brother of a former attorney-general, announced that unlimited amounts of British capital were available for investment in the province, on the condition that the socialists did not gain power. Throughout the 1930s, the CCF in B.C. particularly in the person of E.E. Winch acted as a constant prod to the Liberal Party on questions of social welfare and social reform.[38]

The Conservatives, who had had thirty-five members elected in 1928, were eliminated completely. According to Margaret Ormsby, "the real issue in the election was socialism versus capitalism"; the Liberal Party had managed, through its progressive stance, to steer a middle course between what was believed by many to be revolutionary socialism and reactionary Toryism. "Pattullo was the first of the radical premiers of the '30s' to emerge and the first significant figure in the modern Liberal Party to sense the appeal of progressive Liberalism," writes Ormsby.[39]

In the year following their election victory, the Liberal government hired Harry Cassidy to be the first director of social welfare for the province. Since 1929, Cassidy had been an assistant professor in the Department of Social Science (Social Work) at the University of Toronto. He was a founding member in 1931-32 of the Toronto branch of the League for Social Reconstruction, the first organization of left-wing intellectuals in Canada, which was intended to be a kind of Canadian Fabian society. When the CCF was formed later in 1932, the LSR became known as a brains trust to the party. In 1932 Cassidy had published a study, *Unemployment and Relief in Ontario 1929-1932* and had participated in several other studies with F.R. Scott on labour conditions in the men's clothing industry in Montreal and Toronto, and with other University of Toronto faculty on housing conditions in Toronto. Until he moved to British Columbia, he was also the editor of the LSR's proposed book, *Social Planning for Canada* published in 1935. Cassidy's social philosophy was similar to Pattullo's, and it is not suprising that he was attracted by the opportunity in 1934 to put some of his developing ideas on social welfare and social reform into practice. "Clearly the time had come," Cassidy remarked, "for a provincial government to turn from the easy-going frontier politics of roads and bridges and construction contracts and patronage and the spoils of office to the politics of social welfare in order to retain the confidence of the people."[40]

The position of director of social welfare was a new one, created by the reform-oriented Pattullo government. In 1934, British Columbia's social services were divided among three jurisdictions: the Departments of Labour (responsible for unemployment relief), Education, and the Provincial Secretary. Historically, most of the health and welfare services in the province had been concentrated under the provincial secretary, and it was to this minister that Cassidy reported. The Provincial Secretary in the new government was George M. Weir, who was also the Minister of Education; Weir had been head of the Department of Education at the University of British Columbia. Cassidy described him as a person who "was well known throughout Western Canada as an able teacher and educational leader who held progressive views not only on his own subject but also on social questions in general."[41] The journalist, Bruce Hutchinson, described him as having "the zeal of the real reformer." Weir was regarded by the reform elements in the Liberal Party as being the person "who would provide British Columbia with a modern system of welfare services, and pave the way in Canada for the introduction of social security legislation." In Cassidy,s opinion, Weir's involvement in Pattullo's government was "one of the chief guarantees offered to the electorate that the party was really committed to a policy of reform."[42]

When Weir met with Pattullo to discuss Cassidy's possible appointment, he recommended that Cassidy's responsibilities be to supervise social welfare and to organize state health insurance "as feasible." Weir assured the premier that Cassidy was "not a member of (the) CCF and did not attend (the) Regina Convention." He reported that Cassidy had been "recommended as (the) ablest authority in Ontario on social problems." As well, he told Pattullo that, even though Cassidy was "inclined to be radical in economic views," he was nevertheless "honourable and loyal."[43]

Cassidy, on his arrival in Victoria in September 1934, discovered a ramshackle system of social services that had developed one by one in response to particular needs; there had been little or no consideration given to central planning or long-term policy. Cassidy lost little time in drawing up a new and progressive program which was based on four major principles: 1) the need for reorganization and coordination to avoid overlapping, waste and inefficiency; 2) the value of preventive work in both health and welfare; 3) the expansion of services as quickly as possible; and 4) the importance of "economy," of limiting government to the most essential expenditures.[44]

In the next four years Cassidy was instrumental in overhauling, reorganizing and extending the provincial health and welfare services in British Columbia. A number of local health units were established, the tuberculosis services were expanded, and a division of venereal disease control was set up. The provincial system of mothers' pensions was substantially reformed: monthly allowances were increased, eligibility requirements were broadened, and an advisory board was set up. More humane and scientific policies for dealing with juvenile delinquents were developed.

A welfare field service was set up to bring together within one division all of the department's skilled social workers, whose services could then be used over a larger geographic territory or by more than one division of the health and welfare branch. The Welfare Field Service was, wrote Cassidy, "a unique development in Canadian public welfare organization." As well, a residence and responsibility act was passed in 1936; this guaranteed uniform residence rules across the province for those who were entitled to public assistance of various kinds. The financial position of hospitals was improved and the position of inspector of hospitals was established. Overall, the administration of the province's social services was completely revamped.[45]

The reform closest to Cassidy's heart, however, was a program of health insurance, and the government's failure to implement it was one of the reasons Cassidy left provincial government service early in 1939. The Health Insurance Act of 1936 and the establishment of the Health Insurance Commission in British Columbia were the first definite steps in North America to institute state health insurance. Cassidy was responsible for preparing the health insurance legislation and for planning the implementation of the scheme. A preliminary plan in the form of a draft bill was presented to the legisature in 1935; in July of that year a "hearings committee" of representative citizens was appointed to give initial consideration to the provisions of the draft bill. Wide public support for the plan soon became evident. The hearings committee's report did, however, recommend a more limited plan than the one contemplated in the draft bill, and its recommendations formed the basis for the Health Insurance Act which was passed in 1936.

By 1937, however, it had become apparent that it was going to be difficult to obtain assurances from the medical profession that doctors would provide services to insured persons at the rates and under the conditions proposed. Because of the determined opposition of the medical profession, the government considered it necessary to postpone implementation of the plan, despite the fact that a plebiscite, held at the same time as the 1937 provincial election (which also returned the Liberal Party to power), indicated popular support for the plan. In the spring of 1938 the plan was abandoned because of the loud and sustained objections of the province's doctors.[46]

As elsewhere, British Columbia's major social problem during the 1930s was unemployment. By the winter of 1931-32 the province and its municipalities were engaged in ambitious public works programs costing about $12 million. Unemployed transients and single men were moved to the province's 237 relief camps. In 1930, the provincial government established a cabinet committee on unemployment relief which "formulated policies on a day-to-day basis, often with little regard to principle or consistency." By March of 1933 there were 128,358 relief recipients in the province; from 1931 to 1934 relief expenditures exceeded $8 million per year.[47]

British Columbia's Department of Labour had the main responsibility for administering relief during the 1930s, through its unemployment relief branch. After the Dominion government changed its relief grant arrangement in 1934 from a percentage-of-cost to a lump-sum basis, the B.C. government contributed, for 1934-35, 60 percent of the costs of unemployment relief to the municipalities; from 1935 on, the province contributed

80 per cent. Only those who were employable and their dependents were covered, however; therefore, the municipalities were completely responsible for "indigent" or "poor" relief until 1938, when the province also assumed responsiblity for this group.[48]

Other provisions for the unemployed were made. From 1936, when the Dominion government closed the work relief camps, to 1940, the province again established work relief camps for the single unemployed. There were farm employment plans, youth training projects in forestry, land settlement schemes, and schemes for the rehabilitation of older workers. Transients were a particular problem for British Columbia during the Depression. When the Residence and Responsibility Act was passed in 1936, it guaranteed that residents of British Columbia would not be refused relief if they had moved from their local community. Out-of-province transients were not covered, however, and "provincial policy regarding relief for such people was predominantly negative and severe." The government placed advertisements in prairie newspapers in 1936 and 1937 that no public assistance was available for transients from other provinces.[49]

From 1935 on, it was usual throughout British Columbia to require the able-bodied unemployed to "work out relief," on sewer, park or road construction work, at the rate of forty cents per hour, until they had paid off their public assistance allowance. Table 1 shows the average number of persons receiving public assistance each month, by years, from 1932 to 1943. From 1930 to 1941 the total cost of the province's unemployment relief program was more than $91 million; the province and the municipalities contributed approximately $60 million. There were many serious problems associated with the administration of provincial relief during the 1930s. A large part of the difficulty was that three separate agencies were responsible: the welfare branch of the provincial secretary's department; the unemployment relief branch of the labour department; and the old age pensions branch of the Workmen's Compensation Board.[50]

After 1935 the labour movement's demands for legislation were concerned chiefly with health insurance and with a trade union act guaranteeing the right to organize. The B.C. Industrial Conciliation and Arbitration Act of 1937 guaranteed the right to organize, "but restricted collective bargaining to committees of employees rather than with unions, thus encouraging the growth of company unionism." The labour movement's strident oppostion to the act finally brought about an amendment allowing international unions to engage in collective bargaining. The CCF played a role in the growth of the union movement in British Columbia. Several CCF MP's and MPP's, such as Harold Winch, Grant MacNeil and Colin Cameron, helped in organizing workers in the relief camps and in the province's many mines.[51]

When unemployment increased again in British Columbia in September 1937, there was an accompanying increase in the organization of the

Table 1

Average Number of Public Assistance Recipients, British Columbia, 1932-1943

Year	Unemploy-ment Relief	Provincial Poor Relief	Municipal Poor Relief	Mothers' Allow-ances	Neglected Children	Old Age and Blind Pensions	War Veterans' Allow-ances	War Veterans' Unemploy-ment Assistance	Total
1932	79,003	936	3,400	5,287	421	6,610	2,610	3,681	101,948
1933	108,686	830	2,200	4,983	540	7,328	3,410	3,958	131,935
1934	96,272	793	1,800	4,699	568	8,300	4,310	3,942	120,684
1935	90,624	940	1,700	4,624	577	9,327	5,330	4,290	117,412
1936	81,237	1,359	2,285	4,882	655	10,268	6,440	4,309	111,435
1937	60,669	1,590	2,749	5,259	737	11,121	7,900	3,955	93,980
1938	54,531	3,141	7,101	5,641	864	12,020	10,036	3,667	97,001
1939	62,034	1,024	2,548	5,867	958	13,008	14,232	2,920	102,591
1940	47,311	77	593	5,762	1,025	13,880	15,968	1,893	86,509
1941	21,799	153	532	5,422	1,043	14,432	16,482	890	60,753
1942	11,042	153	415	4,698	1,021	14,700	16,710	297	49,036
1943	7,316	—	373	3,833	1,009	14,719	16,686	77	44,013

Source: Harry M. Cassidy, *Public Health and Welfare Reorganization: The Postwar Problem in the Canadian Provinces*, Toronto, 1945, 116.

jobless. In 1937 and 1938, the Relief Project Workers' Union demanded minimum wages and an eight-hour day. When the provincial government closed some of the relief camp projects and curtailed relief grants to municipalities, six thousand unemployed men, many of them homeless transients, congregated in Vancouver in May 1938. Inspired by communist leadership, they organized demonstrations, and when the government cut off all relief they occupied the Vancouver Art Gallery, the Georgia Hotel and the Post Office. In evicting the men a month later there was a certain amount of police brutality, and a number of demonstrators were arrested; several thousand then converged on the Parliament Buildings in Victoria at the end of June 1938. Although the city provided three abandoned hotels for their use for ten days, neither work nor relief was offered by the Liberal government. There were also arrests for street begging, as there had been several weeks earlier in Vancouver. After a demonstration in Victoria's Beacon Hill Park on July 8, the Pattullo government relented and announced that relief would be granted on certain conditions: British Columbia residents were offered two days' work at $3.20 per day every ten days, on the condition they provided evidence of seeking private employment; transients were given temporary relief, on the condition that they sign an agreement to move to the prairie provinces by August 15 to seek employment in harvesting.[52]

During June 1938, when these unemployment protests were occurring, the Sixth Canadian Conference of Social Work was held in Vancouver. Attending the conference were Paul Kellogg, editor of the *Survey*, an influential American social welfare publication, and Margaret Bondfield, who had been Britain's Minister of Labour in Ramsay MacDonald's Labour government, from 1929 to 1931. While they were in Vancouver, Cassidy arranged for them to have a meeting with Premier Pattullo and British Columbia's Minister of Labour, George S. Pearson. Both Kellogg and Bondfield apparently pressed the government to abandon its "hard-boiled" relief policies, and Cassidy attributed the government's policy change in July 1938 largely to their intervention. Although the Pattullo government was re-elected in June 1937, it was Cassidy's contention "that our local New Deal...is petering out...depression pressure for social change has become very much weaker and there is no longer much disposition on the part of the government to go forward with new schemes."[53]

Conclusion

In this chapter, a multi-cause explanation for the rise of a provincial welfare state in British Columbia has been offered. First, Pattullo's "socialized capitalism" was an attempt to mediate between and among various class demands. Pattullo once insisted that "there is no system that can be devised that is not capitalistic including socialism."[54] Martin Robin notes that, historically, "the British Columbia government has been the grantor and regulator of the greatest material prizes this economy has to offer and businessmen have striven, in large measure successfully, to influence governments as a prelude to capturing economic resources."[55]

What the "industrializing elite" wanted in B.C. above all else was "social stability"; this could be achieved through "the free flow of capital into the province, providing employment and high wages for the workers as well as profits for the employers." The central functions of the state were to protect private property, to facilitate the flow of capital through grants of timber and mining rights, to endow the railways and to restrict trade unions. Only secure and stable governments could ensure the right climate for investment. "The pursuit of stability," writes Robin, "became an enduring theme of twentieth century British Columbia politics."[56]

Second, the struggles of the working class and the unemployed were another contributing factor to the development of social legislation during this period. In the years before World War I, we have seen how protests of the unemployed extracted certain concessions from the City of Vancouver for improved forms of relief; again in the 1930s, working class agitation was a constant reminder to the provincial government that the relief being provided was far from adequate. Unions too, played a part in many of these protests.

Third, the role of women's groups in pushing for social reform, particularly in the mothers' pensions issue, was yet another significant element in the development of social policy in the province. Fourth, the CCF in the 1930s kept up constant pressure on the government to enact more progressive social welfare measures.

Fifth, the role of progressive politicians and civil servants, such as George Weir and Harry Cassidy, in fashioning many of the province's social services during the 1930s was another important response to the obvious need of an industrial society in the throes of a severe and prolonged economic depression. Cassidy ultimately experienced the all too familiar limits of social reform in a capitalist culture when the Pattullo government refused to push through the health insurance plan.

What has been suggested here is that there can be no one explanation for the development of a provincial welfare state in liberal capitalist society. Many factors were at work in British Columbia during the years 1900-1939 so that by the end of the depression, British Columbians perhaps were entitled, as Harry Cassidy suggested, to boast about their social services.

NOTES
1. Harry M. Cassidy, *Public Health and Welfare Reorganization: The Postwar Problem in the Canadian Provinces*, Toronto, 1945, 35.
2. For several examples, see Ian Gough, *The Political Economy of the Welfare State*,

London, 1979; Norman Ginsburg, *Class, Capital and Social Policy*, London, 1979; John Carrier and Ian Kendall, "Social Policy and Social Change - Explanations of the Development of Social Policy," *Journal of Social Policy*, 2:3, July 1973, 209-244; John Carter and Ian Kendall, "The Development of Welfare States: The Production of Plausible Accounts," *Journal of Social Policy*, 6:3, July 1977, 271-290.

3. For a discussion on the functions of the state in Canada, see Leo Panitch, "The Role and Nature of the Canadian State," in Leo Panitch ed., *The Canadian State: Political Economy and Political Power*, Toronto, 1977, ch. 1.

4. Martin Robin, "British Columbia: The Company Province," in Martin Robin ed., *Canadian Provincial Politics: The Party Systems of the Ten Provinces*, 2nd ed., Toronto, 1978, 42, 31. On the close alliance in Ontario, see H.V. Nelles, *The Politics of Development: Forests, Mines and Hydro-Electric Power in Ontario, 1849-1941*, Toronto, 1974.

5. Peter Leonard, "Introduction" to Gough, *Political Economy of the Welfare State*, ix. On the struggles of the working class in British Columbia during the period under discussion, see among others Paul A. Phillips, *No Power Greater: A Century of Labour in British Columbia*, Vancouver, 1967, chs. 6 & 7; and Carlos Schwartes, *Radical Heritage: Labour, Socialism and Reform in Washington and British Columbia, 1885-1917*, Vancouver, 1979.

6. Martin Robin, "The Social Basis of Party Politics in British Columbia," *Queen's Quarterly*, 72, Winter 1965-66, 676.

7. Robin, "British Columbia," 30.

8. For many examples of this influence see Elsie Gregory MacGill, *My Mother The Judge: A Biography of Judge Helen Gregory MacGill*, Toronto, 1955.

9. On the CCF in British Columbia, see Walter D. Young, "Ideology, Personality and the Origin of the CCF in British Columbia," *BC Studies*, 32, Winter 1976-77, 139-162; on other socialist movements, see A.R. McCormack, "The Emergence of the Socialist Movement in British Columbia," *BC Studies*, 21, Spring 1974, 3-27.

10. See A. Ross McCormack, *Reformers, Rebels, and Revolutionaries: The Western Canadian Radical Movement 1899-1919*, Toronto, 1977, 18.

11. Cassidy, *Public Health and Welfare Reorganization*, 40.

12. Martin Robin, *The Rush for Spoils: The Company Province 1871-1933*, Toronto, 1972, 172; Margaret A. Ormsby, "T. Dufferin Pattullo and the Little New Deal," *Canadian Historical Review*, 43:4, December 1962, 277-297; Jean Mann, "G.M. Weir and H.B. King: Progressive Education or Education for the Progressive State?" in J. Donald Wilson and David C. Jones, eds., *Schooling and Society in Twentieth Century British Columbia*, Calgary, 1980, Ch. 4; Allan Irving, "Canadian Fabians: The Work and Thought of Harry Cassidy and Leonard Marsh, 1930-1945," *Canadian Journal of Social Work Education*, 7:1, 1981, 7-28; Dorothy G. Steeves, *The Compassionate Rebel: Ernest E. Winch and His Times*, Vancouver, 1960.

13. Cassidy, *Public Health and Welfare Reorganization*, 41-43, 48, 49. See also Michael Clague et al., *Reforming Human Services: The Experience of the Community Resource Boards in B.C.*, Vancover, 1984, ch. 1.

14. Ibid, Cassidy, 45,49, 51, 52, 53; on the Provincial Industrial School and Boys' Home, see Diane L. Matters, "The Boys' Industrial School: Education for Juvenile Offenders," in Wilson and Jones, *Schooling and Society*, 53-70.

15. This and the previous paragraph are based on Patricia E. Roy, "Vancouver: 'The Mecca of the Unemployed,' 1907-1929," in Alan F.J. Artibise (ed.), *Town and City: Aspects of Western Canadian Urban Development*, Regina, 1981, 393-395.

16. Cassidy, *Public Health and Welfare Reorganization*, 44-45; Diane L. Matters, "Public Welfare Vancouver Style, 1910-1920," *Journal of Canadian Studies*, 14:1, Spring 1979,

3, 6, 8, 13; Roy, "Vancouver: 'The Mecca of the Unemployed,' 1907-1929," 396-402.

17. Martin Robin, *The Rush for Spoils: The Company Province 1871-1933*, Toronto, 1972, 178.

18. Ibid, 171, 172.

19. See Veronica Strong-Boag, "'Wages for Housework': Mothers' Allowances and the Beginnings of Social Security in Canada," *Journal of Canadian Studies*, 14:1, Spring 1979, 24-34.

20. MacGill, *My Mother the Judge*, Ch. 7.

21. This description of mothers' pensions is based on Cassidy, *Public Health and Welfare Reorganization*, 46; Matters, "Public Welfare Vancouver Style," 9; Dennis Guest, *The Emergence of Social Security in Canada*, Vancouver, 1980, 53-60.

22. See D.L. Matters, "A Report on Health Insurance: 1919," *B.C. Studies*, 21, Spring 1974, 28-32; on the flu epidemic and its impact on public health measures see Margaret W. Andrews, "Epidemic and Public Health: Influenza in Vancouver, 1918-1919," *BC Studies*, 34, Summer 1977, 21-44.

23. Robin, *Rush for Spoils*, 176; Margaret A. Ormsby, *British Columbia: A History*, Toronto, 1958, 400.

24. McCormack, *Reformers, Rebels and Revolutionaries*, 159.

25. Stuart Jamieson, *Times of Trouble: Labour Unrest and Industrial Conflict in Canada, 1900-66*, Ottawa, 1971, 186.

26. Robin, *Rush for Spoils*, 177.

27. Ibid, 183, 185.

28. Ibid, 189,212. For details on unemployment policy see Roy, "Vancouver: 'The Mecca of the Unemployed'",402-411.

29. Cassidy, *Public Health and Welfare Reorganization*, 50.

30. Ibid, 54, 55.

31. Ibid, 47.

32. Robin, *Rush for Spoils*, 227, 228.

33. See Ian D. Parker, "Simon Fraser Tolmie: The Last Conservative Premier of British Columbia," *BC Studies*, 11, Fall 1971, 27, 28, 29.

34. Jamieson, *Times of Trouble*, 236, 237, 238. On the B.C. work relief camps and the On-to-Ottawa trek see Ronald Liversedge, *Recollections of the On-to-Ottawa Trek*, Toronto 1973, edited by Victor Hoar; Victor Howard, *"We Were the Salt of the Earth": The On-to-Ottawa Trek and the Regina Riot*, Regina, 1985.

35. Robin, *Rush for Spoils*, 233, 236, 237.

36. Cassidy, *Public Health and Welfare Reorganization*, 57-59; *Robin, Rush for Spoils*, 240. On Whitton's position on the mothers' pensions issue, see Guest, *Emergence of Social Security*, 55-59.

37. Ormsby, *British Columbia: A History*, 456; Martin Robin, *Pillars of Profit: The Company Province 1934-1972*, Toronto, 1973, 11.

38. Ormsby, "T. Dufferin Pattullo and the Little New Deal," 278; and Robin, *Rush for Spoils*, 260, 261, 262. On Winch see Dorothy Steeves, *Compassionate Rebel*.

39. Ormsby, "T. Dufferin Pattullo," 278, 295. It could certainly be argued that MacKenzie King sensed the appeal of progessive Liberalism long before Pattullo. The 1919 federal party platform advocated a number of social welfare measures such as unemployment insurance and old age pensions.

40. On the LSR and Cassidy's role, see Michael Horn, *The League for Social Reconstruction: Intellectual Origins of the Democratic Left in Canada*, Toronto 1980. On Cassidy's career see Allan Irving, "A Canadian Fabian: The Life and Work of Harry

Cassidy" Ph.D., University of Toronto, 1982; Cassidy, *Public Health and Welfare Reorganization*, 64.

41. Cassidy, *Public Health and Welfare Reorganization*, 65. For a detailed discussion of Weir's life and social philosophy, see Robert England, *Living, Learning, Remembering: Memoirs of Robert England*, Vancouver, 1980, 177-180; and Jean Mann, "G.M. Weir and H.B. King," in Wilson and Jones, *Schooling and Society*, Ch. 4.

42. Ormsby, *British Columbia: A History*, 456; Ormsby, "T. Dufferin Pattullo," 285-286; Cassidy, *Public Health and Welfare Reorganization*, 64.

43. Public Archives of British Columbia, T.D. Pattullo Papers, Vol. 67, Folder 6, Memorandum: "Conference with Premier re Social Welfare Appointments," G.M.Weir to Pattullo, May 29, 1934.

44. Cassidy, "New Developments in Health and Welfare, 1933-1937," *Proceedings of the Fifth Canadian Conference of Social Work*, Ottawa, 1937, 21.

45. See Cassidy, *Public Health and Welfare Reorganization*, Part II; and Cassidy, "New Developments," 19-30.

46. Cassidy, "New Developments," 21, 22. For an account of the health insurance issue in B.C. see Margaret Andrews, "The Course of Medical Opinion on State Health Insurance in British Columbia, 1919-1939," *Histoire Sociale/Social History*, 31, May 1983, 131-143.

47. Cassidy, *Public Health and Welfare Reorganization*, 60-62.

48. Ibid, 107.

49. Ibid, 106-109. See also Cassidy, "Relief and Other Social Services for Transients," in L. Richter, ed., *Canada's Unemployment Problem*, Toronto, 1939, Ch. 4.

50. Cassidy, *Public Health and Welfare Reorganization*, 113, 115, 123. These administrative problems are discussed in detail by Cassidy in his book, 123-130.

51. Phillips, *No Power Greater*, 115, 116, 117.

52. Ibid, 118, 119; University of Toronto Archives, H.M. Cassidy Papers, Box 61, Cassidy to Paul Kellogg, July 27, 1938. See also Pierre Berton, *My Country: The Remarkable Past*, Toronto, 1976, Ch. 10 for an excellent description of the eviction of the unemployed from the post office and art gallery.

53. University of Toronto Archives, Cassidy Papers, Box 61, Cassidy to Margaret Bondfield, December 14, 1938; Cassidy to Paul Kellogg, July 17, 1938; Cassidy to Helen Wright, April 28, October 6, 1937.

54. Robin, *Pillars of Profit*, 10.

55. Robin, "British Columbia," 38.

56. Robin, *Rush for Spoils*, 41.

History According To The Boucher Report: Some Reflections On The State And Social Welfare In Quebec Before The Quiet Revolution

B.L. Vigod

In December 1961, the Quebec Government appointed a Committee to study the prevailing system of social assistance, or as it was still quaintly but revealingly called, "assistance at home." The members of the committee were J. Emile Boucher, Chairman of the Board of Directors of the Société nationale de fiducie, Marcel Bélanger, an accountant teaching in the Laval University Faculty of Commerce, and Claude Morin, teaching in the Social Sciences faculty at Laval. The two secretaries, Jean-Paul Labelle and Marcel Lemieux, were provincial welfare administrators. The committee therefore included no historians, it lacked the status of a Royal Commission (unlike the Parent Inquiry into education) and its mandate was very precise and limited. It was to examine the size and criteria of benefits, means of cooperation between government and private agencies and "the overall problem of financial assistance at home, its financial and social implications, prevention and rehabilitation." So one would hardly have expected the Report of such a committee to contain a historical treatise. But the Boucher Report of June 1963 attached a great deal of importance to the history of its subject. It argued that the unsatisfactory nature of existing arrangements for social assistance was the product of a unique historical development stretching back to the very birth of Quebec society. And it very strongly implied that to reform its social welfare system in the 1960s, Quebec had to escape from its institutional and ideological past.[1] This is a fine, indeed classic example of the historical mythology created by the authors and partisans of the Quiet Revolution: "avant nous, rien." The history of modern Quebec is divided into "the uniform bleakness of the pre-Quiet Revolution years (la grande noirceur) and the long-delayed liberation of the post-Quiet Revolution period."[2] As is the case in other spheres of public activity, this generalization about the evolution of social assistance in Quebec distorts the historical record. On the other hand, it sheds considerable light on the outlook and interests of these particular reformers at the time they mapped out the future of social service in Quebec.[3] Historians of the Quiet Revolution are in that sense indebted to documents such as the Boucher Report.

The Boucher Commission and the History of Social Welfare

According to the Boucher Report, the history of social assistance in Quebec was one of remarkable continuity. Institutional developments from the early seventeenth to the late nineteenth century conformed closely to the teaching of the Roman Catholic Church. The system which evolved, was, in the words of Esdras Minville's earlier study for the Rowell-Sirois Commission, which are quoted approvingly, "the concrete expression of a doctrine [of social justice and charity]." Under the French regime, the state was "too busy with quarrels...to pay attention" to social needs; and in any case most people considered their problems too intimate or personal to confide to royal officials. Thus, even the forerunner of "assistance at home," the so-called Committees for the Poor established in the mid-17th century, were an exercise in community responsibility organized by the Church, albeit under Royal authority.[4]

Although French Canada was briefly subject to the Elizabethan Poor Law, and although the Committees for the Poor tended to wither away, the effect of the British Conquest was essentially to strengthen community bonds and private and personal notions of charity. This, the Boucher Report attributed on one hand to French Canadians' fear of the new alien authorities, and on the other hand to the re-establishment of French Civil Law under the Quebec Act. In the first half of the 19th century, St. Vincent-de-Paul societies arose to assume responsibilities for local relief, and there was a gradual expansion of institutions caring for indigents: hospitals, asylums and orphanages. There was some state support for these, but they were largely the work of religious orders recently imported from France.

Because the state's role was so limited, Confederation had no special impact on social assistance: it merely established the theoretical jurisdiction of the provincial government. What did alter the system were the economic changes of the late nineteenth century, which found private [i.e., religious] charitable agencies unable to cope with urban, industrial society. Herein lies the great tragedy, according to the Boucher Report. Responding to a "historical necessity," the Provincial Legislature passed the Public Charities Act of 1921 to increase and regularize state support for institutions which cared for indigents. But despite this promising initiative, neither the concept of indigence nor the range of state activity was brought into line with social reality thereafter. The system failed to acknowledge that economic weakness, not utter destitution, was the prevalent social problem; and it therefore failed to shift the emphasis from institutional support to "social assistance at home." Although some modest allowances were introduced during the late 1930's, this basic failure created a vacuum soon filled by federal legislation of "Anglo-Saxon inspiration" which was ill-suited to Quebec needs, and which itself contributed to the postwar malaise.[5]

How did the Boucher Committee explain the failure to modernize social assistance? Basically, with the categorical statement that "there had long existed in Quebec a profound misconception of the true role of the state in welfare matters..." The misconception was that the state should play an inferior, supplementary role vis-à-vis private initiative, limited in effect to channelling funds through private agencies. When social realities began to threaten this doctrine, the private sector "froze in a rigid and suspicious attitude." For its part, the public sector (i.e., the provincial government) had its own motives for respecting the doctrine and maintaining the fiction — even while assuming the lion's share of costs. The result was a "composite administrative organization over which neither [sector] has full authority." Social needs weren't being met, but the private institutions were too satisfied with their power and status to notice.[6]

The state's acceptance of a subordinate role had dire consequences. Its administrative personnel thought only in terms of controlling public funds; in times of restraint they could be a positive hindrance through false economies. They did not evaluate the quality or adequacy of social services. Indeed, when the Department of Social Welfare finally did hire some professionals in social welfare, their presence was deeply feared by the lawyers and accountants in place. In the same way, legislation never reflected any fundamental changes in thinking about social assistance. Amendments to the Public Charities Act were mere houskeeping: changes in categories of assistance, absorption of new federal-provincial programs, and so on. Even the Great Depression produced only emergency relief and a grudging addition of "institutions without walls" to the list of agencies which could be subsidized. The essentially rural notions of indigence, community responsibility and the role of extended families were never formally abandoned. The Committee conceded that there is always a time lag between changing realities and appropriate legislation. But Quebec's failings could not be considered normal in this sense: the resistance to change was determined, even obsessive.[7]

Thus, the Boucher Report not surprisingly recommended an explicit rejection of these anachronistic ideas. "The Quebec Government should acknowledge in theory and practice an increasingly dynamic and creative role in social security matters...[and] accept in a positive and realistic manner all consequences resulting from this necessary role."[8]

Quebec Social Welfare, 1920-1950: An Alternative View

How should a professional historian react to this version of the past? For the pre-1921 period, he can point to a few contradictions and misconceptions, but nothing terribly serious. Most of them derive from an overemphasis on continuity — the assumption that since religious doctrines were always involved, there were no significant alternations in the relative importance of Church and State in the realm of social assistance. Thus we have a significant downplaying of the powers and initiatives of the civil authority in New France after 1663, and little sense of the impact of the ultramontane triumphs of the mid-19th century, both institutional and ideological. The Report even contradicts itself on this subject, claiming at the outset that Church teaching brought about the acceptance of family and community responsibility without civil compulsion, but later suggesting that the re-introduction of French Civil Law in 1774 created "legal norms [which were] a powerful instrument assuring cohesion and continuity of the family's responsibilities in welfare matters."[9]

But these are minor quibbles. More surprising is the failure to acknowledge the complexities of the period after 1921. A study of the period between 1921 and 1945 reveals something other than "uniform bleakness." There were discernible advances in thinking about social assistance and the role of the state, and if the system in 1960 was unbelievably antiquated and chaotic, the explanation lay in the immediate rather than the distant past. Perhaps the Committee did not want to sound politically partisan, or perhaps it was using history to undermine the legitimacy of the clerically-dominated structure whose displacement it was about to propose. Whatever the reason, it ignored the possibility that the villain was no older than the postwar Duplessis regime itself, which conducted a self-serving but shortsighted and unconscionable resistance to many forms of political modernization. True, a threatened clerical and lay elite in the private sector acquiesced, permitting their agencies to become "dispensing organisms" for Union Nationale patronage.[10] But they were given little choice, and there were just as many people in the Church who warned against the ultimate consequence. By assigning primary responsibility to the welfare institutions and not to the government which had the duty and authority to introduce reforms, the Boucher Commission was turning the situation upside down.

Superficially, the Public Charities Act of 1921 was the Quebec government's reaction to a temporary crisis, the severe postwar depression. The network of private (in most cases religious) and municipal institutions which sheltered and treated helpless and destitute individuals could not cope with a sudden deluge using traditional sources of revenue. At the same time, it had become clear that neither a recently enacted poor law in the Elizabethan tradition, obliging municipalities to care for indigents residing within their borders, nor the Provincial Secretary's custom of making ad hoc grants to individual benevolent institutions, was adequate in the circumstances.[11] Premier L-A Taschereau argued that the Act was an emergency measure which signalled no fundamental change in philosophy. "Voyez-vous par vous-mêmes toutes les affreuses miséres à soulager, et dites-moi si le gouvernement n'a pas le devoir impérieux de venir en aide à nos institutions pour leur permettre de réaliser leur oeuvre."[12]

Critics, however, saw far more than an expansion and regularization of subsidies in the legislation. By spelling out categories of assistance in minute detail and creating a Bureau of Public Charities to administer the grants, the Act raised the spectre of increasing state control and the decline of the "moral" aspect of charity. The sensitivity of the Church is a matter of some complexity. It no doubt resulted in part from insecurity about its own ability to provide adequate services, as well as from legitimate fears about the partisan manipulation of provincial assistance. In addition, some Quebec churchmen were in a state of near paranoia after the war because of anticlerical policies adopted in several European Catholic countries. In any case, there resulted a bitter five year dispute pitting the Liberal government against the Roman Catholic hierarchy and its political and journalistic allies, with religious orders frequently caught in the crossfire.[13] Although the government eventually made some minor concessions to religious authorities, other initiatives soon followed.

Provincial authority and activity expanded dramatically in the field of public health under the direction of Dr. Alphonse Lessard, who served simultaneously as Director of the Public Charities Bureau. In fact some of Lessard's health initiatives contained strong elements of social service, such as the temporary removal of children from tubercular surroundings and an educational as well as a treatment campaign against venereal disease.[14] In 1924, the government also passed an adoption law which finally gave legal and emotional protection to children and adopting parents. Although the nuns who operated orphanages and foundling homes had urged some legislation, it caused a new storm of protest from religious militants. Technically, they objected that as originally worded the law did not guarantee that Catholic children would be adopted into Catholic homes; more fundamentally, critics complained that the state was further invading the sacred domain of the family. Henri Bourassa insisted that the legislation "allongera la liste des atteintes portées à tout ce qui a fait la force et la vitalité de notre ordre social. Elles se sont singulièrement multipliées, depuis quelques années."[15]

By the middle of the 1920s, the reforming zeal of the Taschereau government was rapidly dissipating. The postwar depression was giving way to a period of industrial expansion, the government did not want to increase its financial commitments unnecessarily, and Premier Taschereau was anxious for a truce in what he called "religious warfare." For these reasons and in a classic defence of provincial rights, Taschereau strongly opposed the federal Old Age Pensions Act of 1927. For this he was warmly congratulated in business, ecclesiastical and nationalist circles. However, not everyone in Quebec was satisfied with the traditional, very restrictive definition of social assistance embodied in the Public Charities Act (effectively, the care of indigents within institutions), or with the virtual absence of legislation to mitigate the poverty and vulnerability of the urban working class. In the latter half of the 1920s, voluntary agencies in Montreal began to recognize the need for a variety of social services "outside walls," and for more effective ways of raising funds necessary to provide them.[16] While the Protestant and Jewish communities often set the example, as in launching federated appeals and recognizing the profession of social worker, the parish-based St. Vincent-de-Paul Societies of Montreal began their own extensive inquiry into the nature of their future services to

Catholics.[17] Meanwhile, organized labour and its sympathizers seized an opportunity to introduce the question of income security.

This opportunity arose from a combination of circumstances: the provincial government's refusal to participate in the federal old age pension scheme, and a debate concerning workmen's compensation. The non-confessional Montreal Trades and Labour Council strongly favoured the modest federal initiative, which required provincial governments to contribute half of a twenty dollar monthly pension for needy persons over seventy years of age, and to undertake the costs of administration. More suprisingly, support for Quebec's participation in the scheme came also from Pierre Beaulé, lay president of the Catholic Labour Confederation.[18] Even the Abbé Fortin, clerical advisor to the catholic organization, disputed the claim that Quebec had no need of old age pensions. "Il faut être contre l'étatisme," he agreed, "mais il faut aussi secourir les malheureux. Et aujourd'hui on est rendu à un état de choses tel qu'il faut prendre des mesures nécessaires pour aider les indigents." The only way to avoid "statism" was to pay wages which would enable the working class "d'éléver une nombreuse famille et de prendre soin aussi en même temps de leurs vieux parents."[19] The very fact that Premier Taschereau continued to denounce Old Age Pensions on philosophical as well as constitutional grounds in 1928 and 1929 indicates his awareness that the plan appealed to many Quebecers.

The government had appointed an inquiry into the system of workmen's compensation in 1922, and enacted its unanimous recommendations in 1926. Taschereau at first rejected labour's proposal to remove compensation claims from the courts and transfer the authority to make awards and the administration of the system to a permanent commission. He was forced to change his mind, however, when insurance companies suddenly and drastically increased premiums for the liability insurance employers were required to carry. A commission was created in 1928 to accept liability deposits, make awards and recommend and enforce improved industrial safety standards.[20] As Taschereau had expected, the existence of the commission encouraged labour to press for a greatly expanded definition of "risks" subject to compensation. The argument was disarmingly simple. Seasonal unemployment and poverty in old age were as much "occupational hazards" for the urban working class as were industrial accidents. Politically, this argument was difficult to reject: it proposed a form of old age security without federal intrusion into the constitutional domain of the province and, if workers as well as employers and the government all contributed a share of the "premiums," it was a form of social insurance which did not encourage "reliance on the state." In 1929, growing pressure led Labour Minister Galipeault to admit that "le temps est venu d'étudier le système qui conviendrait pour établir l'assurance social dans cette province... La loi préférée...serait une loi contributoire à la mise en oeuvre de laquelle contribueraient le patron, l'ouvrier et le gouvernement."[21] In 1930, Taschereau appointed Edouard

Montpetit to chair a royal commission inquiry into social insurance. Thus, although the recommendations of the Montpetit Commission were inevitably influenced by the Great Depression, it must be remembered that the inquiry was launched in response to growing demands and expectations in the preceeding decade.

The effects of the Depression were arguably more severe in Quebec than in any other province. Barely able to provide its share of relief under federal unemployment relief legislation, especially when it had to assume a large number of municipal obligations as well, the Quebec government could not seriously consider permanent or more elaborate social security measures. On the contrary, Premier Taschereau emphasized the need for fiscal responsibility and unwisely began denoucing the proponents of reform.[22] Still, the Boucher Report seriously under-estimated the impact of the Depression on clerical, political and public thinking about social assistance. For one thing, the inadequacy of traditional attitudes and existing arrangements was clearly demonstrated. The experience of the St. Vincent-de-Paul societies in Montreal provides a classic example. Since the city had no formal mechanism for administering unemployment relief when the Depression struck, the societies initially agreed to take on the responsibility. As the visible relief agencies, however, the societies found themselves blamed for delays and insufficiencies which they were powerless to control; in fact they became the targets for general discontent and frustration. The laymen and clergy who directed the work of the societies concluded that their original mission, charitable work of the parish level, could be permanently damaged by the loss of prestige. In 1933 they withdrew their services, forcing Montreal City Council to establish its own relief administration.[23]

From a number of quarters, meanwhile, came proposals for reform linked to the realities of the prevailing economic system. The Papal Encyclical *Quadragesimo Anno* (1931) received far more prompt attention in Quebec than had the first great social encylical, *Rerum Novarum*, after 1891. Now that the Pope had declared governments responsible for protecting the economically weak members of industrial society, rejoiced Father J-P Archambeault of the Ecole Sociale Populaire, Quebec clergy need no longer fear being accused of "meddling in politics" simply because they called for social reform.[24] Study sessions organized by Archambault produced the *Programme de Restauration Sociale*, whose reformist content historians often ignore because of the ultimately conservative motives of the authors. There were actually two versions of the *Programme*. The first, written by priests and published in the spring of 1933, called in general terms for a redistribution of wealth in favour of the masses through such state initiatives as accident, sickness, old age and unemployment insurance, crop and other kinds of farm insurance, minimum wage laws related to the cost of living and special grants for large families and the very poor.[25] The second *Programme* published in late 1933 was a more comprehensive document co-authored by lay leaders of the Catholic Action movement.

The section on labour legislation, written by union official Alfred Charpentier, called for a contributory social insurance scheme, old age and needy mothers' allowances, an experimental family allowance system, salaries sufficient to support average-sized families, a law requiring employers to pay wages before dividends, a minimum wage for day labour, slum clearance and increased bargaining rights for unions.[26] In the same year, Cardinal Villeneuve publicly invited the state to elaborate a program of social reform based on papal teaching.[27] All of these demands reinforced the recommendations of the Montpetit Commission, which had exceeded its original terms of reference in a series of reports submitted in 1931 and 1932. In addition to regulatory laws protecting workers and wider provincial support for charitable institutions, Montpetit proposed such direct support programs as needy mothers' and family allowances, old age pensions, unemployment insurance and subsidized health insurance.[28] Even before the second *Programme de Restauration Sociale* appeared, various proposals for income security had reached the political arena. The election platform of the opposition Conservatives in 1931 promised "collective insurance" and increased compensation for accidents at work, general minimum wage legislation, allowances for large families and pensions for the blind, for widows and for orphans.[29] These policies were reconfirmed at the 1933 leadership convention which chose Maurice Duplessis to succeed Camillien Houde, however much Duplessis downplayed them afterward. On the Liberal side, Premier Taschereau's continuing rejection of the more far-reaching Montpetit Commission recommendations was apparently decisive in driving Action libérale reformers out of the party.[30] The leader of the group, Paul Gouin, was an unsigned co-author of the second *Programme*, which was adopted almost verbatim as a platform by his new political party, the Action libérale nationale (ALN). The same platform was supposedly that of the electoral alliance between Gouin and Duplessis in 1935.

Although Taschereau agreed to implement old age pensions only as a form of deathbed repentance, and Duplessis enacted practically none of the social legislation contained in the ALN platform,[31] it would be wrong to conclude that the desire for improved social assistance simply vanished. Duplessis' decision to call a provincial election in 1939 on the issue of Canadian participation in the Second World War was almost certainly an attempt to divert attention from the record of his government. In fact, several of the deceived reformers returned to the Liberal fold for the campaign and one of them, Oscar Drouin, played a central role in the reforms of the Godbout administration. While better known for the introduction of compulsory education and female suffrage and for the nationalization of Montreal Light, Heat and Power Company, the wartime Liberal government also laid the groundwork for an expanded role in social assistance. Without directly challenging the domain of the private institutions, Godbout responded to an acknowledged lack of coordination by creating a Ministry of Social Welfare. At the same time, he extended the needy mothers' allowance and established family courts to deal with juvenile delinquency and other family problems.[32]

Godbout only hinted at an expanding role for the new Department;[33] his immediate dilemma was created by federal initiatives. The Report of the Rowell-Sirois Commission, the ensuring transfer of constitutional authority over unemployment insurance to Ottawa, and the introduction of Family Allowances were anathema to traditional nationalist opinion in Quebec and vindicated Duplessis' prophesies. Yet Godbout and his colleagues probably favoured the new forms of state intervention and believed they were in tune with public expectations. They were undoubtedly less enthusiastic about the expansion of federal authority, regarding it simply as inevitable in the context of wartime fiscal centralization while dreading the eventual political consequences. It is interesting to speculate what would have happened if the Godbout government had not borne the brunt of French Canadian anger over conscription, and instead been re-elected in 1944. For although the "official" social thought of Quebec remained fundamentally different from that of English Canada, practically speaking the gap in terms of public expectations of the state had closed dramatically by the end of the Depression. Despite their distrust of federal authority, after all, Quebec voters supported the welfare state policies of the federal Liberals as strongly as they did the provincial rights platform of the Union Nationale during the postwar decade. And if Godbout was prepared to defy the Roman Catholic hierarchy over education and female suffrage, he was perfectly capable of expanding the state's role in social assistance in response to demonstrated needs. Like Jean Lesage fifteen years later, he would undoubtedly have profited from autonomist sentiment in conflicts with Ottawa: even the Tremblay Royal Commission admitted implicitly that the vacuum in provincial social policy was contributing to the expansion of federal authority during the late forties and early fifties.[34]

Of course 1945 was not 1960. Neither the bureaucratic expertise and ambition, nor the provincial financial resources, nor what Jean-Louis Roy refers to as "social knowledge" were nearly as strong as they would become.[35] Conversely, the "private" sector might have resisted change far more effectively at an earlier stage. Still, it has become almost a commonplace that the Quiet Revoluton was not really very revolutionary: rather, it was a period when public policy and institutions caught up with social and economic change.

This is especially true in the case of social assistance. The inadequacies of the prevailing structure and philosophy were widely recognized, and a public desire for social security measures had already been created by the end of the war. In fact some proponents of reform during the 1930s were considerably more radical than the Boucher Committee, in that they explicitly linked social injustice with the economic system. Of course Boucher and his colleagues knew that poverty and insecurity were rooted in the system, but their response was not to challenge the system. The "bureaucratic revolution" they proposed would not fundamentally alter the course of Quebec history; it would merely cure fifteen years of stubborn neglect, while fulfilling the ambitions of a class whose presence, training and outlook were the product of a perfectly normal evolution.

NOTES

1. Government of Quebec, *Report of the Study Committee on Public Assistance,* Quebec, 1963, 27, 117, [Hereafter, *Report*].
2. Ralph Heintzman, "Image and Consequence," *Journal of Canadian Studies,* 13:2, Summer, 1978, 2.
3. See the remarkably perceptive contemporary analysis by Hubert Guindon, "Social Unrest, Social Class and Quebec's Bureaucratic Revolution," *Queen's Quarterly,* LXXI:2, 1964.
4. *Report,* 27-8.
5. Ibid, 29-33.
6. Ibid, 107-9.
7. Ibid, 110-15.
8. Ibid, 117.
9. Ibid, 27, 30.
10. Conrad Black, *Duplessis,* Toronto, 1977, 687-8.
11. B.L. Vigod, "Ideology and Institutions in Quebec: The Public Charities Controversy 1921-1926," *Social History,* XI:21, May 1978, 168-9.
12. *Le Devoir,* 14 avril, 1921.
13. Vigod, "Public Charities."
14. B.L. Vigod, "Responses to Economic and Social Change in Quebec: The Provincial Administration of Louis-Alexandre Taschereau 1920-1929," Ph.D., Queen's University, 1975, 306-16.
15. Ibid, 291-7; Bourassa citation from *Le Devoir,* 7 mars, 1924.
16. Serge Mongeau, *Evolution de l'Assistance au Québec,* Montreal, 1967, 49-50.
17. Robert Rumilly, *La Plus Riche Aumône: Histoire de la Société St. Vincent de Paul,* Montreal, 1946, 134-148.
18. *Canadian Annual Review,* 1928-29, 386-7; Confédération des Travailleurs Catholiques du Canada, *Procès Verbal,* 1926, 34-5; *La Vie Syndicale,* février, 1928.
19. *L'Evénement,* 18 janvier, 1928.
20. Quebec, *Report of the Investigation Commission on the Compensation in Labour Accidents,* Quebec, 1925; *Canadian Annual Review,* 1927-28, 414-15; Roger Chartier, "La réparation des accidents du travail et la commission du salaire minimum des femmes," *Relations industrielles,* janvier, 1963.
21. Confédération des Travailleurs Catholiques du Canada, *Procès Verbal* 1929, 15-16.
22. B.L.Vigod, "The Quebec Government and Social Legislation During the 1930's: A Study in Political Self-Destruction," *Journal of Canadian Studies,* 14-1, Spring, 1979, 62-5.
23. Robert Rumilly, *Histoire de la Province de Quebec* XXXIII, 150-1, 176.
24. "Avant Propos," *Ecole Sociale Populaire,* No. 232-233, mai-juin, 1933, [Hereafter ESP].

25. L. Chagnon, "Directives sociales catholiques," *ESP*, No. 232-233 mai-juin, 1933.
26. "La question ouvrière," *ESP*, No. 239-40, décembre 1933-janvier 1934.
27. *Action Catholique*, 28 avril, 1933.
28. Commission des assurances sociales de Que'bec, *Rapports*, 1932-33. Recommendations summarized in Mongeau, *Evolution de l'Assistance...*, 60-2.
29. Jean-Louis Roy, *Les Programmes Electoraux du Québec*, Montreal, 1971, Vol. II, 246.
30. Patricia G. Dirks, "The Origins of the Union Nationale," Ph.D., University of Toronto, 1974, 226.
31. The exceptions were modest allowances for blind persons and needy mothers. Duplessis' Fair Wage Act became a cruel joke on labour, since it was used to restrain wage increases.
32. The immediate cause of action, according to Mongeau, *Evolution de l'Assistance...*, 70-2, was a scandal regarding health conditions in commercial daycare facilities; this provoked a wide ranging Inquiry whose recommendations were heeded.
33. It had been established partly to administer a new health insurance program and partly "d'étudier et de resoudre de façon pratique les graves problèmes du bien-être social..." Roy, *Programmes Electoraux* II, 319.
34. Quebec, Royal Commission of Inquiry into Constitutional Problems, *Report*, Quebec, 1956, e.g., Vol. I, 258-60. See also René Durocher et Michèle Jean, "Duplessis et la Commission royal d'enquête...," *Revue d'histoire de l'Amérique française*, 25:3, décembre 1971, 354-55.
35. Jean-Louis Roy, *La Marche des Québécois: Le Temps des Ruptures 1945-1960*, Montreal, 1976.

Forestalling the Welfare State:
The Establishment of Programmes of Corporate Welfare

Neil Tudiver

...as (occupational social services) grow and multiply they come into conflict with the aims and unity of social policy; for in effect their whole tendency...is to divide loyalties, to nourish privilege, and to narrow the social conscience.

Richard M. Titmuss
Birmingham, England, 1955

Profit-sharing (for employees) is one of the niftiest capital-raising tax shelters ever devised.

J.L. Biddell
Chairman of Clarkson Co.,
Toronto, 1978.

Social services have been used in industry to motivate workers towards increased production, to placate angry employee groups, to forestall attempts at unionization, to soften the harsh effects of poor working conditions and to direct workers' loyalty to their employers' interests. Such programmes have often served to subdue worker unrest and reduce total labour costs. Employers have preferred to offer welfare benefits and services in favour of the more costly alternatives of higher wages, low productivity due to low moral, or improvements to workplace health and safety conditions.

A popular illustration of these dynamics appears in the film *9 to 5*. An authoritarian and chauvinist male manager is conveniently removed from the workplace for several weeks by three female clerical workers. In his absence, these captors cleverly institute some workplace reforms in his name. After escaping confinement the manager returns to an office painted in bright colours where workers can dress as they please, move around at their convenience, display family photos and other personal items and even drink coffee at their desks. They also have access to day care and may participate in such programmes as flexitime and job-sharing. Aghast at the horrors of happy workers, the manager prepares to fire his three subordinates. He is thwarted by the chairman of the board who pays a special visit of congratulation to discover the causes for recent improvements in productivity. The obvious conclusion is that happy workers are indeed productive.

These "humanizing" developments have mainly served the interests of employers. Capitalists have used occupational welfare programmes to tighten their control over the labour process, to facilitate efforts at improving the productivity of labour and to combat collective organization by labour. Corporate welfare has been an important means for social control and economic domination.

Employers have installed programmes for profit-sharing, accident, sickness and life insurance, pensions, recreation, health care, education, housing and workplace restructuring in their historic struggle with employees over control of the production process and distribution of surplus. For those employees who qualify, they have obtained increased access to funds for vacation, retirement, health care, dental care, education, recreation, or housing. Compensation packages have been sweetened through plans for profit-sharing, bonuses or stock subscription. Conditions of work have been moderately reformed to reduce monotony and drudgery, or to add creative challenges to the requirements of the working day. Employers have also initiated counselling and training programmes for valued employees who suffer from the tensions and stresses of their jobs.

Origins of Welfare at Work, 1880-1920

Craft production, in which workers exercised significant autonomy over the work process, was the dominant form of organization for much of North American industry in the mid-nineteenth century. By the 1920s it was virtually eliminated. Management had won the power to plan the entire work process and to dominate its detailed execution.[1] Workers' power was being expressed in strategies of resistance and collective organization. Such an immense shift in the balance of power was not captured with ease. There was intense struggle between labour and capital over the fruits of rapidly rising production and productivity.[2]

Management's assault on worker autonomy was aimed at the central factor of work organization and process. With the spread of scientific management, developed by people like Frederick W. Taylor (Taylorism), workers confronted jobs which were divided into smaller and smaller pieces. Skills and trades which were previously required became less and less necessary; former teams and work groups were being destroyed by detailed division of tasks and functions; mechanization was rapidly altering daily work experience.[3] Taylorism was an important step towards the modern assembly line form of manufacture.

Scientific management altered the conception and organization of work in the interests of capital. It allowed for phenomenal increases in total output and in productivity per worker.[4] New problems emerged for management as workers opposed their initiatives. The simplified and homogenized skill requirements did weaken workers' autonomy. Yet as tasks became more routinized, inherent interest in the job declined. Management faced serious problems of reduced motivation and increased turnover of workers. They responded by designing incentive programmes to increase motivation and reduce turnover.

Welfare was often used to combat and undermine worker resistance in firms which had instituted scientific management. Its adoption in a large number of iron and steel companies allowed them to undergo intense mechanization by the turn of the century.[5] By the early 1900s the extensive worker autonomy of the 1880s and 1890s had declined considerably. Systems of inside contracting, which prevailed in mining, steel and cotton through the 1870s and 1880s were reduced significantly by 1900 and eliminated by World War I. Employers faced higher turnover among dissatisfied workers, many of whom were trained operators of expensive machines. Unionization was also increasing.

Employers in the United States were often first at the starting gate in instituting welfare programmes at work. Their counterparts and subsidiaries in Canada shaped many of their programmes on the basis of these U.S. precedents. Scott[6] suggests that most Canadian corporate pioneers of employee representation began their plans at the same time as their U.S. parents. These included such giants as Imperial Oil, International Harvester, Bell Telephone, Canadian Consolidated Rubber, and Swift Canadian. The steel industry was an important pacesetter. Katherine Stone has described how developments in steel took the form of wage incentive programmes based on individual piece work; new promotion policies and job ladders designed to create a sense of vertical mobility out of the growing number of dead-end jobs; and welfare policies. Welfare policies of the U.S. Steel Company included: a stock subscription plan for workers; profit-sharing for executives; pensions; accident insurance; safety and sanitation campaigns; company-built housing; and education and recreation facilties. By the 1920s the company was spending an average of $10 million per year on these benefits, most of which had tight restrictions designed to bind the worker to the company. The stock subscription plan, set up in 1903, sold stock at reduced rates to company employees through payroll deduction. Bonuses were given to employees who stayed with the company for a minimum of five years. To be eligible they had to show a "proper interest" in the company. Any union activity or support for struggles of employees in other companies were included in the list of undesirable behaviours. According to Stone, these new employment policies were partly responsible for delaying eventual unionization. The first collective agreement between U.S. Steel and the Steel Workers Organizing Committee was not formalized until 1937.[7]

Where workers' autonomy held on more tenaciously, employers' responses were more blunt. For example, iron moulders in Toronto retained significant shop control from the mid-nineteeth into the twentieth century. Through a strong closed shop union — the Iron Moulders Internation Union (IMIU) — they negotiated the price for moulding new patterns with the boss; dictated the daily production per worker; controlled the terms for hiring; and determined the number of apprentices and helpers. Employers responded to such worker strength with coercion and the power of the law when necessary. In the early 1890s some firms tried to destroy the IMIU by shutting down their moulding shops and pressing workers to accept reduced rates.[8]

The widespread use of welfare work in the U.S. was supported by major business coalitions such as the National Civic Federation (NCF). Formed in 1900 by leaders in business, politics and academia to promote industrial harmony as a national objective, the NCF had a welfare department by 1904. The actions of the welfare department were directed by prominent employers.[9]

Unlike Taylorism, which attacked workers' control directly, most welfare work concentrated on workplace improvements such as sanitation and ventilation, as well as external factors such as housing, recreation, health and education. They served to bind workers more securely to the company through creating dependencies on employer-provided benefits. As Nelson and Campbell point out, "Welfare work...was usually found in firms that either employed large numbers of women or were geographically isolated."[10] Services provided addressed the demands of employers to retain stable work forces.

The early welfare programmes spread rapidly in industries which faced labour problems. They introduced new methods of social control for management to use over their labour force. As such they were the forerunners of later personnel and industrial relations departments which were concerned mainly with employee control.

Employee Welfare in the 1920s
By the mid-1920s, welfare capitalism, that is, "any service provided for the comfort or improvement of employees which was neither a necessity of the industry nor required by law,"[11] reached its peak in the United States. In 1926, a survey of 1500 of the largest firms determined that 80 percent had adopted at least on aspect of welfare and that over 50 percent had comprehensive programmes. The Bureau of Labor Statistics estimated that expenditures on employee welfare ranged from a low of $14 per employee in the clothing industry to a high of $67 in shoemaking. The average was $27, or approximately two percent of the average industrial wage.[12] By the late 1920s employee representation itself covered over 1.5 million U.S. workers.[13]

In Canada, concern by business and government leaders for industrial peace became more prevalent as the prospects of widespread class war rose during the second decade of the twentieth century. Union membership, strikes and militant labour action had reached a peak by 1919,[14] prompting many businessmen to respond with liberal programmes based on co-operation.[15] These changing approaches toward labour, which began during World War I, were influenced considerably by the earlier work of the NCF in the U.S. and the industrial representation plan promoted by MacKenzie King. King first developed and implemented his plan with the Rockefeller owned Colorado Fuel and Iron Co. in 1915, one year after company-directed militia violently defeated a strike, in which they killed three male strikers, two women and eleven children.

King's plan contained four key elements: a corporate welfare system, a grievance procedure, an employees' bill of rights, and a plan for joint councils containing both worker-elected and management-appointed representatives. The joint council was most appealing to employers since it enabled them to undermine unions as the representatives of employees. The popularity of these plans were widespread. By 1920, between 40 percent and 54 percent of all unionized workers were covered by industrial councils.[16]

Early in 1920, the Social Service Council, a national alliance of church and labour groups, did a survey of fifty-three "representative industries," to determine "...the extent of co-management or welfare work being promoted by employers throughout Canada".[17] Of the fifty-three plants, twenty provided recreational facilities, nine had educational programmes, largely in technical subjects, eighteen had profit-sharing or bonus systems and fourteen had well-developed works councils. Subsequent reports on these findings applauded the employers' sense of responsiblity for providing benefits, yet criticized their paternalism and avoidance of the more basic industrial problems.[18] They further suggested that the industrial councils had a tendency to discourage labour organization. In the early 1920s most of the industrial councils were being established in open shop industries.[19]

One of Canada's earliest comprehensive plans was developed by Massey-Harris. By 1918 they had a company cafeteria directed jointly by workers and managers which offered meals at cost; a full-time first-aid nurse hired by the company; and thirteen acres of land divided into garden plots for the use of employees. In 1919, the company set up an industrial council with equal representation from employee-elected and management-delegated members.[20] The council's mandate was to meet monthly and submit recommendations to the company president on,

...all questions relating to working conditions, protection of health, safety, wages, hours of labour, recreation, education and other matters of mutual interest to the employees and the management.[21]

The council was most successful in matters of safety and health. It was, "...one area where workers found concessions easy to ask for and management found them easy to grant."[22] Its achievements included the hiring of a plant doctor in 1920; installation of drinking fountains and wash basins in two warehouses; and the placing of guards on exposed machinery. Far more contentious were discussions around hours of work, rates of pay and lay-offs. In October, 1919, management defeated the workers' proposal to allow five minutes for washing up before plant closing. A worker's motion to grant one week's paid holiday after five years' service was tabled indefinitely. In 1921, during a recession, management's wage cuts of 20 percent could not be reversed by the council. Although business conditions had improved substantially by 1923, the 20 percent cuts were not reinstated despite attempts by worker members of the council to regain some portion. In 1924, the council obtained more safety improvements, including special shoes and installation of lockers and showers, but the lowered wages prevailed. According to Scott, the council

> ...helped to achieve a decade (1919-1929) of relative labour peace, holding off the spectre of union organization, smoothing difficult wage reductions, ironing out grievances, and inspiring some genuine enthusiasm in at least a minority of employees.[23]

The council "won" only those material concessions which management had been prepared to offer to its employees.

By the middle and latter 1920s, employee benefit plans were widely available among large employers. Some plans were fairly elaborate. A 1928 inquiry by the Ontario Department of Labour surveyed 300 firms with 185,187 employees. The majority of employees had access to some form of in-plant or employer-subsidized medical services which went beyond the legislated requirements of workmen's compensation. They ranged from minimum provision of first aid kits, part-time duty nurses and treatment rooms to establishment of clinics with full-time salaried doctors who were available for all employees' health matters. Regular pension schemes existed in forty-nine firms with a total of 100,000 employees. Another twelve firms made individual provision for their favoured long-term workers. The vast majority of these retirement programmes required minimum service of twenty to twenty-five years. Also, 212 firms had some scheme for group sickness and health insurance. Joint councils existed in 21 percent of the firms, with 48 percent of the employees (Tables 1 and 2).[24]

State provided social security was not advancing during this period, despite considerable pressure. Finkel has pointed out that throughout the 1920s,

> ...the Trades and Labour Congress pressed unsuccessfully for universal old age pensions, unemployment insurance, sickness insurance and disability insurance. And the only program passed by the Federal Government was a pension scheme for needy poor.[25]

This one scheme was a concession to the labour group in the House of Commons under the leadership of J.S. Woodsworth, in exchange for support of MacKenzie King's minority Liberal government.

TABLE 1
Employee Benefits In Ontario, 1927 (1)

	EMPLOYEES		FIRMS	
	#	%	#	%
REGULAR PENSION PLANS	100,000	54.0%	49	16.3%
INDIVIDUAL RETIREMENT PLANS	3,700	2.0%	12	4.0%
SICKNESS INS: - GROUP	51,850	28.0%	105	35.0%
SICKNESS INS: - NONGROUP	92,600	50.0%	78	26.0%
JOINT COUNCILS	88,890	48.0%	63	21.0%
COMPANY CAFETERIA	92,600	50.0%	89	29.7%
RECREATION	138,900	75.0%	123	41.0%
ANNUAL PAID HOLIDAY	59,260	32.0%	60	20.0%
MALE	142,374	76.9%		
FEMALE	42,813	23.1%		
TOTAL SAMPLE	185,187	100.0%	300	100.0%

(1) From a survey conducted by the Ontario Department of Labour in 1927. Data obtained from a summary published in Findlay (1928).

TABLE 2
Hours of Work for Ontario Workers, 1927 (1)
Based on Hours per Week

	Total Workers		Male Workers		Female Workers	
	#	%	#	%	#	%
Over 55 Hours	6,940	4.1%	6,100	4.9%	840	2.0%
49 - 54 Hours	37,786	22.5%	28,129	22.4%	9,657	23.0%
48 Hours or Less	122,908	73.3%	91,417	72.8%	31,491	75.0%
Total Sample	167,634	100.0%	125,646	75.0%	41,988	25.0%

(1) From a survey conducted by the Ontario Department of Labour in 1927. Data obtained from a summary published in Findlay (1928).

These early programmes of welfare and employee representation supplanted other potential forms of social security provision. They were designed to overcome worker resistance, improve worker motivation and undermine workers' collective action. Employers' fundamental positions regarding workers' rights and welfare had been stated nationally in 1919, during discussion of the recommendations of the Royal Commission on Industrial Relations. The Commission's proposals included providing state insurance against unemployment, sickness, disability and old age; the fixing of minimum wages for women, girls and unskilled labour; the eight-hour day; a weekly day of rest; and the right to bargain collectively. At a national meeting of representatives from management, labour and the general public to consider the recommendations,

> ...the postwar agenda of business and industry was revealed as a stand-pat position. Employers refused to make any concession on two of the most important questions from labour's standpoint — collective bargaining and the eight-hour day. The social security recommendations were dealt with innocuously by a recommendation that a "Board or Boards be appointed to enquire into the subjects of State Insurance."[26]

By the mid and latter 1920s business people were generally opposed to welfare outside the workplace, where it served no useful purposes for retention, motivation and discipline of workers. Social security was not a necessary priority for employers.

The employers' position in the U.S. was presented succintly in a 1933 publication of the National Industrial Conference Board, on the experience with welfare work and employee representation:

> It facilitates quick adaptation to special or changing conditions, when passive opposition would bring about the failure of plans. It engenders greater interest in the job, which leads to the offering of suggestions as to short cuts and improvements that in the aggregate may mean considerable savings to the company...(it succeeds in) welding together management and working force into a single, cohesive productive unit.[27]

In Britain, schemes of employee participation, especially those emphasizing profit-sharing, experienced several cycles of popularity between 1865 and World War I, leading to the eventual establishment of the Whitley Councils which were first proposed in 1917 by a government sub-committee chaired by J.H. Whitley. It advocated, "formation of joint standing industrial councils to deal in particular with wages, conditions, unemployment and the means of advancing labour-management cooperation."[28] At its peak in 1920-21, the Whitley Council system covered 3.5 million British workers.[29]

Recent accounts of these schemes demonstrate their direct use to "...combat labour organization, improve labour productivity and overcome resistance to change."[30] Another commentator has observed, "If one examines the subsequent history of profit-sharing down to World War I it is possible to identify a direct relationship between the introduction of profit-sharing or co-partnership schemes with a high level of employment and labour unrest."[31] Aspects of employee welfare were crucial to weakening worker strength and unity when they became problematic for management.

Management's assault on the crafts was thus waged on two fronts. First, direct control, or de-skilling, strategies were developed by capitalists to break down worker strength based on their skill and knowledge of the work process. Secondly, employers attempted to undermine worker resistance and collective action with occupational welfare schemes and employee representation plans. These eventually began to lose their effectiveness where unionization became prevalent among unskilled and semi-skilled workers. Worker strength was shifting from the earlier control over skills to collective unity and union organization. In response management began to alter some of its strategies towards employment and social policy.

The 1930's - Planting the Seeds of Change

While some industrial councils and employee welfare programmes survived through World War II and beyond, many began to be phased out by the 1930s.[32] The councils had served employers by containing worker organization; however their operation was inconsistent with the principles of trade unionism and the practices of most trade unions. They fostered employer benevolence and employee acceptance since worker participation was usually token at best. Having worker representatives on councils and committees often served to legitimate decisions already taken by management. Even where workers were involved in the process prior to decisions being taken, their roles were usually limited to advisory. Senior management retained final decision-making authority.

Longer-term survival was also improbable through the Depression years when the token nature of most of these programmes became increasingly clear. As lay-offs rose and wages fell, the rapidly deteriorating conditions of work could not be addressed through industrial councils. Workers turned more and more towards trade unionism. From the mid-1930's on trade union membership grew substantially. In the early years of the Depression membership in Canada fell to a low of 281,000 or 14.5 percent of non-agricultural paid workers. It increased steadily to 462,000 or 18 percent in 1942, 1,006,000 or 29.5 percent in 1949, and stayed at approximately 30 percent through the end of the 1960s.[33] Previous paternalist provisions by the corporations were replaced by collective agreements; the co-optive joint councils were becoming supplanted by the collective bargaining process. Growing union strength picked away at employers' powers to maintain tight control over workers and the workplace. Managers began to consider less direct and more subtle practices for maintaining their supremacy.

By the mid-1930s new patterns of industrial relations initiatives were becoming clear. As Baritz has observed, "Personnel matters, once considered the private prerogative of employers, were becoming part of an institutionalized pattern...."[34] With large concerns, personnel departments were used to feel the pulse of workers' attitudes and monitor the nature of their activities. This was essential intelligence for management in fighting the growing threats of unionization. The personnel function also served management by reducing the costs of labour during the Depression through standardizing the provisions for hiring and lay-off; gearing training more closely and systematically towards production needs; and pruning welfare programmes to those most useful in motivating employees.

Human relations management began to provide partial solutions to the problems of controlling worker behaviour. Employers saw workers as lacking in motivation to produce; their loyalty to corporate objectives was questioned. New methods were sought for improving the productivity of workers. By the early 1930s investigators at the Hawthorne works of Western Electric announced findings with profound implications for management theory and practice.[35] According to their claims, productivity and motivation were a function of the social group at work. Factors such as compensation, physical amenities of the job, or the detailed forms of work organization were far less significant. These claims broke ground for new directions in social science research. Industry could use social scientific inquiry in ways which were previously unforeseen.[36] Managers became attracted to human relations approaches since improved worker satisfaction, usually led to increased worker commitment to their corporate employers and to increased productivity. It served to substitute "enterprise consciousness" for class consciousness.[37] As such it would become a significant wedge which managers could drive between workers and their unions.

While the seeds of human relations management were planted in the 1930s, little programming was developed in this period. The fear of unemployment was a strong enough motivator during the Depression. But as the legacy of the 1930s hardships were reversed during World War II and the succeeding boom years, employers could no longer count on high unemployment to induce worker submission. The combination of relatively low unemployment, increasing union strength and unemployment compensation began to improve workers' measure of security. They could more readily resist distasteful initiatives by their bosses. It was during these periods — the 1950s and 1960s —that management's intensive social scientific research on human motivation was applied. Employers had to seek new forms of motivation and control in response to pressures from union and workers.[38]

In the area of social security during the 1930s the only major initiative by the Federal government was for unemployment insurance. The government of R.B. Bennett introduced an unemployment insurance bill in 1935, in response to considerable pressure for legislation. The bill was rejected in 1937 by the British Privy Council on constitutional grounds. Working class agitation had been building over the previous five years; there was also pressure from Parliamentarians like J.S. Woodsworth and from some sections of the business community.

While organized labour was united in support of unemployment insurance, positions differed on the form and strategy. The Trades and Labour Congress pressed for a contributory plan, while other groups such as the communist controlled Workers' Unity League favoured a non-contributory system.[39] Business was divided on the issue. The Canadian Manufacturers' Association strongly opposed unemployment insurance, voicing concerns of many of their members that it would increase production costs and reduce worker motivation and mobility. Some chartered banks supported unemployment insurance to replace existing relief measures which were so overburdened that they threatened to bankrupt municipal and provincial governments. Business people who favoured unemployment insurance argued that it would raise the floor of consumer demand, which was so essential to an economic recovery. According to Finkel, it also promised to ease the mobility of labour and to weaken the political opposition of the left.[40]

State Welfare and Occupational Welfare, 1940 to 1950

During World War II, the size and nature of government influence on the economy changed considerably. As federal spending rose dramatically to finance war production, the fiscal impact of government became more significant. Many other initiatives represented new directions for government activity. For example, it quickly became the largest and most important employer of labour, provided moving expenses for war workers, built homes for workers where shortages existed, and financed half the cost of provincial day-care programmes. Extensive post-war manpower planning was undertaken to handle the 800,000 armed forces and 900,000 civilian war workers to be absorbed into the labour force. The federal government also instituted rationing, as well as wage, price and rent controls. Unemployment insurance and family allowance programmes were introduced. Discussions began around the planning of a comprehensive social security system although nothing was accomplished until after the war. The role of social welfare in economic planning was being reconsidered. As Dennis Guest has argued,

...the federal and provincial governments came to understand that social services were not a luxury to be dispensed with in a time of more pressing need but were a vital element in the smooth functioning of the wartime economy.[41]

This view was most clearly demonstrated with passage of the Unemployment Insurance Act of 1940 and its subsequent implementation. MacKenzie King had been pressing the provinces for an amendment to the B.N.A. Act to satisfy the requirements of the Privy Council decision of 1937. King maintained that unemployment insurance was necessary in the crisis of the Depression. Following passage of the Act in 1940, to begin on July 1st, 1941, Kings's government was able to show how the unemployment insurance fund would quickly accumulate large sums of capital for war purposes. By the end of the war, the Unemployment Insurance Act had transferred approximately $280 million from the wages of workers to the coffers of the state.[42]

Business lobby groups like the Canadian Manufacturers' Association and the Canadian Bankers' Association objected to the legislation. They maintained that: it was a tax on employers; it increased the wage demands from workers to cover their contributions; it resulted in reduced consumer purchasing power during a period of rising prices and low unemployment; and there would be upward pressure on prices, since business would try to pass on the cost.[43] They argued that business was capable of caring for the needs of their unemployed workers through private savings plans. Eligible workers could accumulate savings to be received upon separation from their employers. Funds already in existence ranged from straight profit-sharing plans to systems of forced saving, which were neither designed for, nor suited to, unemployment compensation. Rather, they were geared to retaining and disciplining employees and to using their accumulated savings as pools of cheap capital controlled by the employer.

The experience of World War II, especially with wage controls and unemployment insurance, marked a new stage in the state's management of relations between labour and capital. Provisions previously under the domain of private capital would come increasingly under state influence or intervention. As the social security system developed and expanded, it would inevitably invade the private territory of occupational welfare.

Even during World War II, federal government policy exerted considerable influence over employee welfare provisions. The wage control program, administered through the National and Regional War Labour Boards, kept wage rises in check during a period of relative prosperity. The Boards encouraged the establishment of contributory pension and sick benefit plans in lieu of wage increases. From 1941 to 1946, the Boards processed 4,398 new plans covering 785,084 employees.[44]

A national survey of employee benefits was conducted by the Dominion Bureau of Statistics in 1947.[45] Plans covered were: pensions; group life insurance; sickness and disability insurance for wage loss and for medical and hospital services; and in-plant medical services. The survey reached 14,452 firms with 1.8 million employees. Fifty-five percent of the employers reported having no plans at all. Of those with plans, it was determined that the most popular were group life insurance, followed by pension plans and accident and disability plans.[46] The majority of plans were selective, typically covering between half and two-thirds of total employees on a payroll.

Some of the most interesting findings regard financing and adminis-tration of the plans. The vast majority received contributions from both employers and employees. Yet very few plans were administered jointly by employers and employees. Administration was usually determined by employers. They either controlled the plans directly or hired commercial firms for the task.[47] Although most employee groups financed their benefit plans jointly with their employers or entirely by themselves, they rarely participated in controlling the plans. Sole administration by employees or unions was virtually non-existent.

Most employers also managed to keep the setting of these benefits outside the collective bargaining process. The number of plans covered by collective agreements was extemely small, ranging from two percent to six percent.

While the sheer amount of corporate welfare provisions grew during World War II and after, the nature of these programmes, and of their relation to state policy began to shift. Until this period, corporate welfare had developed as part of management strategy for controlling labour relations. Business enjoyed fairly little interference from government in this regard, with exceptions such as the enactment of workmen's compensation legislation and the setting of extensive regulation during World War I. The limited provision of welfare programmes by the state favoured the interests of employers over those of workers. Despite the paternalism and anti-union stance of corporate welfare, employees found it necessary to cooperate with the programmes. They were dependent on employers' benevolence for some measure of social security, since few alternatives were made available by the state.

Corporate welfare had penetrated the lives of workers from the cradle to the grave and from the bedroom to the factory, performing functions later assumed by the federal and/or the provincial governments. Their main area of focus was production, and in particular the behaviour of workers on the job. Many firms were also concerned with social reproduction. They developed programmes which addressed all manner of social and family life in order to ensure a stable home environment for the producing worker.

It is interesting to note how these functions of occupational welfare correspond to some of the social reproduction functions which were taken up later by the welfare state. Business people had recognized the importance of the family and school in maintaining their employees and in socializing succeeding generations of workers.

Conclusion
Industry has developed elaborate and imaginative schemes of employee welfare. They have been in response to a number of factors, including conditions of the economy, the state of the labour markets, the nature of

technology and the organization of work, and the extent of worker strength and organization. Occupational welfare has proved to be an important part of the corporate accumulation process by serving to manage the stabilitiy and productivity of employees.

Early management practice concentrated on developing factory organization and on coercing workers to perform in these new environments. To this end, employers undermined craft production and rationalized the organization of work. This was accomplished at the expense of worker autonomy. Occupational welfare became important to combat the negative effects of work rationalization such as reduced motivation to work, collective association of workers into unions and rapid turnover of employees. It was also used to address social, psychological, household and family problems where they have seemed to interfere with production on the job. Where relatively closed or tight labour markets existed, programmes have been implemented to influence the future labour supply. Occupational welfare has thus been concerned with social reproduction as well as production.

As the modern welfare state developed, it influenced the content of occupational welfare. Welfare policies of corporations and of the state became more closely connected. The experience of welfare benefits during World War II illustrates the direct effect of state policy on corporate provisions. As the federal and provincial governments became more extensively involved in the management and supply of labour during World War II and after, they performed some of the functions previously tackled by corporate welfare programmes. They also established a more stable economic and social environment for business. The counter-cyclical effects of expenditure on programmes like unemployment insurance and income security, promised an end to devastating economic depression. They allowed some measure of national scope for programmes which was not previously possible. As well, the state was becoming more and more a mediator between labour and capital, although serving the interests of the latter more than the former.

Canadian workers also enjoyed an additional measure of security during the early 1940s and through the 1950s and 1960s due to the increasing social welfare commitments of governments in a period of high employment and growing union strength. They were marginally less dependent on the whims of employers' paternalism. It thus became more difficult to control workers with welfare at the workplace. Although some of the tried and true methods for disciplining employees were becoming less effective, industry still needed measures for discipline. The stage was set for serious consideration of new patterns for management which scholars and business schools had been investigating since the Hawthorne experiments of the 1930s. Human relations management was on the agenda for business by the 1950s. New techniques were being developed to manipulate the social environment at work in the interests of profit.

NOTES

1. See for example, David Montgomery, *Workers Control in America*, Cambridge 1979; Greg Kealey, *Toronto Workers Respond to Industrial Capitalism, 1860-1892*, Toronto, 1980; Katherine Stone, "The Origins of Job Structures in The Steel Industry," *Review of Radical Political Economics* 6, Summer 1974, 61-97; Dan Clawson, *Bureaucracy and The Labour Process*, New York, 1980.

2. There is now a growing literature on workers resistance. See for example Richard Edwards, *Contested Terrain: The Transformation of the Workplace in the 20th Century*, New York, 1970; Carter L. Goodrich, *The Frontier of Control: A Study of British Workshop Politics*, London 1920; Bryan Palmer "Class, Conception and Conflict: The Thrust for Efficiency, Managerial Views of Labor and The Working Class Rebellion, 1903-22," *Review of Radical Political Economics*, Summer 1973, 31-49; Andrew L. Friedman, *Industry and Labour: Class Struggle at Work and Monopoly Capitalism*; Michael Burawoy, *Manuracturing Consent: Changes in The Labor Process Under Monopoly Capitalism*, Chicago, 1979.

3. Harry Braverman, *Labor and Monopoly Capitalism*, New York, 1974; David Noble, *America by Design; Science, Technology and The Rise of Corporate Capitalism*, New York, 1979; Daniel Nelson, *Managers and Workers: Origins of The New Factory System in The United States, 1880-1920*, Madison, 1975.

4. Jack Russell, "The Coming of the Line; The Ford Highland Park Plant, 1910-1914," *Radical America*, 12, May-June, 1978, 29-45.

5. Daniel Nelson and Stuart Campbell, "Taylorism Versus Welfare Work in American Industry: H.L. Gantt and the Bancrofts," *Business History Review*, 46, Spring 1972, 1-16.

6. Bruce Scott, "A Place in The Sun: The Industrial Council at Massey-Harris 1919-1929," *Labour/Le Travailleur*, 1, 1976, 158-192; and also, "Cultivating The Workers' Smile: Works Councils in Canada," *This Magazine*, Jan.-Feb. 1977, 30-33.

7. Stone, "The Origins of Job Structures...;" David Brophy, "The Rise and Decline of Welfare Capitalism," in D. Brophy ed., *Workers in Industrial America: Essays on The 20th Century Struggle*, New York, 1980, 48-81.

8. Kealey, *Toronto Workers*.

9. James Weinstein, *The Corporate Ideal in The Liberal State, 1900-1918*, Boston, 1968; National Civic Federation, "What is Welfare Work?" *Monthly Review* 1, August 1904, 5; and "How The Welfare Department Was Organized," *Monthly Review*, 1, June 1904, 14.

10. Nelson and Campbell, "Taylorism versus Welfare Work...."

11. Stuart D. Brandes, *American Welfare Capitalism 1880-1940*, Chicago, 1970, 5-6.

12. Ibid, 20.

13. Brophy, "The Rise and Decline...."

14. Stuart Jamieson, *Times of Trouble: Labour Unrest and Industrial Conflict in Canada, 1900-66*, Study No. 22, Task Force on Labour Relations, Ottawa, 1968; "1919: The Canadian Labour Revolt," *Labour/Le Travail*, 13, Spring, 1984, 11-44.

15. Scott, "A Place in The Sun...."

16. Ibid, 160.

17. The Social Service Council grew out of the Social gospel movement. It was formed in 1907 as The Moral and Social Reform Council of Canada with membership mainly from Church organizations, and some farm and labour groups. See Richard Allen, *The Social Passion: Religion and Social Reform in Canada, 1914-28*, Toronto, 1973. Quote from page 141.

18. Social Service Council of Canada, *Social Welfare* 1, August 1920, 316-17.

19. Allen, *The Social Passion.*
20. Scott, "A Place in The Sun..."
21. Ibid, 162.
22. Ibid, 168.
23. Ibid, 178.
24. Marion Findlay, "Industrial Relations," *Social Welfare,* August 1928, 245-47, 259.
25. Alvin Finkel, *Business and Social Reform in The Thirties,* Toronto, 1979.
26. Dennis Guest, *The Emergence of Social Security in Canada,* Vancouver, 1980.
27. Brophy, "The Rise and Decline...," 56.
28. Harvie Ramsay, "Cycles of Control: Worker Participation in Sociological and Historical Perspective," *Sociology,* 11, 1977, 487.
29. E. Halevy, "The Problems of Workers' Control, 1921" in E. Halevy, *The Era of Tyrannies,* London, 1967, 123-40.
30. Ramsay, "Cycles of Control...," 485.
31. R. A. Church, "Profit-Sharing and Labour Relations in England in the Nineteenth Century," *International Review of Social History,* 14:1, 1977,10.
32. Brandes, *American Welfare Capitalism.*
33. Canada, Department of Labour, *Union Growth in Canada, 1921-1967,* Ottawa, 1970.
34. Loren Baritz, *The Servants of Power: A History of The Use of Social Science in American Industry,* New York, 1970, 120-21.
35. Elton Mayo, *The Human Problems of an Industrial Civilization,* New York, 1960; F.J. Roethlisberger and W.J. Dickson, *Management and The Worker,* Cambridge, U.S.A., 1947; Henry Landsberger, *Hawthorne Revisited,* Ithaca, U.S.A. 1958.
36. The Hawthorne studies are important because of the major influence they exerted. However, the research itself was unfavourably reviewed, methodically weak and analytically unsound. For critical commentary see the works of Charles Perrow, *Complex Organizations: A Critical Essay,* Glenview, U.S.A., 1973, and Alex Carey, "The Hawthorne Studies: A Radical Criticism." *American Sociological Review,* 32, June 1967, 403-16. In reviewing the original data, Franke and Kaul have argued that most of the increased output (78.7%) was due to tighter discipline. See R.H. Franke and J.D. Kaul, "The Hawthorne Experiments: First Statistical Interpretation," *American Sociological Review,* 43, 1978, 623-43.
37. E. Bristow, "Profit-Sharing, Socialism and Labour Unrest," in K.D. Brown ed, *Essays in Anti-Labour History,* London, 1974, 262-89.
38. It is important to note that until the mid-1970s, most corporate programmes for work humanization or human resource development were in non-union plants and offices. Where they did appear in unionized workplaces, union participation was weak. See Ted Mills, "Human Resources-Why The New Concern?" *Harvard Business Review,* March-April, 1975, 120-134.
39. C. Cuneo, "State Mediation of Class Contradictions in Canadian Unemployment Insurance, 1930-1935," *Studies in Political Economy* 3, 1980, 37-65.
40. Finkel, *Business and Social Reform*: Cuneo and Finkel take somewhat different positions on the role of business in social reform. Cuneo (1980) argues that between the 1920s and 1940s capitalists generally opposed unemployment insurance, except during the Depression when splits occurred temporarily in their ranks. Finkel (1979) suggests that business had a much more unified position favouring unemployment insurance and other social reforms. For another thorough discussion of these issues, see James Struthers, *No Fault of Their Own,* Toronto, 1983.

41. Guest, *The Emergence of Social Security...*, 105.
42. C. Cuneo, "State Class and Reserve Labour: The Case of the 1941 Canadian Unemployment Insurance Act," in J. Paul Grayson, ed., *Class State Ideology and Change: Marxist Perspectives on Canada*, Toronto, 1980, 130-53.
43. Ibid, 139-40.
44. Dominion Bureau of Statistics, *Survey of Pension and Welfare Plans in Industry, 1947*, Ottawa, 1950.
45. Ibid.
46. Thirty-five percent of employees were covered by group life insurance; 26 percent by pension plans; and between 13 and 33 percent by accident and disability plans.
47. Eighty-one percent of group life plans and 82 percent of pension plans were financed by joint contributions. Less than 8 percent of all plans were jointly administered. Sole direction by the employer accounted for 88 percent of group life plans and 58 percent of pension plans.

PART IV

A Welfare State Established

World War II and the Welfare State in Canada

Dennis Guest

If we had to select one period in Canadian history most amenable to the development of the Canadian welfare state, the years of the Second World War, 1939 to 1945, would be a reasonable choice. This follows from the fact that the pressures and demands of war have a number of consequences, both positive and negative, for developments in social policy. It is not part of this paper (although it would make an interesting study) to compare the effect on social policy in Canada of both the First and Second World Wars. One could hypothesize that whereas the First World War retarded the development of Canadian social policy, the Second World War provided the milieu for advances in social programmes.

The positive forces in the 1939-1945 era arose from a number of sources but the first that should be acknowledged was the government's need to build and maintain the morale of its fighting forces and civilian population. This coincided with a deeply-felt longing on the part of the average citizen, soldier or civilian, for a better and more secure future as compensation for the sacrifices demanded in the present.[1] The desire on the part of Canadians for a better future was particularly intense in the World War Two period because of the bitter memories left by the economic depression of the 1930s. The same young men who had been herded into labour camps or treated as pariahs by provincial and municipal welfare officials as they drifted across the country in search of work were now being asked to fight for their country. To give people something to fight *for*, the Canadian government set into motion plans for a postwar society that would raise the hopes and aspirations of the people.

The degree to which this longing for a better life in the postwar world was present in the minds of Canadians in the early 1940,s can be judged by the reception accorded in Canada to the British proposals for peace and reconstruction contained in the celebrated Beveridge Report.

"One of the discoveries of the year 1942" according to the report's author, Sir William Beveridge, "was the deep and vivid interest of the people of Britain in the kind of Britain which is to emerge when the floods of war subside."[2] The interest created by the report was not confined to Britain but spread worldwide, with a pronounced impact on North America. The report, with the prosaic title of *The Report on Social Insurance and Allied Services* was published simultaneously in London and New York, late in 1942 (in itself a unique event in publishing history given that the report was an official British government document). It was, by all counts, the best seller to that date among British offical reports (250,000 of the full Report, 350,000 of the official abridgement and 42,000 of the American edition).[3] Within weeks of its release, postwar planning in Canada underwent rapid advancement.

One can contrast the reception given to the Beveridge Report in Canada in December 1942 with that given to the Rowell-Sirois Report in May 1940. The Rowell-Sirois Report, formally titled The Report of the Royal Commission on Dominion-Provincial Relations, was the most comprehensive study of federal/provincial relations since Confederation, and dealt with significant Canadian issues arising out of the depression. These included the allocation of jurisdiction between the federal and provincial governments of such pressing responsibilities as unemployment insurance, contributory old age pensions and minimum wages and hours of work. It was also concerned with regional disparities, with the means of achieving a national standard of social services and with the restructuring of financial arrangements between the two senior levels of government. However, if public interest can be likened to a pond, the Rowell-Sirois Report caused scarcely a ripple; the Beveridge Report, on the other hand, created waves.

The difference in public reaction had to do with the fact that the Beveridge Report tapped into the well-spring of Canadian aspirations for a post-war world. The principal aim of the Beveridge Report was "Freedom from Want" but Want was only the first of five giant evils to be overcome: the others, all familiar to Canadians, were Disease, Ignorance, Squalor and Idleness.[4] In a radio address over the national network of the Canadian Broadcasting Corporation in May 1943, Sir William Beveridge described his report as falling under three main headings: a comprehensive scheme of social insurance to maintain incomes when they are interrrupted by any cause; a comprehensive health service; or, as Beveridge expressed it in another context, "an all-in scheme of medical treatment of every kind for everybody." As well, a system of children's allowances paid to parents regardless of whether or not they are earning money. These three programmes were to be buttressed by a policy of full employment, a task which, Beveridge emphasized, was too important to be left to the private market.[5]

Beveridge claimed three advantages for his plan: it called for contributions from all who were gainfully employed and thus could not be said to provide something for nothing; it was universal in its application thereby expunging any notion of charity and it was a first step toward giving those who were fighting a positive aim and not merely a negative one of avoiding defeat.[6]

The Beveridge Report not only tapped the core of Canadian aspirations for a postwar world but it also addressed, with unaffected simplicity and directness, the anxieties engendered in urban-industrial employment, the costs associated with illness and disability, and of the penury of old age or retirement. It spoke to the concerns of families for raising and educating their children and of finding suitable and affordable housing. It provided the assurance of a decent burial — hence, the notion of "cradle to the grave" security. But, preeminently, having in mind the mass unemployment of the 1930's, the Beveridge Report called for government planning to ensure full employment.

Notice of the Beveridge Report's release first appeared in the British press on December 1, 1942. The *London Times* hailed it as "a great social measure."[7] The *Vancouver Sun* carried a small item on its front page on December 1, which noted that "particulars of one of the great documents of these times were laid before the British Parliament today..." Further details on inside pages bore the heading "Great Britain's Epochal Plan for 'War on Want'."[8] The *Toronto Globe and Mail* gave full coverage to the Report under the headline "Britain Free of Want Envisaged in Report Written by Beveridge," and with a sub-heading indicating that the Report was an "Outline of the most sweeping plan for government-sponsored social security ever set forth."[9] At a memorial service for Lord Beveridge in May 1963 at Westminster Abbey these words recalled the impact of the release of the Beveridge Report:

> "He spoke: and the whole free world stopped to listen: after a time, as it was bound to happen, it turned again to other occupations; but never to be the same again..."[10]

The Rowell-Sirois Report, by contrast, failed to touch a responsive chord in the Canadian public. The press reports following the Report's release, May 16, 1940, were headlined "Roundtable Agreement Required to Implement Commission's Findings" and "Greatest Demand Was For Simplification of Government Machinery."[11] The following day, May 17, 1940, the *Toronto Globe and Mail* had more extensive coverage with the headline "Sweeping New Deal in Public Finance Advised For Dominion."[12] An editorial on May 18 said "If and when the terrible storm passes (referring to the battle of Dunkirk), it may be the foundation of a recreated Confederation."[13] Given the sombre news from the European war front, it all seemed of little consequence. Although published in 1940, the Report, prepared between 1937 and 1940, was a product of the Depression and reflected the pessimism of that era. D.V. Smiley has referred to it as a "somewhat cautious document,"[14] and M.G. Taylor has said that "except for the restructuring of financial arrangements, the Commission carefully avoided recommendations on substantive policies."[15] The Report also fell victim to one of the common negative consequences of war for social policy —the view that planning for anything other than the prosecution of the war should be postponed until the enemy has been vanquished. Thus, when a Dominion-Provincial Conference called in 1941 to discuss the Rowell-Sirois Report broke up in disagreement on the second day, further acrimony was easily postponed on the pretext that the prosecution of the war must have priority. Beveridge, however, anticipating attempts to delay plans for peacetime reconstruction, argued strongly that planning for peace was part of the wartime job:

"...democracies, like Cromwell's armies, need to know what they fight for and to love what they know."[16]

One of the discoveries, then, of the year 1942 for Canadians as well as for Britons, was the concept of comprehensive social security. The diaries of Prime Minister Mackenzie King indicate that he and Franklin Roosevelt "had quite a talk about Beveridge's Report" in December 1942 and Roosevelt told King that the Report "had made a real impression" in the United States. Mackenzie King recorded Roosevelt's thoughts on the political appeal of social security: "The thought of insurance from the cradle to the grave. That seems to be a line that will appeal. You and I should take that up strongly. It will help each of us politically as well as being on the right lines in the way of reform."[17]

It was into this environment in March 1943 that Leonard Marsh's *Report on Social Security in Canada* was released. The time was auspicious for other reasons as well. In 1943, the social security landscape in Canada was relatively moon-like in its lack of prominent features. Although the Unemployment Insurance system was put into place August 7, 1940 and by July 1, 1941 contributions were being collected and benefits began to be paid in Februray 1942, this social benefit was more than offset by the winding down at the end of fiscal 1941 of the federal programme of aid to the unemployed — the largest federal-provincial welfare programme up to that time. Apart from the federal-provincial old age pension programme, and its small appendage, pensions for the blind, as well as pensions for war veterans and war veterans' allowances, the only other social programmes of consequence were provincial programmes of Workmen's Compensation and Mothers' Allowances and what was termed "relief" for the unemployables. The health and welfare empires we see today were not in place in 1943 and, therefore, planning a social security system was probably easier and less contentious with this relatively clean slate.

Kevin Collins takes an opposing view, arguing that the absence of programmes has two disadvantages.[18] Firstly, vested interests such as commercial insurance companies occupied certain of the territory and could be counted on to mount opposition to the development of public programmes. This view was supported by a knowledgeable contemporary writer, Harry Cassidy, who wrote in 1943:

"The commercial insurance companies may have their life and superannuation businesses curtailed considerably by a full-fledged scheme of social insurance; and many non-commercial agencies will also be affected. Under the circumstances it will not be surprising if they throw their great power and influence against a really comprehensive scheme. The well-known opposition of the medical profession to broad plans of health insurance or 'socialized medicine' need only be mentioned."[19]

Secondly, Collins argues that the administrative experience required to operate a comprehensive social insurance programme was almost entirely lacking. But these arguments can be countered by pointing out that the political attractiveness of "social security" was at least a match for commercial interests during this period. One can also argue that business and commercial interests were not necessarily monolithic in their attitude toward social programmes. Some business representatives could see the value of income maintenance programmes as economic stablilizers. When the Unemployment Insurance Bill was before a special committee of the House of Commons in 1940, for example, the Canadian Chamber of Commerce implicitly opposed the legislation by urging that the legislation could wait until the war's end. However, another business group, the Canadian Life Insurance Officers Association, went on record as "very sympathetic" to the principle of social insurance and congratulated the government for introducing the measure. Support was also voiced by the Retail Merchants' Association and the British Columbia Lumber and Shingle Manufacturers' Association.[20] Later, in 1943, the Canadian Medical Association and the Canadian Life Insurance Officers Association approved in principle the idea of public health insurance.

As far as organizational expertise, the effort required to mobilize manpower and material to wage a war had built up the confidence and experience of senior federal civil servants which prepared them for large scale social programmes.

A more significant issue posed by the relative absence of social security structures was that Canadians were, by and large, unfamiliar with modern techniques of social security, notably, social insurance, which was the keystone of the Marsh Report. This is a problem that Sir William Beveridge did not face in submitting his Report to the British people. England had pioneered social insurance against unemployment in 1911, and health insurance covered many British workers prior to World War One. The Beveridge proposals, in part, spoke of extending and making more universal certain social security protections that were already in place for some of the population. Marsh, on the other hand, was obliged to educate Canadians about the various techniques of social security and to explain the rationale for having a comprehensive system, a concept which was new and unfamiliar to most Canadians. Would Canadians read and learn from his Report? Would Marsh's arguments be sufficiently persuasive to generate the political support necessary to overcome the thinly veiled hostility toward comprehensive social security from a majority of the federal cabinet and the powerful business interests they represented? Or would Canadians view social security as an issue that would be adequately addressed by the prospect of a steady job, bolstered when necessary by the country's unemployment insurance scheme, but without the range of social protections recommended by Marsh?

Another reason for the war years being a congenial time for social security planning for Canada was that the war had shifted the locus of power from the provinces to the federal government. Ottawa was leading the country in the war effort and it therefore seemed appropriate to most Canadians that planning for the postwar period would also take place in Ottawa. This provided an opportunity for plans of a national character to be drawn up at a time when federal-provincial rivalries had been curtailed in the interest of a united war effort.

An additional spur to social security planning was, of course, the fact that the desire for a better future was sharpened by the memories of the mass unemployment of the 1930's. By October 1943, returns tabulated by trade union organizations indicated that only .3 per cent of their membership were unemployed, down from a high of over 17 per cent in 1939.[21] The number of persons filing claims for unemployment insurance benefits was 26,924 in 1942 (the first year in which benefits could be claimed), rising to 36,660 in 1943 and 77,127 in 1944, only just over 3 per cent out of an estimated two and a half million covered workers.[22]

The contrast between the active stance of a wartime federal government which was able to find the money to finance any project to further the war effort and the apparent helplessness of governments during the Depression to fight that particular battle was not lost on Canadians. There would be no return to the bad old days. This was made increasingly clear as the CCF, which had campaigned for social security measures since the party's inception in 1933, picked up strength politically in province after province as well as increasing their representation in parliament.[23] The Conservative Party convention of December 1942 adopted a social security platform calling for full employment, collective bargaining, social security and medical insurance. To mark this transformation the word "Progressive" was added to the party's name.[24] Only the Liberals appeared to be lagging in their support of social security planning and this was soon to be remedied. Within two weeks of the release of the Beveridge Report, plans were made to prepare a report on social security for Canada. Ian MacKenzie, Minister of Pensions and Health spearheaded this effort but he undoubtedly acted with the full knowledge and support of Mackenzie King.

The appearance of the *Report on Social Security for Canada* in March 1943, together with the *Health Insurance Report*, followed a year later by the *Report on Housing and Community Planning* is testimony to the interest manifested by Canadians in planning for a more secure future.[25]

The Genesis of the Marsh Report

Postwar planning in Canada first began as early as 1940, with plans for the eventual demobilization of the armed forces and for such programmes as veterans' medical and other benefits. As Marsh had noted "it soon became apparent that the problem of demobilization could not be assessed without reference to the total postwar economic situation...and a separate Advisory Committee on postwar reconstruction was established in September 1941, headed by the president of McGill University."[26] The Advisory Committee on Reconstruction then established six sub-committees covering such topics as: Post-war Employment Opportunities, Agriculture, Conservation and Natural Resources, Postwar Construction Projects, Housing and Community Planning; and on the Special Postwar Problems of Women. A total of eighteen research projects were developed by the Committee to further the work of the six sub-committees. Most of these projects were completed and published either separately or as part of the reports of the Advisory Committee on Reconstruction and its Subcommittees.[27]

Canada was extremely fortunate to have in its midst an individual of the calibre and training of Leonard C. Marsh. British by birth, Marsh had been a prize-winning student at the London School of Economics in the 1920s when Sir William Beveridge was head of that institution. In early 1930, McGill University principal, Sir Arthur Currie, convened a series of meetings and consultations from which evolved the McGill Social Science Research Project. Currie and his social research council members began searching for a research director. They hired the twenty-four-year old Leonard Marsh after Beveridge had written in reply to Currie to confirm Marsh's suitability for the post. He arrived in Montreal in September 1930 to help prepare an application for funding to the Rockefeller Foundation. In December 1930, after receipt of the grant, Marsh was confirmed as Director. He then began almost ten years of teaching and research on various aspects of employment, unemployment and related issues, providing him with an invaluable background of study and publication in Canadian social policy prior to his taking on the role of research director to the Advisory Committee on Reconstruction.[28]

He also had numerous contacts with leading authorities in the fields of social insurance, social work and other related professions in Canada and the United States. The International Labour Office, a centre of research and publication on worker-related concerns such as social insurance schemes, had moved its headquarters from Geneva to Montreal at the outbreak of the Second World War and its officials were at Marsh's disposal. With the help of a small team of experts, Marsh drew up his "blueprint" for Canadian social security within the space of a few weeks. Critics of his plan charged that it was hastily drawn. But they overlooked the years of apprenticeship that Marsh had undergone in the study of social security issues. The Marsh Report was the product of a mind that had synthesized the most current research and ideas relating to social security programmes from the world's leading industrialized countries, adapted to Canadian conditions. It was an unparalled achievement, but carried out in wartime, when such efforts were more commonplace.

The Marsh Report
The Marsh Report, entitled *Report on Social Security for Canada,* appeared on March 15, 1943. It was Canada's first anti-poverty programme as well as a comprehensive social security plan. In relation to social security, the Report contained six main proposals:

A National Employment Programme
Like most economists of the day, Marsh expected large-scale unemployment at war's end based upon the experience after World War One. Therefore, a policy of full employment had to be a priority of the government. To this end, the Marsh Report recommended a billion dollar a year in public works, conservation projects and other public investment as a means of ensuring full employment.

Supplementary Occupational and Training Schemes
These would be required to equip people to find work or to train people for better paying jobs as one method of attacking the problem of inadequate income. In the light of more recent proposals to supplement the incomes of the working poor,[29] the following quotation from the Marsh Report is food for thought:

> "The proper approach to intolerably low wages, and easily the most desirable in the long run, is to raise the efficiency of the worker himself; either by improving his training, education or skill or — a remedy whose importance is frequently forgotten — by placing him in an environment in which his efficiency will be improved. This environment may necessitate reform of his home conditions or of the organization and equipment of his place of work. The latter is the real argument for the minimum wage forced upon industries which exploit cheap labour; they must become more efficient so that they can pay better wages, if they are to stay in business at all. Supplementation of poverty-line incomes, without any reference to constructive attacks on the problems are merely palliatives if indeed they do not delay reform."[30]

A Comprehensive System of Social Insurance Protection
Two plans were visualized: one covering the so-called employment risks — unemployment, sickness, maternity and industrial disability or death, financed by employers and employees, administered by the federal government and paying wage-related benefits. The exception would be the provincial programmes of Workmens' Compensation which would remain under provincial jurisdiction. The second insurance plan would cover all gainfully occupied persons against such common risks as old age or retirement, permanent disability, the death of insured persons and funerals. This scheme should be financed by contributions from insured persons and the government and would pay flat-rate benefits (all beneficiaries within defined categories would receive the same amount of

benefit) for individuals or couples with child care costs covered by a separate system of family allowances.

Medical Care
A comprehensive system of public medical care for the whole population to be financed by contributions from the gainfully employed and from both federal and provincial governments. Administration was to be in provincial hands. A separate report prepared for the Advisory Committee on Health Insurance (the Heagerty Committee) appeared at the same time as the Marsh Report. It is important to note that Marsh, was a member of the Heagerty Committee and worked closely with the Committee when integrating his proposals for a comprehensive system of medical care into his social security scheme.

Children's Allowances
Marsh also argued strongly for a system of universal children's allowances to be paid to all parents. He recommended a payment of $7.50 per child, with the cost of the allowances and the administration to be carried by the federal government. The system of family allowances as visualized by Marsh, would have contributed greatly to the administrative efficiency and overall coordination of his social security plan, if it had been adopted. Under the Marsh scheme for children's allowances, all income maintenance programmes that presently have their own scales of benefit for child dependents — such as Workers' Compensation, pensions for war veterans, the Canada and Quebec Pension Plans, War Veterans' Allowances and provincial social assistance programmes, would be unnecessary. Instead the children's allowances would be used to meet this category of financial need. Income maintenance programmes could then be designed for adult beneficiaries and their adult dependants, if any. The basic case for children's allowances in Marsh's words is that "the needs of children should be met as a special claim on the nation, not merely in periods of unemployment or on occasions of distress but at all times."[31]

Public Assistance
Marsh proposed a federally financed and administered program of unemployment assistance for those who had exhausted their benefits or who were for some reason not working in employment covered by unemployment insurance. In 1943, only about 70% of the work force was covered by unemployment insurance. This part of the plan reflected the conviction that a postwar recession was inevitable.

While Marsh was unable to make any close calculation of the total costs of a comprehensive social security scheme, the experience of more advanced welfare states led him to suggest that the cost would be on the order of one billion dollars, or something less than 12 percent of the national income. A further billion-dollar job creation programme in the postwar year was also visualized. These amounts were considered by Marsh to be a "reasonable commitment."[32]

The Heagerty Report: The Report of the
Advisory Committee on Health Insurance

The Health Insurance Report, which was released to the public on the same day as the Marsh Report, was the work of the Advisory Committee on Health Insurance established in February 1942, and headed by Dr. J.J. Heagerty, director of public health services in the federal Department of Pensions and National Health. The Committee consulted with a variety of national groups representing the medical profession and other helping professions, business groups, labour and women's groups. A majority of these groups advocated a provincially administered health insurance plan aided by federal grants.

The Report, consisting of 558 pages, was the most comprehensive treatment of the subject of health insurance prepared in Canada up until the Royal Commission on Health Services in the 1960s. It traced the growing interest in Canada in health insurance, from the 1920s on, and recorded how the depression of the 1930s had aggravated the problem of paying for medical care at a time when thousands of Canadians were having trouble paying rent and putting food on the table. The Report also discussed the growth in the interest in health insurance in the United States and the intransigence of the organized medical lobby in that country.[33] The Report contained a review of national health insurance schemes in operation world wide at the time (1942), and compared the various schemes by type of administration (public or private through approved societies), method of paying the practitioner, method of financing the plans, and by the scope of coverage. The practice of providing compensation for wages lost due to illness in various countries was also reviewed. More significantly, the Report included a survey of Canadian health statistics over the period 1926 to 1940 and demonstrated that adult, infant and maternal mortality rates and the sickness toll in Canada were "excessive."[34]

The Report linked the provision of adequate medical services for all Canadians, and a more even distribution of public health services to all parts of Canada, with the maintenance and security of a democratic state (a reasonable theme for a country at war):

> "A Society or state cannot maintain a democratic form of government without a mentally and physically healthy and well-informed electorate... It naturally follows then that there are reciprocal duties toward its citizens on the part of the state...One of these duties would appear to be the provision of educational and health facilities of such calibre and in such quantity that each person may be prepared mentally and physically to perform his duty toward safeguarding the security of that state..."[35]

In preparation for more than a year, the Report was specific in its proposals, and included a model provincial and federal act for the guidance of the governments who would be charged with the financing and administration of health insurance. It called for a national, compulsory system of health insurance, provincially administered, and a comprehensive public health system of a preventive nature. The influence of the Beveridge Report was evident in the framing of the Report's recommendations. The key words were universal, contributory and comprehensive.

As recommended by the Report, the whole population was to be eligible for a full range of medical benefits including medical, dental, pharmaceutical, hospital and nursing services. The plan for financing involved contributions from the federal and provincial governments as well as the insured. The annual insurance registration fee for all persons sixteen years and older was to be twelve dollars. In addition, all income tax payers would contribute a health insurance tax up to a maximum amount depending upon marital status. This formula raised the ire of labour representatives who objected to the regressive registration fee (a head tax, it was called) and who felt that the cost of the scheme should be raised from income taxes and levied on the ability to pay. Labour also advocated much more lay participation in the plan's operation and expressed concern about the domination of the medical profession in the proposed plan's administration.[36] The Canadian Medical Association approved health insurance in principle but statements by CMA leaders at this time indicate their unswerving ambition to be in control of the plan's operation.[37]

The Heagerty Report was overshadowed by the much more comprehensive Marsh Report (much to the reported chagrin of Ian Mackenzie, Minister of Pensions and National Health, who had hoped the Report and resulting public health insurance measures would provide a noteworthy climax to his political career).[38]

The Curtis Report

The Subcommittee on Housing and Community Planning, under the chairmanship of C.A. Curtis, was asked to review the existing legislation and administrative organization relating to housing and community planning, both urban and rural, throughout Canada, and to recommend those changes in legislation, organization or procedure which would provide an adequate housing programme for the postwar years.[39] Despite the extensive scope of the Committee's mandate, within fifteen months the first comprehensive treatise on housing and town planning in Canada was published. The Report was divided into three sections: Experience, Measurements and Requirements. The first section, Experience, included a review of housing legislation in Canada, in Britain and in the United States. Part II, Measurements, discussed the dimension of urban housing, the critical relationship between incomes, rentals and the costs of ownership and estimates of postwar housing needs. The Report's third section, Requirements, provided some answers for the problems identified in the first two sections. Policies and programmes to promote home ownership, low rental housing, farm housing and the reduction of housing costs were discussed. The Report's findings were supported by careful statistical analysis.

A contemporary review of the Report noted that it argued strongly for public intervention in the housing market, where, as a result of the free play of market forces, aggravated by the depression, a serious deficiency in housing existed for about one-third of the population.[40] This deficiency was typified by overcrowding, substandard construction and excessive rents.

The Report emphasized the importance of town planning: "Town planning is essentially the matter of using land in its most efficient and socially desirable way."[41] Clear warnings were posted about the effects that would flow from a lack of planning in this area - effects which are painfully visible throughout Canada today.[42]

Following publication of the Report, the federal government passed the second National Housing Act in 1944 (the first having been passed in 1938). Rose points out that the principal reason for this legislation was to promote employment in the postwar era. The Report's comprehensive approach to housing and town planning and in particular the provision of low-rental housing was ignored.[43]

The Eclipse of Social Planning, 1943-45

The Advisory Committee on Reconstruction began its work as early as 1940 but accelerated its efforts in September 1942, when the Advisory Committee on Postwar Reconstruction was formally established under the chairmanship of Principal Cyril James of McGill University. Between that date and early 1945, when the James Committee and its radical notions of comprehensive planning were reined in by a powerful committee of senior civil servants,[44] three landmark studies in the areas of comprehensive social security, health insurance, and housing and town planning in Canada were published. All three were notable for the way in which they illuminated social conditions in Canada and for their clear and unequivocal recommendations for action. The problem of poverty, its measurement and a comprehensive plan for combatting it were presented for the first time in the Marsh Report. The problems of paying for health care and the uneven distribution of public health services in Canada were revealed and reconciled by the Heagerty Report's proposals for health insurance and the development of public health services. These proposals have been described by a present day authority as "bold, imaginative and comprehensive and compared with what we now have, extraordinarily enlightened."[45] Added to these two was the Curtis Report, a Canadian primer on housing and town planning and as Rose has typified it, "a milestone in the enunciation of social responsibility by government."[46]

There were, in addition, supplementary reports on subjects that are of front-rank importance in the late 1980s — an ecological approach to natural resources, as one example,[47] and the role of women, as another. The latter report, the work of the Subcommittee on the Postwar Problems of Women, contained a number of recommendations for improving working conditions, opportunities for advancement, freedom of choice for married women, improved coverage for women in social security programmes and better protection under labour codes. These suggestions were brushed aside and would not surface again until the Report of the Royal Commission on the Status of Women in 1970.[48]

Despite the powerful political appeal of comprehensive social security, the plan for postwar reconstruction was dictated by a group of conservative-minded individuals in Ottawa, comprising a majority of the federal cabinet supported by an elite group of civil servants.[49] They attacked the Marsh Report's proposals as beyond the powers of the British North America Act because of the commanding role assigned to the federal government but they were probably most offended by the emphasis on social responsibility and the Report's implied criticism of the individualistic, free-enterprise system.

The cabinet was divided on what the nature of postwar economic conditions would be. The Minister of Munitions and Supply, C.D. Howe, one of the most able men in the government and with strong ties to the corporate world, saw the immediate postwar years as a time of shortages. Canadian industry would be hard-pressed to meet the backlog of consumer goods which had built up over the depression decade and the war years. The critical issue for Howe was to see that Canadian industry was reconverted to peacetime production with the fewest impediments and the least delay. Other voices in the cabinet argued that the postwar problem would be that of unemployment and recession, as had occurred following World War One. Radical political parties such as the CCF would grow and prosper under these conditions and the free enterprise system itself might be threatened. Therefore, plans for public works, housing, and social security programmes were supported to maintain purchasing power and to help blunt the electoral success of the CCF. In the debate between these two points of view, any notion of comprehensive social security was largely irrelevant. The prime minister, Mackenzie King, vacillated between the two positions but with his usual caution supported both sides by appointing C.D. Howe as Minister of Reconstruction for the immediate postwar era and by introducing a system of family allowances. In addition to maintaining spending power in the case of a recession, family allowances would also improve Liberal fortunes at the polls. A number of other economic stabilizers such as improved old age pensions, federal unemployment assistance aid and federal sharing in the costs of provincial health insurance plans were offered to the provinces at a Conference on Reconstruction in August 1945. The provinces thought the price too high, i.e., ceding the lucrative fields of personal and corporation taxes to the federal government and so the federal proposals for health insurance and income security were withdrawn.

C.D. Howe's prediction of a booming postwar economy proved correct. Under his direction Canada moved from a system of public management of the war back to private management of the peacetime economy. The transition was facilitated by generous tax provisions for business, and by equally generous re-establishment benefits for veterans. Plans for health care, housing and comprehensive social security were set aside. In their place, Canadians were offered the agenda of a resurgent capitalism — the promise of full employment and the flood of consumer goods. With the joblessness and deprivations still green in their memories, a majority of Canadians accepted this substitution without protest. In the rush to plan a collectively oriented postwar society, had there been any time to build a supporting political constituency? Apparently not, if we are to judge by the ease with which the glittering prize of comprehensive health, housing and social security was withdrawn from public gaze.

However, the seeds planted by the Beveridge and Marsh Reports and by the Heagerty Report continued to grow, despite the unfavourable postwar environment in Ottawa. Several years after the federal health insurance programme was withdrawn, T.C. Douglas, premier of Saskatchewan, decided to introduce hospitalization insurance without federal aid. Canada's march toward prepaid health care quickened its pace.

As for the comprehensive system of social security and the plan for eliminating want in Canada, that remains tantalizingly out of reach as the presence of food banks in the 1980s testify. Many of the programmes recommended by Marsh are now in place; but because they were developed in a piece-meal fashion, Canada's social security system suffers from some serious gaps despite (and partly because of) the existence of an array of federal, provincial and municipal programmes. Much of the most recent planning and thinking about social security in Canada has had a sombre, if not pessimistic character. The MacDonald Commission's proposal for a Universal Income Security Programme is cast against a louring background of unemployment and under-employment.[50] In sharp contrast to the Beveridge and Marsh Reports, the MacDonald Commission appears willing to tolerate unemployment, under-employment and low wages. These were conditions considered capable of eradication in those heady war years when people believed in, and social reformers planned for, the new Jerusalem.

NOTES

1. One indication of this is Granatstein's mention of wartime surveys of public opinion in Canada which asked people to select items from a list of twelve topics that they would like to know more about. The survey indicated that "plans for after the war" was the most frequently requested topic. J.L. Granatstein, *Canada's War: The Politics of the Mackenzie King Government, 1939-1945*, Toronto, 1975, 251.

2. Sir William H. Beveridge, *The Pillars of Security*, London, 1942, 10.

3. *The Pillars of Security*, 203

4. Abolition of Want meant a national minimum of income assured to all as a matter

of right; disease would be tackled by a comprehensive universal health service; ignorance would require educational reform; squalor would be dealt with by housing and community planning; idleness was to be vanquished by public planning for full employment.

5. *Globe and Mail*, Toronto, 24 May 1943, 2, report of speech given by Beveridge in Ottawa; the quotation by Beveridge relating to medical care is from his book *The Pillars of Security*, 53.

6. Ibid.

7. Reported in the Toronto *Globe and Mail*, 2 December 1942.

8. Vancouver *Sun*, 1 December 1942.

9. Toronto *Globe and Mail*, 2 December 1942.

10. Cited in Philip Beveridge Mair, *Shared Enthusiasm*, Surrey, 1982, 135.

11. Toronto *Globe and Mail*, May 16, 1940. The report was in the newspaper's second section.

12. Toronto *Globe and Mail*, May 17, 1940.

13. Ibid, 6.

14. D.V. Smiley, "The Rowell-Sirois Report, Provincial Autonomy and Post-War Canadian Federalism." *In* J. Peter Meekison, ed., *Canandian Federalism: Myth or Reality*, Toronto, 1968, 66.

15. Malcolm G. Taylor, *Health Insurance and Canadian Public Policy*, Montreal, 1978, 7.

16. *Pillars of Security*, 11.

17. J.W. Pickersgill, *The Mackenzie King Record*, Vol. 1. Toronto, 1960, 433.

18. Kevin Collins, "Three Decades of Social Security in Canada," *Canadian Welfare*, 51, January-February 1976, 5.

19. Harry M. Cassidy, *Social Security and Reconstruction in Canada*, Toronto, 1943, 186-187.

20. Alvin Finkel, *Business and Social Reform in the Thirties*, Toronto, 1979, 96-97.

21. This was out of a total of 483,933 members. *Labour Gazette*, 44:1, January, 1944, 101.

22. The rise in unemployment claims was a result of shortages of material, not jobs, which idles some people from time to time. *Labour Gazette*, 45:1, January 1945, 76. The small percentage of claims underlines the point made earlier that Canadians had little experience with social insurance.

23. Dennis Guest, *The Emergence of Social Security in Canada*, revised edition, Vancouver, 1985, 125.

24. Granatstein, *Canada's War*, 252.

25. Canada, *Report on Social Security for Canada*. Prepared for the Advisory Committee on Reconstruction, House of Commons, Special Committee on Social Security; *Health Insurance*, Report of the Advisory Committee on Health Insurance, Ottawa, Minister of Pensions and National Health, 1943. It was known as The Heagerty Report. L.C. Marsh was a research advisor to this committee; Canada. Parliament, House of Commons, Advisory Committee on Reconstruction, *Housing and Community Planning, Final Report of the Sub-Committee*, March 24, 1944, Ottawa, 1946, 339. It is known as The Curtis Report. L.C. Marsh was research advisor to this committee and wrote much of the report.

Adding to the public discussion on social security was the appearance in late 1943 of "an extended memorandum" on social security by Charlotte Whitton, one of Canada's most prominent social welfare authorities. Under the title *The Dawn of Ampler Life*, Ms. Whitton offered a critique of the Marsh and Heagerty Reports and put forward some alternative ideas. For a discussion of her proposals see Dennis

Guest, *The Emergence of Social Security in Canada*, revised edition, Vancouver, 1985, 117 ff. In addition, Harry M. Cassidy produced two books on social security programming and planning between the years 1943 and 1945. *Social Security and Reconstruction in Canada*, Toronto, 1943; and *Public Health and Welfare Organization in Canada*, Toronto, 1945.

26. Leonard Marsh, *Report on Social Security for Canada 1943*, Toronto, 1975, xviii.

27. Marsh, *Report on Social Security for Canada*, xix.

28. For details of Marsh's appointment as Director and his work with The McGill Social Science Research Project see Allan Irving, "Leonard Marsh and the McGill Social Science Research Project," *Journal of Canadian Studies*, 21:2, Summer 1986, 6-25. Major publications of the Project include A.G. Fleming and C.F. Blackler, *Health and Unemployment*, Toronto, 1938; Leonard C. Marsh, *Canadians In and Out of Work*, Toronto, 1940. Marsh was also prominent in the League for Social Reconstruction (LSR) in the 1930's.

29. See for example Marc Lalonde, *Working Paper on Social Security in Canada*, Ottawa, 1973 which includes "An Income Supplementation Strategy." More recently the MacDonald Commission's *Report on the Economic Union and Development Prospects for Canada*, Ottawa, September 1985, contained plans for a Universal Income Security Program.

30. *Report on Social Security for Canada*, 57-58.

31. Ibid, 67; see also Brigitte Kitchen, "The Introduction of Family Allowances in Canada," in this book.

32. Ibid, 263 ff.

33. *Health Insurance*, 72.

34. Ibid, 182.

35. Ibid.

36. Labour's point of view is represented in H.A. Chappell, "The State's Responsibility for Health Services." *Proceedings of the Ninth Canadian Conference on Social Work*, Winnipeg, 1944, 49.

37. See the comments of T.C. Routley, General Secretary, Canadian Medical Association, to the *Ninth Canadian Conference on Social Work*, Ibid, 51-56.

38. See *MacLean's*, April 15, 1943, "Backstage at Ottawa," 14-15.

39. Advisory Committee on Reconstruction, *Housing and Community Planning*, Final Report of the Subcommittee, Ottawa, March 24, 1944, 4. The Committee acknowledged the "very heavy task of preparing the final text...aided by the Research Adviser." The Research Adviser was Leonard Marsh.

40. *The Social Worker*, 13:2, November 1944, 22-23.

41. *Housing and Community Planning*, 9.

42. Ibid, Chapter 7. The usurption of prime agricultural land in the Fraser River delta in British Columbia for housing and related development is an example of the folly of ignoring this report.

43. Albert Rose, *Canadian Housing Policies 1935-1980*, Toronto, 1980, 28.

44. Robert Bothwell, Ian Drummond, John English, *Canada Since 1945*, Toronto, 1981, chapter 7; Robert A. Young, "Reining in James: The Limits of the Task Force," *Canadian Public Administration*, 24:4, Winter 1981, 596-611.

45. Malcolm Taylor, "The Canadian Health Insurance Program," *In* C.A. Meilicke and Janet L. Storch, eds., *Perspectives on Canadian Health and Social Services Policy*, Ann Arbor, Michigan, 1980, 186.

46. Albert Rose, *Canadian Housing Policies 1935-1980*, 28.

47. A.H. Richardson, *The Ganarska Watershed*, Toronto, 1944.

48. See Gail Cuthbert Brandt. "Pigeon-Holed and Forgotten: The Work of the Sub-Committee on Post-War Problems of Women, 1943," *Social History*, XV, 29, May 1982, 239-259.

49. See J.L. Granatstein, *Canada's War*, Toronto, 1975, Chapter 7, and Robert Bothwell, et al., *Canada Since 1945*, Chapter 7.

50. Royal Commission on the Economic Union and Development Prospects for Canada, Ottawa, 1985.

The Introduction of Family Allowances in Canada

Brigitte Kitchen

Early Interest in Family Allowances

Discussions about family allowances in Canada were, from the beginning, closely related to the issue of wage levels. The stage had been set by Charlotte Whitton in her capacity as the Canadian delegate to the Child Welfare Committee of the League of Nations which had been formed in 1925. She reported to the readers of the *Child Welfare News*, a publication of the Canadian Council for Child Welfare, that:

> "...the system of augmenting wages by special allowances based on the size of the workman's family is entirely unknown in the practice of Canada and the United States...it has been recommended by the British Coal Inquiry Commission, etc... The system being entirely foreign to Canadian and U.S. practice will doubtlessly arouse considerable interest on this side of the water."[1]

If the practice of paying family allowance was unknown in North America, its principle was not. The Chicago economist Paul Douglas, whose main concern with the practicality of a "living wage" had led him to examine the various family allowance schemes in operation in Europe, had proposed a family wage for the United States in his book, *Wages and the Family*, in 1923. He had based his proposal on the French modes of employment-related compensation funds for married workers with children.[2] Charlotte Whitton thought family wages were prevalent in industrially weaker countries where wage levels were generally lower than in Anglo-Saxon countries where workers' earnings were comparatively high. Drawing a distinction between the economic and social reasons for the payment of family allowances and their political implications, she wrote:

> "Family wages have proved their value and are constantly expanding in those countries where they were introduced for economic as well as social reasons; for instance, in France, as a means of raising the birthrate and in Belgium for preventing the exodus of workers to France. In countries where they were introduced merely as a social welfare measure, as in Germany, the Netherlands, Sweden and Czechoslovakia family wages have never become very prevalent."[3]

There was a school of thought which believed that higher wage levels to support a man, his wife and three children adequately, would make the payment of family allowances unnecessary. An Australian Royal Commission found, however, that wage levels sufficient for the support of a family of that size would have exceeded the total wealth produced in the entire country in 1919, and therefore concluded that such a scheme was economically infeasible. Furthermore, the Royal Commission felt that basing wage levels on a particular family size was inefficient, since it did ' nothing for families which had more dependents to support and too much for those which had fewer dependents or no dependents at all. For these reasons, the Royal Commission rejected an increase in wage levels and recommended family allowances instead.[4]

In Great Britain, Eleanor Rathbone had become interested in family allowances when she discovered that, during the first world war, the separation allowances paid to the families of enlisted men had greatly improved their conditions. She found that in spite of the war and the absence of the main breadwinner, working class children were better-fed and clothed and healthier than they had ever been before. This convinced her that such payments should be continued after the war, and that they should be paid to mothers.

In Canada, Dr. George F. Davidson, the first Deputy Minister in the newly founded Department of National Health and Welfare could reflect in 1949 with the wisdom of hindsight:

"Why were we content to accept the social inadequacies of any industrial wage system through generations of peace and discover only when we went to war that the application of industrial wage principles to our armed services could not be tolerated on social grounds?"[5]

The 1914-1918 war had not provided this experience because the Separation Allowances paid to soldiers overseas included a grant for one dependent only; this was usually the wife or an aging parent. Provisions for children were left to the public through voluntary subscriptions to the Canadian Patriotic Fund.[6] The contingencies of war did not change Dominion government policy which was to consider children the responsibility of their parents and private charity. The presence of children was, however, recognized when Canada introduced its first personal income tax act in 1917. Taxpayers with children were given a two hundred dollar tax exemption for a child under the age of twenty-one dependent on parental support. A parent could claim the same exemption for children under the age of twenty-one who were dependent because of a physical or mental incapacity. This was an important step since it was recognition in principle of the variation in income needs between parents and non-parents.

In the late 1920s Canadians were made aware of the concept of family allowances through the initiative of private organizations and individuals. The Jesuit Father, Léon Lebel, played a particularly crucial role in advocating the benefits of family allowances in a wage economy that fails to recognize family responsibilities.

The Ecole Sociale Populaire in Montreal was the first institution in Canada which recommended the introduction of family allowances, as early as 1927.[7] From that date, the School continued to publish brochures and documentation about the concept and principle of family allowances and advocated their introduction at all its conferences and study sessions.[8]

The Role of Pére Léon Lebel

The person whose name is more closely associated with making Canadians familiar with family allowances was the Jesuit Father, Léon Lebel. He was born on January 8th, 1883, the son of a farmer in Cacouna, in Quebec. Between 1927 and 1929, he wrote a number of pamphlets about the financial difficulties of large families which had been caused by the structural changes in the economic system. In Les Allocations Familiales, published in 1927, he argued that:

"Pour un pays comme le Canada, en plein essor de developpement, qui a besoin de nombreux travailleurs pour mettre en oeuvre les immenses ressources de son territoire, le problème des familles nombreuses devrait être le premier à l'ordre du jour."[9]

He was far-sighted enough to recognize that the question of family allowances was closely and intimately related to the question of income, which again had to be seen as part of the even broader question of the economic system.[10] In Le Probleme de la Famille Nombreuse he attacked the economic liberalism of the 19th century, in which a wage was regarded as just, he pointed out, as long as it had been voluntarily agreed upon between employer and employee, although it may not have been sufficient to support an individual or a family.[11] Lebel's views were supported by the Catholic social school of thinking, which had repudiated the liberal doctrine of wages. Pope Leo XIII in his encyclical Rerum Novarum had stated that "the just wage could not be insufficient to support the honest worker:" and as the same pontifff had also argued that it was the duty of a father to support his children, it followed that the "just" wage had to be sufficient to meet the needs of a family.[12] Yet, to pay men doing equal work according to the number of their children was an untenable proposition. For this reason, Lebel suggested that the principle of "equal pay for equal work", should be placed between the principles of a justice based on "quid pro quo" (justice commutative), which always had to be taken into account in the setting of wage levels. Pére Lebel recognized that these two principles were contradictory, although they both appeared to be eminently reasonable.

"D'une part, le principe de sens commun exprime par Lion XIII: le salaire juste doit être familial; d'autre part, le principe de justice commutative: à travile égal, salaire égal. Comment les concilier?"[13]

He went on to say that Catholic sociologists had come to the conclusion that the solution to the contradictory principles was to be found in the supplementary remuneration of family men in proportion to their family responsibilities.

"La remuneration dont il s'agit est celle qui est due au pére de famille non en tant que travailleur, mais à raison de services qu'il rend à la societe et aux employeurs en leur fournissant des producteurs de richesses et des consommateurs."[14]

This meant, of course, that Lebel could argue that a family man was entitled to family allowances whether he was receiving an income from work or not.

In the 1940s both the Beveridge Report in Great Britain and the Marsh Report in Canada recommended the payment of family allowances regardless of the employment status of the family head. But they did so for entirely different reasons from those proposed by Pére Lebel. It is interesting that both reports anticipated the possibility that a family could be better off receiving unemployment insurance benefits that would provide for the needs of children. Family allowances, however would avoid this possibility since they would be paid regardless of the employment status of the parents.

This could lead to the assumption that parents in such families might prefer not to work. Yet, it should be noted that in the case of family allowances, work disincentive is not an issue. They are payable regardless of the employment situation or earnings levels of the parent(s). Treating family allowances, as Pére Lebel did, as a public token of recognition for the child-raising services parents provide to ensure the continuity of society, clearly divorced them from the wage question but linked them to the issue of procreation and population growth. For Pére Lebel this was a major argument in favour of family allowances.

The Population Question

Pére Lebel's emphasis on child-raising as a service for the benefit of society as a whole was used as a weapon by the opponents of family allowances. They could represent (or misrepresent) the proposal as a scheme to credit parents for their procreative powers. Lèbel was a late mercantilist. His position in relation to the population question led him to the belief that: "le nombre est le grand facteur de prospérité d'une nation."[15] He argued that Germany, in 1870, was generally regarded as a poor country; yet, in the thirty years which preceded the outbreak of the war of 1914, she would double her wealth with the growth of her population; whereas France, in spite of her resources, the progress in her disposable capital, her scientific inventions and all the ingenuity of the Gallic mind, had remained more or less stagnant in both wealth and population.[16]

In 1928, there was great concern about the number of Canadians who left Canada to settle in the United States, attracted by the higher wages and higher standard of living there. Premier Tolmie of British Columbia described emigration as the biggest social problem facing Canada.[17] Although Canada was receiving a great number of immigrants every year, the realization grew that it was impossible to build up a stable population size if emigration continued to equal immigration. Pére Lebel believed that the inadequacies of Canadian wage levels (in the late 1920s) were not only the principle reasons for the lowering of the birthrate in Canada but also for the exodus of Canadian citizens to the United States.[18]

It was true that Canada could make up for their loss by admitting more and more immigrants from abroad. But Lèbel went on to point out that the main supplier of immigrants, Great Britain, was herself suffering from a drastic decline in the birthrate and that therefore, it was more than likely that this source would dry up. Moreover, Canada, in order to have any immigrants at all, would have to resign herself to accepting everyone who would want to come "l'élèment morbide comme l'élèment sain."[19] From the complaints that had come from various provinces of the Dominion, it was obvious that this state had already been reached, and that among the latest arrivals from Britain, there had been a large portion of undesirables.

It seems that he was alluding here to the 150,000 or so children sent to Canada from Great Britain between 1869-1924 unaccompanied by parents and guardians. The Bondfield Commission (1924) in Great Britain, investigating the fate of British emigrant children in Canada, had found that children lacking "normal moral stamina and self-control" were poorly suited to adjust to the social conditions of life in Canada.[20] The findings of the Commission were readily accepted in Canada and led to increasing criticism of this country's immigration policy.

Lébel also pointed out the difficulties involved in assimilating a large immigrant block to the Canadian way of life; and he asked whether this did not involve the risk of having colonies of strangers living in Canada who were different in language and customs, whose affinities were not the same and who were putting Canada in danger of losing her "physionomie actuelle et son unité."[21] One may wonder whether he was reminding the xenophobic elements of French and English Canada that the best form of population growth was still achieved by a high birthrate.[22]

Between 1921 and 1926, the birthrate in Canada had declined from 26.4 to 22.0 per cent. The decline in the province of Quebec had been even more drastic over the same period of time. There, the birthrate had fallen from 37.6 in 1921 to 32.1 in 1926.[23] Pére Lebel was seriously concerned about this decline, given his view that population size was an important factor for the prosperity of a nation. He argued that in different countries economists had attempted to translate the value of a man's material production into money terms.

"Au Canada," les statisticiens de la compagnie d'assurance "Dominion Life" estiment qu'un adulte de 35 ans qui gagne $50.00 par semaine a une valeur economique de $36,982; un enfant americain au berceau representerait déjà pour le pays une valeur pecuniaire de $9,333.00. Sans doute il peut y avoir de l'exageration dans ces calculs, mais en divisant par trois et en donnant $3,000.00 comme valeur au nouveau-né canadien, il s'ensuivrait qu'une augmentation de 100,000 naissances verserait au pays un capital de $300,000,000.[24]

According to him, Canada needed population growth in order to develop her resources. He pointed out that Canada would rely in vain on the continuation of immigration from Europe. Quoting the evidence of unidentified economists to support his point he stated:

"Economists anticipate, not only for Canada, but elsewhere a stabilization of the white population. They are fearing — especially those in Europe —that the white race is impoverished and in danger of seeing its population go down...For a few years yet European countries may be partly overpopulated with adults, but our chances to secure more are dwindling steadily day by day. It requires no prophetic foresight to conclude that the time limit, within which Canada may solve her population problem in terms of millions of new citizens is coming to an end."[25]

He also warned that the decline in the birthrate of Great Britain and the recovery of British industry would cease to make Britain "a population exporting" country.[26] In view of the resistance to the introduction of family allowances in 1944, among certain sections of English speaking Canada who feared becoming out-numbered particularly by French Canadians, it seems ironic that in 1928, Pére Lebel, a French-Canadian, expressed the warning that a combination of a declining birthrate in Great Britain and anglophone Canada "would mean a danger for the future of Canada as a British country."[27]

First Government Interest in Family Allowances.
The first official interest in family allowances was shown in the House of Commons on February 13th, 1929, when Mr. J.E. Letellier (Member for Compton) moved a resolution, seconded by Mr. J.S. Woodsworth (Member for Winnipeg North Centre):

"That, in the opinion of this House, the question of granting family allowances should be studied, taking into consideration the respective jurisdiction of both federal and provincial parliaments in the matter, and that the said question should be referred to the Committee on Industrial and International Relations."[28]

The Select Standing Committee on Industrial and International Relations had been set up a year earlier in order to investigate and report on insurance against unemployment, sickness, and invalidity. The opening words of the Minister of Labour, the Honourable Mr. Heeman, on February 26th, 1919, at the first hearing of evidence for and against family allowances, throws an interesting light on the social climate of the time. In 1927, the long debated Old Age Pension Act, a means-tested, non-contributory pension scheme had finally been enacted. When the Select Standing Committee on Industrial and International Relations approached the provinces as to their reaction to the question of unemployment, sickness, and invalidity insurance, Mr. Heeman had to admit that:

"The attitude of the provinces has not been very enthusiastic...Some provinces, being faced with old age pensions and not knowing how far the provisions will take them in a financial way, hesitate to embark on any new scheme."[29]

The committee heard the evidence of five individuals. Pére Lebel and Mr. Robert Daoust, a shoe manufacturer from Quebec, argued in favour of the scheme; and Miss Charlotte Whitton, on behalf of the Social Service Council of Canada; Mrs. Mildred Kensit, Director of the Children's Bureau of Montreal and Mr. Robert E. Mills, Director of the Children's Aid Society, Toronto, argued against the concept of the scheme.

Pére Lebel outlined basically the same arguments in favour of the introduction of family allowances in Canada as he had developed in his pamphlets. His most significant point was his perception of parenthood as a social service for the country. He compared the service of parenthood with the service the King, politicians and judges provided. They were not paid by the hour, but they rendered a service without which society could not subsist, and so "society gives them an honorarium or a fee in order that they may be able to properly render that service."[30] The payment of family allowances would help parents by providing them with some financial assistance to meet the material obligations of parenthood. According to Pére Lebel, 20th century economic conditions lowered the standard of living of the family man compared to a wage earner unencumbered by family responsibilities. Even such social legislation enacted for the protection and benefit of the child tended to burden the family, since parents were obliged to keep children in school and support them beyond the age at which they had once started to support themselves. He argued therefore, that as the family was the fundamental unit of society, it was the duty of the state when changes in social conditions rendered the economic organization of society unfavourable to the family "to modify economics in order to readapt social conditions to family needs."[31]

Robert Mills, the Director of the Children's Aid Society of Toronto called such action an "unwarranted interference with individual liberty and initiative." He pointed out that having a family could not be considered as a "dire accident that happens to you and, therefore, you are trying to protect yourself against it." Having children was something normal and it was surely not possible to insure against something normal? Furthermore, he felt that the possibility of saving for a decent married life should not be taken away from workers. The state or private industry should not be put into a position where they had to do the saving for workers; and he thought that it was impossible to subsidize the married couple without making some sort of reduction from the unmarried group. The payment of family allowances would undermine the pillars of North American civilization: responsiblity for oneself and responsibility for the family group as an entity. He felt that it was the duty of the social work profession to oppose this danger as it stood in sharp contrast to the cherished values of the profession.

> "Social workers are tremendously interested in people. That is our job. We are particularly interested in their material prosperity and welfare; but we are interested even more, I take it, in their psychological, in their spiritual and their intangible value: the whole of modern social work, I think can be said to be built upon the development of character and personality, whereas in the old days all that social workers thought of was a matter of relief. Relief, of course, sometimes is an essential thing, but the thing we are driving at, the thing that we think is of value in our poeple — of greatest value in our people — are the qualities that make them different from the brute beast, the qualities that make one people different from another, and we are extremely careful that certain of the simpler qualities, certain of the more important qualities should not be lost. Among those that we consider as being very essential are self-reliance and in-dependence."[32]

Mills was, of course, seriously mistaken. Traditionally, the need for relief had been associated for too long with personal pathological deficiencies of the individuals concerned. Liberal elements in the social work profession had to fight a long and bitter battle to achieve a separation of public assistance, or "relief", from psychotherapeutic services. Provincial Mothers' Allowances are a good case in point. The debate about the separation of services has to be seen against the background of a growing awaresnss of the dynamic interrelationship between individual and familial material needs. In the words of Barbara Wooton, "it may well be true that problem families are the victims as much of their economic circumstances as of their own personal shortcomings, and that these shortcomings are themselves, at least in part, the reaction of despair to impossible demands."[33] What is needed is to recognize that the human values of self-reliance and independence cannot be achieved without an adequate provision of material means to do so. The three spokesmen of the social work profession before the Select Committee on Industrial and International Relations indicated by their evidence how far removed they still were from this recognition.

Mr. Mills as well as Mrs. Kensit expressed concern about the possibility of encouraging the birthrate among low income earners who were "frequently physically unfit, verging towards the unemployable with the added liability in many cases of limited intelligence caused by mental defects, which precluded them from higher paid work."[34] Moreover, social workers as a group did not favour large families. They were the families with the most problems; the families with the smallest income had very often the largest families and it was surely undesirable to encourage the birthrate from such stock whose children would inherit poor health and mental defects and thus be consumers and dependents rather than producers.[35]

The large numbers of immigrants living in Canada were pointed to as a serious problem in the consideration of family allowances:

"... different standards of life prevailing among different peoples, and the well-known fecundity of the central European races over women of this continent would inevitably mean the bartering away of the birthright of the basic stock of this country."[36]

This was one of the persistent arguments used by Charlotte Whitton to resist the payment of family allowance. Miss Whitton emerged from the 1929 hearing as the most formidable opponent to family allowances in the country. She was most insistent in her belief that family allowances would stimulate the birthrate. The time she had served as the Canadian assessor to the Child Welfare Branch of the League of Nations, her discussions with Pére Lebel, and the study of his pamphlet on family allowances, had given her that conviction. "It was from that evidence, from that background and from passages in that report that I made the assumption,"[37] she stated emphatically.

Yet her most powerful and most eloquent arguments, which were shared by the majority of the trade unions, were in relation to the question of wages. "Family allowances", she argued, "are an admission by the State that the wages within its areas are not and cannot be made sufficient to support the average family according to minimum standards of health and decency, and that, therefore, the state must, by subsidy, redistribute resources, the equitable development and distribution of which it cannot control."[38] She went on to argue that it was totally unnecessary for Canadians to proclaim to the world that a decent standard of living was only possible through state intervention in the form of the payment of family allowances.

In an exchange of arguments with J.S. Woodsworth during the course of the hearings, she emphasized that it was not the level of wages paid which were insufficient but annual incomes which were reduced by periods of unemployment of wage earners and by the lack of organization in the equalization of employment. For her, the problem consisted in the existence of persons who were either unemployable or who could only be employed at low wages because their services were worth so little to the state or industry. She was contradicted by J.S. Woodsworth on this point when he quoted the statement of the Manufacuturer's Association that steadily employed workers were earning about a thousand dollars a year. "I think you will admit that this is a very low income?" She did.

Mr. Joseph Daoust stated that the average worker in the shoe manufacturing industry would earn between twenty and twenty-two dollars a week or $1,144 per annum. The inadequacy of such a wage level can easily be seen when it is compared to the four budget categories which were drawn up by the Department of Labour at the request of the Select Standing Committee on Industrial and International Relations. In 1929, the poverty level for the average family of five was set at $900; the minimum subsistence level at $1,400; health and decency level at $1,775 and the comfort level at $2,400.[39] According to the Census of 1921, 58.2 percent of Canadian families with children had three or less; 41.8 percent had four or more.

In his pamphlets on the subject of family allowances, Pére Lebel had pointed out that an examination of the "family budget:" (average budget for a family of five persons), as published every month in the *Labour Gazette*, showed that average wages paid in Canada were not sufficient to meet the most conservative family budget.[40] Before the Select Standing Committee, Pére Lebel proposed as a solution to raising the income of families, the payment of a supplementary benefit in proportion to a wage earners' family responsibilities, modelled after the French family allowance system. He pointed out that the cost of family allowances was rather low when compared to the amounts paid out in wages. He drew attention to the psychological effects of family allowances. He argued that its payment would lessen the pressure on employers for wage increases as an income of $1,000 a year was regarded as a "famine wage" largely because the value of wages was regarded in terms of the needs of families. His point was that once children were provided for by family allowances, a wage of $1,000 or even $980 would be considered a fair and reasonable wage, because it was only meant to meet the needs of individuals or a couple.[41]

Pére Lebel argued that Canada was in a position to support the costs of family allowances for the benefit of families with three or more children. Initially, he suggested the payment of fifty dollars per child estimating that the costs would be $47.5 million. Costs could be cut by paying twenty-five dollars a year, as in New Zealand; in that case, the expenditure for Canada would be reduced to $22.5 million. However, when he found out that, according to the 1921 Census, there were 2,850,000 children under the age of fourteen living in Canada, and calculated that the fifty dollar payment a year for each of them would cost $142 million, he consulted with economists, who suggested that in Canada it would be sufficient to begin payments with the third child.[42]

His plan for the financing of family allowance benefits was a very interesting one. He regarded the payment of family allowances as a form of social insurance, and therefore suggested that unmarried men would have to contribute to the scheme. He expected that the unmarried men would complain that they were being fleeced; yet, he argued that:

"Even at the outside figure, the cost on each individual would hardly exceed $20 per year which is 40 cents a week, the value of two packets of cigarettes, and it is for this precisely that the family allowance would be to the greatest advantage to them, because it would serve as an insurance, for which they were paying premiums with the prospect of receiving back in five or six years all they have paid. The idea of insurance is so well known in Canada that it is easy to understand this matter."[43]

The latter appears to have been rather a rash statement, considering the fact that the only social insurance programme in existence in Canada at that time was the provincial workmen's compensation funds. Interestingly enough, the city of Montreal had established a ten dollar a year tax on bachelors, which had been withdrawn in 1929. This tax had not been earmarked and had simply been put into the Treasury, to be used for whatever purpose seemed necessary. Pére Lebel argued that this fact constituted the crucial difference between this scheme and his own.

"...but a tax paid by a bachelor for a special purpose and for a purpose which would be to his advantage, would be something different, and I think bachelors would understand this, especially if it were proposed as part of an insurance system."[44]

As it was, bachelors were never put to the test, nor were Canadian employers who would have paid two per cent of their wage bill into the family allowance fund.

The Committee presented the evidence of the witnesses on the subject of family allowances to the House of Commons on May 31, 1929, with the recommendations that (1) as the proposal was new in Canada and required more careful consideration, no immediate action should be taken; and (2) the jurisdictional question of family allowances between the federal and the provincial governments should be considered by the government. The most important outcome of the hearings of the Select Standing Committee on Industrial and International Relations in 1929, was the fact that the Committee had not actually opposed the proposal.

Moreover, the Committee recommended the publication of its report in both English and French, presumably in order to keep the debate alive.

In November, 1929, the Executive Board of the All Canadian Congress of Labour at its convention in Winnipeg urged its member unions to give earnest consideration and close study to the question of family allowances.[45] The Board gave a number of important reasons for its recommendations. It stated that family allowances involved at least a partial recognition of the principle that each member of the community should receive according to his needs. In a country like Canada with its need for a larger population, it would be desirable that the conditions for the upbringing of families should not involve hardship on either parents or children. From the workers' point of view it was important that his dependents did not suffer because of the existing disparity between costs of living and income, as was unfortunately often the case. The Board also believed that family allowances would lead to an increase in the consumption of stable commodities which in turn would have a positive effect on the employment situation. Altogether the Board felt that family allowances could on these grounds be regarded as a promising palliative for the faults of the existing economic system. However, a resolution which called for support of family allowances was tabled.[46]

The collapse of the New York Stock Exchange, which marked the beginning of the Great Depression, put an end to the discussion on family allowances until the year 1932, when the Quebec Social Insurance Commission reopened the debate. The Commission was not in favour of paying family allowances in Quebec. It entertained grave fears for a population exodus from the rural areas and agriculture into the urban industrial sector of the provincial economy, if family allowances were to be paid only to workers in that sector. It is interesting to note that the Commission could not envision that family allowances could be paid to the whole population, nor could they see them as a state institution.[47]

On the federal level, family allowances were mentioned only once in the Parliament of Canada between 1930-43, in relation to the birth of the Dionne quintuplets.[48]

Yet, in 1938, at the annual convention of the Trades and Labour Congress (TLC), a resolution was introduced by the Toronto District Labour Council favouring the introduction of family allowances. Among the many reasons cited in favour of their payment was the crucial point that the "minimum wage and wage code legislation were drafted not with a view of meeting family needs but rather to assure essentials to the individual worker."[49] Decision on the resolution was deferred at both the 1938 and 1939 convention. But in 1940, the Executive Board of the TLC came out in opposition to the payment of family allowances. The Executive based its decision on its belief that:

"Where family allowances are in effect, the tendency is to keep the standard wage closely related to the requirements of the single person, the family income then being proportionally increased to the size of the family being raised."[50]

This decision was, of course, in line with the past policy of the Canadian Trades and Labour Congress in relation to family allowances. Their attitude had always been that wages sufficient to maintain a worker and his dependents should be paid in return for a man's production. Yet the very fact that in the late 1930's a resolution in favour of family allowances had been presented at a union convention indicates that there were some union members who had understood the need for a "social" wage, in addition to the "economic" wage, based on the criterion of need rather than production.

There can be little doubt that the federal government's decision to pay a special allowance for the dependents of servicemen which guaranteed them a defensible standard of living (based on the cost of living study which had been carried out by the Toronto Welfare Council in 1938), threw a new light on the relationship between income from production and family needs. The introduction of dependents allowances can thus be seen as a major step in bridging the incongruencies between the two. The principle of family allowances had also been previously applied in the form of veterans' and blind persons' pensions by the federal government and in the form of widows' pensions by the provinces.[51]

The Discussion of Family Allowances in the War Years

Dr. L.C. Marsh's Report on Social Security for Canada appeared in March 1943, outlining a comprehensive Canadian social security system. Marsh made the enactment of unemployment and health insurance as well as the group of old-age, survivors, and disability insurances as a priority ahead of family allowances. There were a number of people in Canada who considered the Marsh Report a replica of the British Report by Sir William Beveridge on Social Insurance and Allied Services. After all, the Liberal Government of Prime Minister Mackenzie King invited Beveridge to address the House of Commons in Ottawa during the parliamentary debate on the Family Allowance Act in 1944 and not Dr. Marsh. There can be little doubt that the Marsh Report was not popular in government circles. Government interest in the concept and principle of family allowances was raised because of its committment to its anti-inflationary price and wage stabilization policy, which it had established in the later months of 1941. It soon became apparent that the wage freeze had grave consequences on the standard of living of the lowest paid sector of the economy, i.e. unskilled workers whose wages had been frozen at less than fifty cents an hour. Wage control was administered by a National Labour Board as well as a number of regional boards which had the power to (1) adjust wage levels which were too low by comparison with wages paid for similar work under comparable circumstances, and (2) pay a cost of living bonus if there was need to do so, or prevent such a bonus from being paid in such cases where basic wage levels were considered to be too high. The result was a very complicated structure of different wage levels and cost of living bonuses.

In March 1942 the workers of two steel companies went on strike after their demands for a wage adjustment for unskilled workers had been denied by their respective regional labour boards. Their strike represented a serious threat to Canada's war effort and therefore prompted the Cabinet to act. The Prime Minister blamed the Finance Department on the grounds that they should never have frozen an increasing injustice.[52] Ilsley, the Minister of Finance, on the other hand, agreed that there were indeed injustices inherent in the wage stabilization policy but they could not be amended if the policy was to be maintained.[53] But in order to at least be seen to be doing something Cabinet proposed a minimum wage of fifty-five cents an hour: a 10 percent increase in wages for those working at the lowest end of the income scale, as well as an administrative reorganization of the National Labour Board. Thus, the Minister of Labour, Humphrey Mitchell, was replaced as Chairman of the Board by an Ontario Judge, John McTague.[54] The reorganized board made up of a representative from capital and a representative from labour and chaired by Judge McTague, held public hearings on labour relations and wage conditions throughout the country, between April 15th and June 17th 1943. The result was a split between the other board members and the representative of organized labour, J.L. Cohen. The latter wrote a dissenting Minority Report which reinforced the official union policy from the 1930s that family allowances could be used as an instrument of keeping wages down.

McTague and the representative of capital had favoured the intro-duction of family allowances because they feared that an increase in the minimum wage for all 900,000 low-income earners in Canada would raise the costs of production which in turn would lead to an increase in prices. No mention was made of how family allowances would be financed nor whether the private or the public sector would administer them.

Mackenzie King's government was quite justifiably proud of the success of its ceiling policy. The cost of living between 1941 and 1943 had risen by 6.7 percent. This compared well with the experience of the early years of World War I when it had increased by 34.7 percent.[55] Both McTague and Mackenzie King were well aware that family allowances would have to be kept separate from any discussion on labour policy and would have to be considered in relation to social security coverage. Cohen, for his part, had accepted the principle of family allowances in a general social security network. But how was this objective to be achieved without arousing the suspicion of organized labour?

The Government was forced to act when the coal miners in Alberta and British Columbia walked out on strike. The Cabinet adopted a new orientation towards wage policy which allowed for the correction of "gross inequalities and injustices." Furthermore, the cost of living bonus was to become part of the basic wage rate, and a strict price control policy would be applied to prevent further increases in the cost of living and thus, cost of living bonuses would gradually become redundant.

In a radio address to the nation on December 4, 1943, the Prime Minister outlined the details of the revised wage policy orientation and told his listeners that the Majority and the Minority Report of the National Labour Board would be made public. He did not mention the proposal for the payment of family allowances. To have acted differently would have left Mackenzie King and his Cabinet open to attack that family allowances had been deliberately chosen as a device for the protection of the government's wage and price stabilization policy. It would also have meant that family allowances would have inevitably and possibly forever been associated with low wage levels. By the time of the Speech from the Throne, January 27th, 1944, which introduced the Government's intention to bring in family allowances as the first universal social security programme, it seemed that the Prime Minister had successfully separated the two issues. By allowing for the adjustment of gross inequalities and injustices at the lowest wage-level before he announced the introduction of family allowances, Mackenzie King could confidentaly refute the claim that family allowances had been introduced to save the wage and price control programme. Whether family allowances would have been introduced on a universal basis, if it had not been important to dispel the suspicion of organized labour is, of course, a moot question. But it seems reasonable to surmise that the price the Prime Minister had to pay for his obfuscation of the connection between family allowances and wage control was the payment of universal benefits.

It is important to note that in the discussion of family allowances before the Act was finally passed in July 1944, their importance was buttressed by a battery of economic arguments. The fact that the allowances were meant to extend the same financial benefits to all Canadian families with children which had, until then, been limited to families who were paying income tax, was almost totally ignored. Instead, prominence and emphasis was given to Keynesian economic principles which considered family allowances as a sure and valuable economic primer which would stimulate the economy through increasing the spending capacity of those Canadians with the highest "propensity" for consumption, i.e. low-income families. This would prevent a post-war economic recession, it was hoped, and thus the eruption of social unrest. By that time the relationship between economic and political instability had been understood, and governments in Canada, Britain and the United States, in line with the objectives of the Atlantic Charter were mapping out post-war reconstruction plans.

Family Allowances As A Divisive Wedge

In Canada, family allowance came to be seen as "a further wedge in disunity" if not a serious threat to national survival. C.E. Silcox, for instance saw the Family Allowance Act as a "cause for endless antagonism on religious grounds."[56] The *Ottawa Morning Journal* warned of the vast differences in racial fertility and birthrates which existed between the Quebec and the "foreign" or "new Canadian" element of the population and people of British stock. This was seen as a danger to Canada's survival as British North America. The leader of the Conservative Party, John Bracken described family allowances as a "bribe" to win votes in Quebec, and soon the racial battlecry of the "revanche des berceaux" was sounded to warn Canadians of British stock that French Canadians would soon be reversing General Wolfe's military victory and gaining control of the country by outbreeding the English.

The absurdity of this kind of argument becomes more apparent in economic terms. Family allowance payments, when first paid in 1945, varied between five and eight dollars per month, depending on the age of the child. Although this amount constituted about 8 percent of the average industrial wage in Canada at that time, it would hardly seem a powerful financial enticement to reproduce. The population issue however played an important role in the thinking of Canadians during the war years. The Ontario Federation of Labour, in its journal *The Labour Review*, hailed family allowances as a population policy in the same way as Père Lebel had done it. Future Canadian citizens would arrive by the stork rather than by steamboat.[57] In this way the social significance of the allowances became almost totally obfuscated. The general public saw family allowances as a "baby bonus," rather than the family income support benefit which had been proposed in the Marsh Report.

According to the Marsh Report, all discussions of social security issues had to begin with the level of family income.[58] Marsh believed that families had to have social security coverage to meet the contingencies of working and family life.[59] His "social minimum" was to provide a "desirable level of living"[60] for individuals and families. From his review of existing income support programmes he had realized that there were anomalies in their provisions for children. Provincial Workman's Compensation programmes recognized the needs of children whose father had been killed at work, but in the case of the father who had been disabled because of an accident at work, the amount of his pension would be based on the severity of his disability, and his family responsibilities would be totally ignored. Thus, Workman's Compensation recognized the dependents of dead workers but not of injured and disabled workers. This is, of course, not only a problem for income maintenance programmes; it is also an inherent weakness in the industrial wage-system. The incommensurability of industrial wage levels based on the principle of need and family obligations is of interest to all those who are concerned about the material and psychological welfare of children. For Leonard Marsh, family allowances were one avenue to a solution by which the incongruencies of wage and social security in relation to the dependent children could be overcome. Family allowances were to become the key to consistency between the economic and the social spheres, by recognizing the material needs of children apart from the needs of their parent(s).

Marsh's understanding of the use of family allowances in this way was unique and innovative. In Britain, Beveridge had argued that wage levels were high enough to allow for the support of at least one child. Family allowances were therefore paid only for the second child, or for the first child when the main breadwinner was unemployed. For Canada, given average male wage-rates, Marsh did not recommend the exclusion of the first child from receiving benefits. The *Montreal Star*, reported that "in the years before the war," in normal years, "the average wage earned by all male workers in Canada was less than one thousand dollars a year."[61] The average benefit of $72.48 per child per year would have increased the average male worker's wage in 1945 by 7.2 percent; but, if he had the traditional number of three children to support, then family allowances would have provided him with 24 percent of additional income. Larger families would receive considerably more benefit than those with less children, and the objective of horizontal equity was achieved.

Besides income levels, Dr. Marsh had yet another reason to insist on coverage for all children. This was the relationship of family allowances to other social insurance programmes. Unemployment insurance benefits, for instance, were wage-determined, and thus, like the wage system, did not reflect family needs. To recognize the needs of children separately from those of their parents, Dr. Marsh felt that family allowances should meet the basic subsistence needs of the child. This would allow wage-related contributory social programmes to be limited in their coverage to the married couple which he considered as "the typical contributor unit."[62] Provisions for dependent children within the comprehensive social security system which the Marsh Report had outlined, would have become unnecessary in individual social programmes. Marsh emphasized the necessity to provide a "social minimum" for children as a basic income floor below which no Canadian child should fall. "Allowances for children had to be recognized in relief and social assistance budgets," Dr. Marsh argued, "because they were so near the minimum that there were no margins."[63]

Among social security experts at that time, Marsh stood alone in proposing such a visionary application of family allowances. The International Labour Conference in Philadelphia, in 1944, in its income security recommendations suggested that "family allowances ... should represent a substantial contribution to the costs of maintaining a child."[64] The 1944 Family Allowances Act reflected this recommendation, and family allowances failed to become a social floor for children, and as such the first categorical guaranteed income programme in the history of social security.

Conclusion

Thus, family allowances never emerged as the "greatest single reform since the adoption of free education" as some of their supporters described them in their enthusiasm.[65] The opportunity to develop a comprehensive social security system, wherein social programmes would have been carefully dovetailed to meet the needs of families more adequately was lost. Family allowances had a different meaning for the three men, Pére Lebel, Prime Minister Mackenzie King and Dr. Leonard Marsh, who had been most instrumental in the struggle for their acceptance in Canada. The interests of these three men in family allowances differed substantially, yet they believed they could be met by the same type of social programme. Pére Lebel saw family allowances as a means to counterbalance the anti-family bias of the industrial wage-system, whilst Mackenzie King sought to save his price and wage control programme for reasons of political expendiency.[65] And Dr. Marsh, for his part, wanted to make family allowances the key to consistency in social security in a way that would recognize differences in family size.

Its opponents saw the programme as a possible wage depressant, a bonus for procreation and a wedge pushed into national unity. There are few examples of a social programme proposal that incited such conflicting reactions before becoming a statuatory provision. The particular social and economic significance of family allowances in 1945, as well as today, rests on the impossibility of providing for the needs of children through a wage and a social security system that fails to take into account the varying sizes of family units. In this sense, the Family Allowances cannot be considered a welfare programme for the poor. But if set at an adequate level, they could at least lift the working poor out of poverty. The fact that family allowances as a social security programme are complementary to the wage system was recognized in 1944 by the Montreal branch of the Canadian Association of Social Workers, in their brief on the Marsh Report:

> "In the first place, any true exponent of children's allowances, believes that minimum-wage legislation ensuring decent wages is absolutely essential, and no other device can be substituted for it."[66]

When the connection between family allowances and equivalent living standards for families of varying sizes began to be obscured after 1945, interest in family allowances soon faded away. But as long as the wage system fails to provide families with horizontal equity and the tax system does not provide vertical equity, the case for family allowances remains strong and unshakable.

NOTES

1. *Canadian Child Welfare News,* II:2, May 15, 1926.
2. Paul Douglas, *Wages and the Family,* Chicago, 1925.
3. *Canadian Child Welfare News,* 1:5, January/March 1925, 59.
4. *Labour Gazette,* 29:7, July 1928, 751.
5. G.F. Davidson, "The Economic Welfare of Children: The Role of Children's Allowances." *National Conference of Social Welfare, 1949.* Selected Papers, New York, 1950.
6. Booke Claxton Papers, Public Archives of Canada, Ottawa C 187708.
7. *Relations,* 4, August 1944, 197.
8. Ibid, 197.
9. Léon Lebel, *Les Allocations Familiales,* Montreal, 1927, 2.
10. Ibid, 2.
11. Léon Lebel, *Le Probleme de la famille nombreuse,* Montreal, 1927, 8.
12. Ibid, 8.
13. Ibid, 8.
14. Ibid, 9.
15. Léon Lebel, *Les Allocations Familiales,* 1927 Montreal, 14.
16. Ibid, 16.
17. Léon Lebel, *Family Allowances: as means of preventing emigration.* A plea for the family of the worker so that it may share in the general prosperity of the nation. With a foreword by Frederick Wright, Montreal, 1928, Introduction.
18. Ibid, 28.
19. Léon Lebel, *Le Probleme de la famille nombreuse,* 7.
20. *Canadian Child Welfare News,* IV:3, August 1928, 20.
21. Léon Lebel, *Le Probleme de la famille nombreuse,* 7.
22. Léon Lebel, *Les Allocations Familiales,* 16.
23. Canada, House of Commons, Select Standing Committee on Industrial and International Relations, *Report,* Ottawa, 1928, 7.
24. Léon Lebel, *Le Probleme de la famille nombreuse,* 5.
25. Select Standing Committee, *Report,* 7-8.
26. Ibid, 4.
27. Ibid, 4.
28. *Labour Gazette,* 29:7, June, 1929, 605.
29. Select Standing Committee, *Report,* 2.
30. Select Standing Committee, *Report,* 20. This argument was supported by Mr. Joseph Daoust, shoe manufacturer from Montreal who stated before the committee: "I am willing to protect a man who has a number of children to support because the man is working for his country," 49.
31. Select Standing Committee, *Report,* 3.
32. Mr. Robert Mills, Director of the Children's Aid Society, Toronto, before the Select Standing Committee, *Report,* 71.
33. Barbara Wooton, *Social Science and Social Pathology,*59.
34. Select Standing Committee, *Report,* 68.
35. Ibid, 68.
36. Charlotte Whitton before the Select Standing Committee, *Report,* 66.
37. Ibid, 56.
38. Ibid, 56.
39. Select Standing Committee, *Report,* 39.
40. Léon Lebel, *Family Allowances: as means of preventing emigration,* 27.
41. Select Standing Committee, *Report,* 39.

42. Ibid, 25.

43. Ibid, 21.

44. Ibid, 30.

45. *Labour Gazette*, 29:12, December 1929, 1364.

46. Ibid, 1365.

47. Dorothy Stapler, *Family Allowances for Canada*, Toronto, 1943, 18.

48. Frank R. Breul, *Family Allowances in Canada*: A Discussion of the Social, Economic and Political Considerations which lead to the Passage of the Family Allowances Act of 1944 and a Description and Analysis of its Administration, Ph.D., McGill, 1953, 45.

49. Trades and Labour Congress, *Report of Proceedings*, Ottawa, 1938, 195.

50. Trades and Labour Congress of Canada, *Report of Proceedings*, Ottawa, 1940, 45.

51. Margaret Gould, *Canada Must Choose, Family Allowances in Canada, Facts versus Fiction*, Toronto, 1945, 126.

52. J.W. Pickersgill, *The Mackenzie King Record*, Vol. 1 1939-44, Toronto, 1960, 591.

53. Ibid, 474.

54. Ibid, 471-472.

55. W.L. Mackenzie King, "The Fight Against Inflation," radio broadcast delivered on December 4th, 1943, reprinted in *The Labour Gazette*, XLIII:12, 1599.

56. C.E. Silcox, *Canada Must Choose. The Revenge of the Cradles*, Toronto, 1945.

57. James Magladery, "At Last a Population Policy," *Labour Review*, 6:18, August/September, 1944, 310.

58. L.C. Marsh, *Social Security for Canada, 1943*, Toronto, 1976, 29.

59. Ibid, 19.

60. Ibid, 58.

61. The Montreal Star undated clipping in the Brown Weston Papers, Public Archives of Canada, MS 35B5, Vol. 167.

62. L.C. Marsh, *Social Security for Canada, 1943*, 58.

63. L.C. Marsh, "Family Allowances in Canada," address to the Pacific Northwest Conference on Family Relations, published in *Family Relations*, Washington State College, 1948.

64. International Labour Review, "Report on Family Allowances Schemes in 1947:I," 57:4, April 1948, 323.

65. Harry Cassidy, "Children's Allowances in Canada" *Public Welfare*, August 1945, 4.

66. For a detailed discussion of the role of Mackenzie King in the introduction of family allowances, see Brigitte Kitchen, "Wartime Social Reform: The Introduction of Family Allowances" *Canadian Journal of Social Work Education*, 7:1, 1981.

67. C.A.S.W. Montreal Branch Report quoted in the Social Worker, 13:2, 1944, 2.

Winding Down Social Spending:
Social Spending Restraint in Ontario in the 1970s

Jeffrey Patterson

This paper deals primarily with the pattern and magnitude of government spending restraint in Ontario in the 1970s, especially with respect to social development and human service programmes. It also examines the relationship of spending restraint to current political and economic events in contemporary Ontario and Canada.

Following World War II, and building on the prior experience of the Great Depression, there was an effort to hedge against future dramatic fluctuations in the economy. Attention was turned toward the construction of a social security safety net. Significant sectors of the business community could see the value in such a net, in maintaining purchasing power, in controlling wage demands and the like. Labour had been pushing for many decades for social security programmes for workers, and they continued to mount pressure in the postwar period. Workers wanted some protection against the economic insecurities associated with a free-market economy: unemployment, ill health and retirement. At the same time, no commitment was ever made to labour's demand for full-employment. The social security net can be seen as partial compensation for the continuance of structural unemployment.

At the state level, a variety of administrative, economic and political motivations made for a reluctance to invest in state welfare programmes. Both major levels of government were involved, the provinces holding the constitutional responsibility for social welfare programmes and the federal government controlling a large portion of overall state revenue. In the context of postwar Keynesian fiscal policies, business, labour and the state appeared to be pushing in the same direction, although not for the same reasons. Some would argue that there was a consensus. Others would argue the social legislation that was enacted resulted from class struggles between labour and business, with the state feeling the need to respond to both interests, while maintaining a general allegiance to the prerogatives of business. Keynesian economic attitudes and the general postwar affluence both supported some investment in a social security safety net. Social programme development was slow and reluctant, in part related to the general weakness of class consciousness and organization among Canada's workers. What emerged therefore was a social security safety net that was seen as serving the interests of business as much as, if not more than, those of the workers.

Social programmes required government spending and, for a while, such spending was seen, to an extent, as serving the varied interests of both labour and business. But pressure in the 1970s for the generation of new private capital, in the face of the changing worldwide economic situation, resulted in a shift in the domestic redistribution of income in favour of big business and affluent investors. We have been facing what some have called "a fiscal crisis of the state."[1] State action therefore has tended towards the continual erosion of the social security net. Keynesian economic policies have been criticized and there has been a dramatic shift to spending restraints, income policies, supply-side economics and monetarism. There has been an attack on social programme spending by business and the state. The pressure from private capital has resulted in increased state attention to capital accumulation and a shift therefore, from social programme expenditures to capital investment expenditures.

The primary intent of the balance of this paper is to describe the nature and extent of this social spending restraint in Ontario. It is important to indicate at the outset however, that 1) social spending restraint is national in extent and 2) it has the full participation of both federal and provincial governments.

Federal spending restraints by their very nature occur at three levels. First, they occur with respect to those programmes for which the national government has jurisdiction, mostly income transfer programmes, but also including such important areas as housing. Secondly, they occur with respect to inter-governmental transfers from the federal to provincial and municipal governments. These spending restraints have recently taken on increased importance. Thirdly, they take place with respect to what are increasingly referred to as tax expenditures. Tax expenditures, defined here as extending public support by purposefully foregoing government revenues, have grown in importance in recent years.

Ontario's social spending restraint measures, as well as their relationship to overall provincial government spending, are summarized below, and then placed in the context of the national attack on Canada's social security system. Comparison is made between Ontario's pattern of social spending cutbacks and that of other provinces. Finally, policies of cutback are related to changing patterns of taxation.

The Attack on Social Security Spending in Ontario
Ontario has led the attack on the social security system and social spending by governments. It goes under the names of cutbacks, spending restraints, de-institutionalization and privatization, a manifestation of the same phenomenon. There are several indicators that Ontario has led the attack.

In terms of recent social programme spending, as of 1980/81, examining all provinces, Ontario ranked ninth in per capita spending on human services. It ranked fifth if provincial and municipal spending on human services are combined. With respect to social welfare programmes in particular, Ontario ranked seventh in per capita spending when provincial and municipal spending are combined. Ontario ranked tenth in per capita spending on human service increases in the period from 1979/80 to 1980/81, while at the same time it ranked third in percent increase in all other provincial spending. Ontario ranked eighth in social assistance levels, or a very distant tenth if one relates social assistance levels to per capita income. A 1981 document from the Ministry of State for Social Development (Canada) documents the fact that in the previous five years alone, Ontario had slipped from second to fifth place in per capita spending on health and post-secondary education, the established programmes whose future funding is currently being negotiated by the provincial and federal governments.[2]

Social spending restraint in Ontario involves virtually every programme and is of long duration.[3] Provincial government spending can be characterized as having climaxed with respect to total gross provincial product in 1971 or 1972. It peaked in 1975/76 and has been declining since then. Provincial spending was 9.9 percent of gross provincial product in 1966/67, reached 15.5 percent in 1971/72 and 16.0 percent in 1975/76, and was 15.2 percent in 1980/81.

Social development spending grew more slowly than overall government spending throughout the early 1970s. From 1972/73 to 1975/76, all government spending, following adjustment for changes in consumer prices, increased by nearly 32 percent, while social development spending increased by 20 percent. From 1975/76 to 1977/78, the respective real dollar increases were 17.1 and 10.9 percent. From 1977/78 to 1980/81, overall government spending decreased by 9.0 percent, again following adjustment for consumer price index, while social development spending declined by slightly less, 7.6 percent, small comfort for those in need of social security protection. The only area of spending growth in this latter time period was spending for the public debt.

Spending on colleges and universities has been an area of extremely severe spending restraint throughout the 1970s. Trends in the late 1970s were no different than for the earlier period. From 1977/78 to 1980/81 spending on colleges and universities, following the adjustment for inflation, declined by 8.8 percent, 11.2 percent in the case of the universities and 3.7 percent in the case of community colleges and adult education. Nor did student loans escape provinvial budgetary restraints. From 1975/76 to 1979/80 the fee revenues in Ontario's colleges and universities increased by 68 percent, 33 percent in constant dollars. In the same time period spending for student loans and grants increased by 17 percent in constant dollars.

The Ministry of Culture and Recreation, created in 1973 as Ontario's answer to multiculturalism and the demand for increased quality of life, has perhaps been the worst hit ministry in the provincial government. From 1977/78 to 1980/81, spending declined by over 31 percent in constant dollars.

Spending on libraries declined by nearly 28 percent, although cuts, as in the case of primary and secondary education, are not necessarily passed through to the libraries themselves. Often, local taxpayers pick up all or some of the difference, as has been the case for libraries in Metropolitan Toronto. In these instances, provincial spending restraint becomes a way of transferring the burden of paying for some services from provincial taxpayers to local taxpayers. What is important to observe here is that there will be some shift in revenue from a progressive to a regressive tax source. In addition, there is increased potential for a less equitable distribution of resources. Some local councils will be willing or able to raise the resources required to maintain the services while others will not.

The tendency to shift tax burdens from provincial to local taxpayers is most evident in the funding of the primary and secondary education systems. Education, which in 1980/81 comprised 14 percent of total provincial expenditures, has been one of the primary areas of spending cutbacks and restraints throughout the 1970s. From 1972/73 to 1977/78, while provincial budgetary spending increased by over 54 percent, spending on education increased by only 10 percent. From 1977/78 to 1980/81 spending on education — in constant dollars — decreased by nearly 21 percent.

Again, local school boards reduced the full impact of these cutbacks. In the case of Metropolitan Toronto, for instance, provincial grants to the Metropolitan Toronto School Board increased by only 25 percent from 1972 to 1980, a 37.5 percent decrease in constant dollars. During the same period the Metro school (property tax) levy increased by over 127 percent, 13.8 percent in constant dollars. Toronto was perhaps hardest hit by provincial cutbacks as a result of enrolment decreases.

Notwithstanding that the propaganda from Queen's Park would have us believe that health care costs are breaking the provincial treasury, spending for the Ministry of Health decreased by 1.4 percent from 1977/78 to 1980/81. Provincial spending on health declined from 4.5 percent of gross provincial product in 1972/73 to 4.3 percent in 1980/81. Hospitals, recipients of over two-thirds of provincial health funds, have absorbed most of the cutbacks. From 1975/76 to 1977/78, increases in spending on hospitals almost exactly matched consumer price increases while there was a decrease of almost six percent from 1977/78 to 1980/81.

Spending by the Ministry of Community and Social Services has on the whole not been as subject to spending cutbacks and restraints as many other areas, showing a decrease of 2.2 percent in constant dollars from 1977/78 to 1980/81. However, priorities have changed substantially. Income maintenance spending decreased by 13.2 percent, while spending on social services increased by 9.6 percent. Decreases in spending for income maintenance were directly reflected in the incomes of social assistance recipients, who saw their real spending power decline from 10 to 20 percent from 1975 to 1980.[4] This erosion of spending power would have been greater if changes in federal programmes had not taken place.[5]

Spending on social service increased by nearly 10 percent in real dollars from 1977/78 to 1980/81. Even the latter spending increases can be shown to be more illusionary than real. Some part of the increase is the result of the geographical expansion of services into areas probably less fully served in earlier years. For instance, increases in social service spending in Metropolitan Toronto almost exactly matched consumer price increases from 1977 to 1980. This pattern is little different in Ottawa. Operating grants to residential facilities for the elderly decreased by nearly 6 percent in constant dollars, although spending for residential home support for the elderly continued to increased.

Spending for day nurseries and children's aid societies increased in the reference time period, but this must be qualified as well. The funding formula for the children's aid societies, which is currently based on number of children in care, has not changed in real dollars in spite of a new child abuse and prevention emphasis that has been added to the workload of the societies. Funding per space in day nurseries (day care centres) has declined in real dollars, as new funds have been channelled almost entirely into private, commercial day care centres where employee wages are low and growing much less rapidly than inflation.[6]

Social service spending restraint also shows up as relative rate decreases, after adjusting for consumer price increases for many services, such as family counselling, homemaking and home nursing.[7] While the volume of service may be increasing, as more and more people become eligible for publicly assisted services, and/or begin to take advantage of their eligibility, fee-for-service decreases make it more difficult for service providers to provide quality services.

In summary, the 1970s have witnessed considerable spending restraint and cutbacks with respect to human services programmes in Ontario, and this tendency has intensified since 1975. Parallel tendencies at the federal level are described below, indicating that the erosion of the social security net is national in extent.

Spending Restraints at the Federal Level

Reduction in federal government spending on income maintenance has been a constant threat from the early 1970s onward. Unemployment insurance became a primary target of those unhappy with the extent of income security provided through state financing. This should not be surprising in view of the relationship between income security and work incentives. The defenders of the amended 1971 Unemployment Insurance Act could not muster enough forces to prevent the erosion of some of the principles underlying it. Numerous changes affecting entitlement were made and benefit levels were reduced substantially in 1978. The principle that government, because it has some control of the key economic levers that affect employment and unemployment rates, should itself be a major contributor to the unemployment insurance fund, has been largely foregone. Consequently, contributions required of both employers and employees have been raised. A limited needs and income test has also eroded the insurance principle and benefit reductions have been implemented in situations where other household members are working.

Family allowances have been another target of conservatives. Benefits were increased for the first time in twenty-five years in 1971 when the government was unable to agree on a new income security programme for Canadians. Government efforts to make an income test conditional for receipt of family allowances were thwarted in 1972 only as a result of adroit use of the rules of procedure in the House of Commons by one member. Benefits were again reduced in 1978 as part of the government's budgetary restraint efforts. While old age security programmes and pension systems have escaped budgetary restraint efforts, the need to improve the income levels of elderly Canadians has yet to be addressed, in spite of numerous conferences and reports on the subject, and acknowledgement by both federal and provincial governments. The Government of Ontario has been one of the major impediments to the nationwide reform of this issue. It remains wedded to the principal of individual responsibility in spite of the evidence that only 40 to 50 percent of Canadians can provide sufficient income protection for themselves in their retirement years.

Direct services spending has also been reduced at the federal level. Spending by the Department of National Health and Welfare, other than in income and intergovernmental transfers, has grown at a rate significantly less than inflation since 1978. The same is true for programmes in the Department of the Secretary of State and the federal government has practically withdrawn from the housing field. Amendments to the National Housing Act in 1973, which extended the forms which capital and subsidy contributions could take, actually signalled a withdrawal from new social housing commitments. Crisis level housing shortages, combined with record-low new starts, are currently facing several Canadian housing markets, including Toronto, and the federal government seems unwilling to ameliorate it in any way, a marked departure from policies that were in effect until at least 1975. Currently, the federal government is committed as well to reducing growth in intergovernmental transfer payments to the provinces for health and post-secondary education, both areas critical to the maintenance of the social security net. The Minister of Finance published three year forecasts of spending estimates of major policy areas in October 1980. Spending in the social development areas was projected to increase less than spending in any other area.

Spending restraints in Canada stand out in the context of other advanced western nations, principally those enrolled in the Organization for Economic Co-operation and Development (OECD). As can be seen in Table 1, the expansion of the government sector in Canada increased at about the same rate as it did for the average of the OECD countries in the period lasting from 1960 to 1976. However, in the last four years of this period, 1972 to 1976, the public sector expanded significantly less rapidly than the OECD average, less rapidly than all but three OECD countries.

Table 1

Increase of General Government Expenditure Relative to the Increase of Total Revenue, 1960-1976

	1960-76	1967-71	1972-76
Canada	.995	1.061	1.118
OECD average (weighted by population)	1.036	.927	1.156

Source: OECD, *Public Expenditure Trends*, Paris, June 1978, Table 10

The above has provided a summary of budgetary restraint measures being pursued by federal and provincial governments. A similar catalogue of service reductions could have been provided. It would probably have presented a bleaker picture, as cost inflation in the government sector has outpaced that in other sectors of the economy.[8] Below, the pattern of spending restraints is examined analytically for its important political implications, and its value in reaching a clearer understanding of class relations in Canada today.

Pattern of Spending Restraints

Two outstanding patterns are evident. First, the largest blows of spending restraint have been dealt the poorest of the poor, mostly a group with no more than tenuous connections to the labour force. Most Canadians, including those working steadily at well-paying jobs, have been spared the worst consequences of government spending restraints and cutbacks. The level of the welfare floor which the social security net is supposed to provide seems to be the most serious casualty of the breakdown of the support for such a safety net.

Welfare recipients in Ontario have seen their real incomes reduced over the past five years by 10 to 20 percent. The elderly who are too poor, or whose families are too poor to look out for them when they become too frail to live on their own have been shunted into inferior nursing homes. People requiring mental health treatment have been told to find inferior shelter near an out-patient treatment centre (eg. Parkdale in Toronto) and come in for treatment when they become too depressed about their shelter or with their loneliness. These cuts are about as unkind and cruel as you can get, but they do not involve the majority of the population.

This does not mean that the basic social security net has not been eroded, for it has. That it has is evident from an analysis of spending restraints in Ontario. In addition to those programmes specifically benefitting the poor, those large programmes providing services that are both universal and considered most essential, have been subjected to the most spending restraint. Programmes in education, health and income maintenance, which comprised 46 percent of the provincial budget in 1980/81, experienced an average decrease of 12.1 percent in constant dollar expenditures from 1977/78 to 1980/81. The medical insurance and community health programmes and the social service programmes of the Ministry of Community and Social Service, which together comprised 14 percent of the Ontario budget in 1980/81, experienced expenditure increases averaging 11.0 percent in constant dollars from 1977 to 1980. It is the universal programmes that have generally been subjected to the most severe spending restraints. In fact, it will be asserted that the cuts for programmes benefitting the poor, combined with increased support for lower-cost categorical programmes has legitimated the spending restraint efforts in the view of the majority of the population.

A second conclusion that can be drawn is that the principle of collective social security that was a major part of the postwar national direction is being eroded. In its place we find privatism, the principle that each member of society is responsible for his or her welfare. The following examples illustrate this point:

- Provincial mental health hospitals have been emptied as part of de-institutionalization. The Ontario Minister of Health has told patients that they must fend for themselves in the community. Even the mentally ill are responsible for their well-being.

- The same is true for frail and poor older people. The government of Ontario has had a freeze on new spaces in homes-for-the-aged for several years. The result is that these people take places on longer and longer waiting lists for often inferior private nursing homes.

- Growth in the commercial social service sector is promoted at the expense of the government and non-profit voluntary sectors. Day care and nursing homes are examples.

- The growth of a private medical care system side by side with the public system is condoned. By 1981 over 16 percent of Ontario physicians had opted out of the public medical care system. A much higher proportion had opted out in the case of many critical medical specialties.

- The Treasurer of Ontario in 1981, reflecting as well the views of a provincial royal commission, said that individuals are responsible for their security in old age.

- Government has withdrawn from any responsibility for income security for the unemployed. No matter what the level of unemployment, government is committed to full funding of unemployment insurance by employers and employees.

An often neglected indication of the decline of the national consensus reached following World War II is the extent to which, especially since the Income Tax Act was amended in 1971, the principle of progressive income taxation has been eroded. Increased numbers of tax loopholes and deductions from taxable income, many rationalized as stimulating increased individual saving, have been legislated during the 1970s. Regardless of rationalization, the end result is the same: a reduction in taxes for high income individuals. "Tax expenditures" is the term used increasingly to describe these tax reductions. The postwar consensus is still associated with sufficient legitimacy that overall rate reductions might not meet with societal approval. Such reductions are legitimated by the pronouncement that those receiving them behave in the public interest, that they select their savings and investment opportunities to conform to the requirements of the Income Tax Act, as amended from time to time. Parallel to tax expenditures with respect to the personal income tax have been reductions, both selected and generalized, in corporate income taxation.

In addition to reducing significantly revenues available to government to meet either the full employment or welfare objectives of government, one of the results of these tax expenditures is to restore income differentials that had been declared unacceptable 25 or 30 years ago. These tax expenditures have become great enough and of enough public concern, especially to those opposing them, that the Minister of Finance published Canada's first tax expenditure budget in December 1979. Over $32 billion in "tax expenditures" were listed and classified. A Department of National Revenue Report estimated personal income tax expenditures at from $6 to $9 billion in 1975 using what it terms a "normative" tax structure.[9] The estimate of corporate income tax expenditures totaled nearly $4 billion.

Taxation statistics for the year 1979 show deductions of over $21 billion. Three-fourths of these, nearly $16 billion, stem from amendments to the Income Tax Act in the past decade. Most of the deductions and exemptions go to higher income groups. Nearly 15 percent of the returns for 1979 had total incomes of $25,000 and over. These returns accounted for over 35 percent of all deductions and exemptions. Loss revenues stemming from these exemptions and deductions likely totalled over $4 billion. This does not include revenue lost from indexation of personal income exemptions.

From 1971 to 1980, the ratio of corporate profits to gross national product increased from 9.2 percent to 13.7 percent. Simultaneously the effective rate of federal and provincial corporate taxation declined from 38.4 percent to 29.5 percent. The application of 1971 corporate income tax rates to 1980 profits would likewise have generated an additional $4 billion in revenue.[10]

It does not take much imagination to realize that closing many of the corporate and personal income tax loopholes, together with the additional revenues that could accrue to the federal government as a result of the energy accord reached between the Governments of Canada and Alberta in September 1981, could make it possible to not only erase the federal budgetary deficit, but maintain social spending as well. Thus, tax expenditures and the widening magnitude of income differentials to which they contribute, should be seen as part of the larger attack on the national consensus reached at the end of World War II.

The Legitimation of High Unemployment and Social Spending Restraints

The real question for social policy analysts is why has the erosion of the post-War national consensus, both the full employment and social welfare objectives, taken place? Why has this erosion been accepted by those who stand to lose the most, the majority of Canada's workers? While the answers to these questions are complex, they are not so complex that we cannot venture some preliminary observations. The most profound observation is simply that a level of class consciousness that would have led to effective opposition from Canadian workers has not existed. If it did the full employment objective would not have been set forth in a government white paper, as it was in 1945, and then almost immediately disowned. It was not honoured because it did not have to be.

The establishment of an effective social security net remained in the interests of all sectors of society and hence remained in place as an objective of Canadian policy makers. That it took nearly thirty years to implement it is evidence that those who stood to gain the most from the establishment of a floor under private consumption could not demand the immediate fulfillment of their self esteem. It is therefore no wonder that social spending restraints have been difficult to resist. The level of consciousness and organization prerequisite to such resistance does not exist. If this is not sufficient explanation, there are other factors working against the materialization of the required opposition.

First, the cuts are largely marginal. As outlined above, they are especially so when their impact on mainstream workers — those who are somewhat organized, such as the trade union sector — is analyzed in detail. The most critical spending restraint measures have been those affecting the poor, those who are largely unorganized. In large part these people have also born the largest burden of high unemployment. As well, the recent pattern of social development in Canadian society seems to have favoured an upper-middle income professional class. Inspection of income distribution data reveals that those in the fourth quintile have seen their income share grow in recent years. Many of the tax expenditures described above have been designed to benefit this group as well. This group collectively controls much of society's knowledge development, a fact which is also critical to the acceptance of the breakdown of the postwar national consensus. In addition, state taxation policies have also benefitted mainstream Canadian workers. The indexation of personal exemptions, under the Income Tax Act, beginning in 1972, one of the largest causes of government's contemporary revenue crisis in Canada, primarily benefits the bulk of the working class.

Finally, the mainstream of Canadian society seems to have accepted the notion that there is currently a crisis in capital accumulation and that everyone will have to make some sacrifices to assure economic growth and productivity gains in the future. The Canadian Labour Congress, the Ontario Federation of Labour and the New Democratic Party have all accepted the notion, probably correct as far as it goes, that government must become more actively involved in guiding economic development if the current crisis in economic growth is to be overcome. Having accepted the basic agreement, it is therefore difficult to oppose state economic intervention, no matter how poorly formulated or carried out. It likewise becomes difficult to effectively oppose social spending restraints and cutbacks.

Conclusion

The above notwithstanding, why have the people of Ontario been subjected to a greater degree of spending restraints than the residents of most other provinces. There are likely several factors involved rather than one all-encompassing explanation. Worker consciousness and organization are obviously involved. Ontario labour always seems to have been more wedded to negotiation, including collective bargaining, than labour elsewhere in the country. Populism amongst both labour and farmers is more common in Quebec and the west. The political arm of labour, the New Democratic Party, has slipped substantially in popularity from the immediate postwar period when it formed the Official Opposition in the Ontario Legislature and came very close to forming a government. The NDP has ranked third in popularity since the 1948 Ontario general election.

Ontario now possesses one of the lowest provincial tax structures in Canada, which serves two purposes. Structurally, it enables provincial businesses to compete with neighbouring states in the U.S.A., and labour may be as wedded to this structure as the corporate sector. Low taxes are popular amongst workers as well, and low taxes ultimately mean less government spending. Finally, incomes are still higher and unemployment still lower than anywhere else except Alberta, even with high unemployment, employer lay-offs and plant shut-downs. Ontarians still benefit disproportionately from national economic policies and this fact is reflected in part by immense social and political stability.

The analysis of social spending restraint by government sheds considerable light on the nature and politics of the welfare state, especially on the ways in which the state makes restraint and cutbacks politically acceptable. While the process is certainly more complex than the present paper presents, some valid initial impressions do emerge.

That the poorest of the poor, those not connected to the labour force have borne the brunt of cutbacks is evidence that one way in which cutbacks are legitimated is to turn poor people into the architects of their own victimization. Such victimization, in addition to reducing spending in the first instance, likely serves to legitimate even modest reductions in spending on programmes and policies that benefit those more a part of the main stream. Reducing spending by large amounts on programmes that are critical to social security is evidently unpopular enough in itself that it has not happened extensively or over a long period of time. Spending restraint in a manner that simply reduces quality without affecting volume or accessibility to a great extent appears to be quite acceptable.

It is quite clear that the federal and provincial governments are engaged in an ongoing campaign to cutback on their financial and political support for the social security safety net that was reluctantly pieced together following World War II. Fiscal resources are being transferred to the corporate sector to enhance capital investment, indicating that the corporate sector is coming out ahead in the current class struggle in Canada. Left unanswered is the critical question of how far cutbacks can be taken. These limits have likely not been tested thus far.

NOTES
1. See for example: J. O'Connor, *The Fiscal Crisis of the State*, New York, 1977; Ian Gough, *The Political Economy of The Welfare State*, London, 1979; Harold Chorney and Phillip Hansen, "The Falling Rate of Legitimation: The Problem of the Contemporary Capitalist State in Canada", *Studies in Political Economy*, 4, Autumn, 1980, 65-98.
2. CANADA. Ministry of State for Social Development, unpublished background materials, Ottawa, 1981.
3. The main source for the following discussion is the provincial spending estimates, published annually, and the provincial *Public Accounts*, published annually as well, usually about two years following actual spending.
4. Social Planning Council of Metropolitan Toronto, *...And the Poor Get Poorer: A Study of Social Welfare Programmes in Ontario*, Toronto, 1981.
5. The initiation of the child tax credit in 1978 doubled the proportion of income which social assistance recipients received from federal sources. Cf. Ibid, 7,8.
6. Social Planning Council of Metropolitan Toronto and Action Day Care Coalition, *Effects of Government Spending Restraints on Day Care Services in Metropolitan Toronto*, Toronto, April 1980.
7. Social Planning Council of Metropolitan Toronto, *Voluntary Sector at Risk: Trends in Government Support of the Voluntary Social Service Sector in Metropolitan Toronto*, Toronto, 1981.
8. At the end of March 1981 the price index for personal expenditures was 219.2 (1971 dollars), while the implicit price index for current expenditures of government was 217.0.
9. U.I. contributions, registered pension plan contributions, retirement savings plan premiums, registered home ownership, interest, dividends and capital gains deduction, pension income deduction, union and professional dues, education

deduction, tuition fees, general expense allowance, standard deductions and deductions transferred from spouse. Cf. Canada, Department of National Revenue, *Taxation Statistics*, Ottawa, 1981, Table 2A.
10. Statistics Canada, *National Income and Expenditure Accounts*, Ottawa, catalogue II 13.001, quarterly, Tables 1 and 84.

The Limits of Health Insurance

Donald Swartz

Health insurance is one of the core elements of the welfare state in Canada, accounting for almost 30 percent of provincial expenditures.[1] This essay is concerned with examining the limits of social reform through an analysis of the Canadian health insurance system established by the 1957 Hospital Insurance and Diagnostic Service Act and the Medicare Act of 1968. Enormously popular among Canadians generally as well as social reform advocates, the declared objective of these two acts was to promote the health of Canadians by making comprehensive health care available to all on the basis of need rather than the ability to pay.

Two issues have dominated recent discussions of the existing system of health insurance. One is its cost, with free enterprise idealogues in particular arguing that widespread abuse by patients has rendered the system unaffordable.[2] The other is the related concern of the erosion of accessibility due to the appearance in several provinces of user fees and extra-billing by physicians. This concern prompted the short-lived 1979/80 Clark Federal Conservative government to ask Justice Emmett Hall to undertake a Health Services Review, and the subsequent Liberal government to pass the Canada Health Act in 1984 to buttress the original legislation.

While I will examine these concerns in some depth, they are not, in my view, the only problems, or even the most important ones to address. The recent controversy is exceedingly narrow in focus, and superficial in its analysis, confined as it is to recent developments in the operation/administration of the original programmes. Virtually without exception it is taken for granted, that health insurance as originally conceived and implemented was fundamentally sound. More specifically, two crucial assumptions have been integral to this controversy:

    a. that health insurance results in ready access to health care for those needing it;

    b. that the health care provided is effective in promoting health.

These two assumptions, of course, are the very foundation upon which health insurance as rational social policy rests. They are, in my view, dubious, and it is by understanding why, that we can begin to grasp the real limitations of health insurance. Consequently, I will attempt to develop a critique of the validity of these assumptions. This critique will form the basis for an analysis of the recent concerns regarding access to health care.

To introduce this analysis, I will first discuss briefly the history of health insurance in Canada.

Health Insurance: Its Origins And Meaning

"The architects of the modern welfare state tried to reform neither the worker nor the economic system in which he (sic) made his living. Rather they required him by law to provide for himself and his family so that he could better withstand the vagaries of capitalism."[3]

Health insurance, both in its origins, and belated arrival in Canada was an outgrowth of working-class struggles against the ravages of capitalist development. For workers, people who are dependent for their living on the sale of their ability to labour, disease and injury, no less than a shortage of buyers for labour generally, posed a threat to their survival. It was a threat that workers could not and did not ignore. One response was to create benevolent funds upon which its contributors could draw under specified conditions, such as sickness. The inadequacies of these undertakings, which were typically localized responses to acute problems — whether initiated by workers or their employers — tended to add credence to another response advocated by workers: the abolition of wage labour and its replacement with a socialist system.

It was with at least one eye clearly focused upon preserving capitalism in the face of a growing working-class socialist movement that health insurance, indeed the whole set of reforms — unemployment insurance, pensions, etc. —comprising the welfare state were conceived. As Kaiser Wilhelm I, the "grandfather" of the welfare state observed:

"The cure for social ills must not be sought exclusively in the repression of social democratic excesses, but simultaneously in the positive advancement of the welfare of the working-class."[4]

A similar logic was at work in Canada, even if it wasn't so bluntly expressed. It was in 1919, in the wake of the state's repressive response to the upsurge in working-class militancy symbolized by the Winnipeg General Strike that the Liberal Party, led by Mackenzie King, first promised a national health insurance programme.

King's rationale for such a programme is instructive:

"Social insurance, which in reality is health insurance in one form or another, is a means employed in most industrial countries to bring about a wider measure of social justice, without, on the one hand disturbing the institution of private property and its advantage to the Community, or on the other, imperilling the thrift and industry of individuals."[5]

It follows that if some measure of social justice was to be established without disturbing the institution of private property and without altering capitalist relations of production and the exploitation of labour that these entail, then it was in the conditions of consumption that reform was to be sought. Within the framework of social insurance then, the issue became not the social conditions giving rise to disease but workers' inability to purchase health services once they were stricken by disease — one of the "vagaries of capitalism." The point to note here is not merely that health insurance was as much about insuring capitalism against socialism as it was about improving workers' health, but that health insurance need not, (and in Canada did not) even imply "nationalizing" the production and distribution of health services.

The long path of health insurance from a 1919 Liberal promise to the final establishment of a nationwide health insurance system in 1971 can be only briefly reviewed here.[6] The Liberal Party's promise notwithstanding, the first concrete step towards health insurance was not taken until 1948, and then only in Saskatchewan. "Ideas," as Leo Panitch has cogently put it, "if they are socially disembodied in the sense of not correlating with the nature and balance of class forces in a society, can themselves have little impact."[7] The working-class was not only relatively small in 1919, but in the following years the balance of class forces tilted sharply in capital's favour as well. It was not until the unprecedented tide of sustained working-class mobilization and politicization of the late 1930s and 1940s that health insurance returned to the national political agenda.

Despite its accomplishments, this surge of self-activity by Canadian working people failed to bring about a national health insurance scheme. Only in Saskatchewan, where the CCF won the 1944 election, were reforms implemented. Yet even these were limited as the Party abandoned its promise of a socialized health system (conceived as including salaried physicians) for a universal hospital insurance scheme (1948) and medical insurance for pensioners in 1950 (administered by a doctor-controlled commission).

In the 1950s, with the reformist unions and the CCF now the chief exponents, pressure for a national health insurance plan continued to grow; not least because in several provinces, notably Ontario, hospitals were incurring substantial deficits. Finally, in 1957, a rather reluctant Liberal government moved to introduce the Hospital Insurance and Diagnostic Services Act, in a futile bid to stave off electoral defeat. In essence, the legislation simply committed the federal government to sharing the cost with any province (health being a provincial responsibility under the BNA Act) of a public prepaid insurance plan covering the costs of acute hospital care for all residents.

With hospital insurance in place, attention then focused on medical insurance; in 1961 Saskatchewan's CCF government again took the first step. In the hope of preventing similar legislation elsewhere, the Canadian Medical Association convinced the Diefenbaker government to establish a Royal Commission on Health Services (known as the Hall Commission after its head Emmett Hall). Before the Commission's report was finished,

Diefenbaker had been swept from office by the Pearson led Liberals, who were now quite committed to public medical insurance. Whether coincidence or not, the Hall Commission's report, when it finally appeared, firmly declared itself in favour of such legislation. The ensuing Medicare Act (C-227), introduced in July 1966, closely followed Hall's recommendations and the earlier hospital insurance legislation. Again the federal government offered to share the cost of any provincial medical insurance plan meeting federal criteria; namely that the plan be universal, cover all physicians services, be financially administered on a public, non-profit basis and portable from province to province. In 1972, when Ontario joined, a national health insurance scheme covering hospital and medical care was finally in place.

What was in place, however, was anything but socialized medicine. The 1958 federal legislation merely socialized the cost of hospital care not its provision. Undoubtedly, Liberal Health Minister Paul Martin had the CCF's precedent setting legislation clearly in mind when he explained the limits of the federal legislation: "In Canada, I do not think anyone seriously proposed that the title to our (sic) hospitals should be transferred from religious or private bodies to the state."[8] The Medicare Act based on the precedent established by the Saskatchewan CCF in 1961 was no different. The CCF's medical care plan did not entail a public medical system modelled along the lines of public education with locally elected boards overseeing salaried physicians as once envisioned. Rather it was based upon the existing model of medicine with individual self-employed physicians selling their services for a fee, while collectively enjoying a legal monopoly over the provision of medical care. Still, it did at least call for a significant public presence in the administration of the insurance scheme, including the setting of fees. Nonetheless, when Saskatchewan doctors undertook their infamous strike of 1961 over this latter issue, the CCF was prepared to compromise to achieve a settlement. The resultant system of health insurance became the model for all the provincial plans which followed the passage of Medicare, with the exception of Quebec. No moves were made to subject either the medical supply or the drug corporations, so intimately involved in shaping hospitals and physicians health care practices to public control.

Health insurance, then, was concerned only with personal health care —medical services to individuals as prescribed by physicians. It did *not* undertake to socialize the production and delivery of these services. Rather it merely socialized the costs of providing them, under conditions, moreover, in which even indirect public control was minimal. In sum, what was in place was precisely what Dr. Norman Bethune had contemptuously characterized 30 years earlier as a "bastard form of socialism produced by belated humanitarianism out of necessity."[9]

This is not to deny that the realization of health insurance was a significant achievement by working people with real benefits for them. Socializing the costs of health care at least weakened the link between individual consumption levels and ability to pay. Working people no longer had to live in fear of medical bills or experience the humiliation of seeking services for which they could not pay. Consequently, their access to health care was improved. Nor should the relative efficiency of public insurance be ignored. By eliminating profits, advertising, etc., inherent in private insurance, public insurance reduced administrative costs from an average of 27% to 5% of revenue, thus providing more medical services for a given level of expenditure.[10]

But, what health insurance failed to change, profoundly circumscribed its efficacy not only in regard to health but also in regard to the narrower objective of equalizing access to health care. In elaborating this argument, I will consider first the effect of health insurance on access to medical care and the relationship between medical care and health, and then explore the contradictions inherent in these reforms.

Access To Health Care

As our concern here is to understand as well as to describe the limited impact of health insurance on access to medical care, it is important to remind ourselves that health insurance itself only addresses the decision of individuals to seek care, and only eliminates the direct cost — the bill — from active consideration. Nothing else has changed. And it is with what has not changed that we must begin.

> "Medicine must be seen as part of the social structure. It is the product of any given social environment. Every social structure has an economic base, and in Canada this economic base is called capitalism, avowedly founded on individualism, competition and private profit... Medicine is a typical, loosely organized, basically individualistic industry in this "catch as catch can" capitalist system operating as a monopoly on a private profit basis."[11]

I will develop the broad ramifications of this quotation from Norman Bethune later. Here I want to concentrate only on certain aspects of it.

To begin with, the vast majority of doctors, as noted, are essentially self-employed business people, who live by selling medical services on a fee-for-service basis. They hold to the dominant values of Canadian society and its acquisitive ethos, probably more so than most in light of their middle class backgrounds, sex (male) and self-employed status. These factors — together with the fact, given the extreme inequality of wealth in Canadian society, that urban areas with a wealthy clientele provide the potential for a higher income — have profoundly shaped physicians' social availability. If medical insurance made it possible to earn a substantial income from treating other people in other places, it was hardly necessary to do so. As Roos *et al.* put it, in explaining why differences in the regional concentration of physicians were unchanged by health insurance: "while universal coverage gives the underdoctored areas more money to spend on health services, it provides the same benefit to overdoctored areas."[12]

The basic issue, of course, is not regional inequalities but class inequalities in medical care utilization. Health insurance ostensibly addressed under-utilization by lower income groups whose needs were not being met (consequently health costs ought to have risen). In fact, if consumption of medical services was based upon need we might expect that utilization rates would vary inversely with income. For there is no doubt that the incidence of morbidity and mortality is much greater among working-class people than the professional / managerial class and the employing class, given the relatively greater health risks associated with working-class life.[13] These risks also include the stress from job insecurity, financial worries and absence of control over one's work circumstances; popular mythology notwithstanding, the so-called "diseases of affluence" are much more common among working-class people than executives.

What is the record of health insurance in this regard? As already suggested, health insurance has resulted in increased access to medical care by lower income people. Professor Beck's[14] analysis of the impact of medical insurance in Saskatchewan confirms this general point, but the consumption of medical services by upper income groups is still much greater than by lower income groups. The former, moreover, seem to have shifted their consumption pattern, away from general practitioners and towards specialists, so much so that income class differences in the use of specialists seem to have widened.

These data are not surprising. In part they reflect the historic concentration of medical services in affluent communities. They also reflect the fact that out-of-pocket costs are not the only financial barrier to visiting the doctor. Since doctors' offices are overwhelmingly run on a 9 - 5 basis, working people must forego income from having to leave work; in addition the costs of transportation and child care also play a role. Further, differential utilization rates may be explained by differential knowledge of disease symptoms, and the formal value of different physicians' treatments. Finally, as Beck cautiously suggests, it appears that since seeing a specialist involves being referred by a general practitioner, such referrals seem to be based in part upon the social class of the patient.

Thus, at its best, health insurance did not substantially alter class-based inequalities in the use of medical care, and certainly did not lead to a consumption pattern which corresponds to the incidence of disease across income classes. I say "at its best" to indicate reference to the time when direct financial barriers to access were minimal. They were *never* wholly eliminated, particularly in provinces like Ontario where coverage was not automatic but required payment of a premium. In the last few years, direct financial barriers have made a comeback, in the form of user-charges levied by provinces, and extra-billing/opting out charges levied by physicians which will be addressed.

The Value of Medical Care

Are you able to heal?

When we come to you
Our rags are torn off us
And you listen all over our naked body
As to the cause of our illness
One glance at our rags would
Tell you more. It is the same cause that wears out
Our bodies and our clothes.

The pain in our shoulder comes
You say, from the damp, and this is also the
reason for the stain on the wall of our flat
So tell us:
Where does the damp come from?

(Bertolt Brecht, "A Worker's Speech to a Doctor")

If the image of workers clothed in rags in Brecht's poignant poem is somewhat dated, his searing criticism of the practice of medicine surely is not. Modern medicine is the product of a lengthy process of development, a development which was neither smooth nor continuous. What we understand as modern scientific medicine emerged to challenge existing theories about the same time as industrial capitalism arose. Now the dominant approach, its theory, no less than the organization of the medical industry, has been profoundly influenced by the society within which it developed.

Scientific medicine is rooted in the notion of the "specific etiology." That is, it views disease as an isolatable "thing." which attacks individuals so as to physically impair the normal functioning of the body (hence the term physician). The underlying theoretical assumption, patently derived from the system of factory-based production, and the machine age it gave rise to was, as Dr. Thomas McKeown has cogently expressed it, that:

A living organism could be regarded as a machine which might be taken apart and reassembled if its structure and function were fully understood. In medicine the same concept led further to the belief that an understanding of disease processes and of the body's response to them would make it possible to intervene therapeutically mainly by physical (surgical), chemical, or electrical methods.[15]

One implication of this conception of the medical task is a dehumanized approach to treatment. Scientific medicine entails not just a tendency to segment people; it also entails establishing an authority relationship in which the patient is treated as a passive and ignorant object to be repaired, the means of which is the doctor's choice and the ensuing record the doctor's property. Its worth adding here that good patients are those who readily acquiesce to their "own objectification" while those (women in particular) who insist on control over their bodies are labelled "difficult." The parallels between the good patient and the good worker here are obvious, suggesting more than science is at work. A second implication is that progress, as with capitalist development generally, is seen to lie with the development of technology; ever more powerful means for intervention in the human body.

The triumph of scientific medicine over contending approaches signified that health primarily would be sought through efforts to cure individuals of disease, rather than by creating the socio-economic (and physical) conditions which could prevent disease and promote health. What has been its record? Here we must consider the impact of scientific medicine *per se* as well as the specifics of the medical system within which it is practiced.

The broad acceptance of the theory of scientific medicine was very much based upon the association of early scientific discoveries with declining mortality rates for infectious diseases — for which scientific medicine was credited. To a large extent this association, however, was spurious. In the last decade there have been several studies, primarily by British epidemiologists, of the decline in death rates due to infectious diseases (diptheria, scarlet fever) between 1850 and 1950.[16] These studies show that the decline in mortality rates was well under way before the discovery of the antibiotics used to treat them, and the trend of the decline was scarcely altered by that discovery. The major reasons for the decline were advances in sanitation and increased resistance to infection owing to improvements in nutrition; in short, prevention was more important than intervention. When one turns to chronic disease, one again finds that socio-economic factors are much more important in explaining reductions in mortality and morbidity. Indeed, Dr. McKeown argues that the scientific medicine paradigm is simply inappropriate to the nature of most contemporary illness.[17]

The point of these considerations is *not* to suggest that antibiotics are useless, or that we would be worse off without physicians; indeed, even better off, as Ivan Illich would have us believe. It is rather that, following McKeown it is necessary to distinguish care from cure, or managing disease from advancing health.[18] Modern medicine can provide care (reassurance and comfort, ease from suffering) and indeed save limb and life particularly through treatment of acute emergency, given technical competence and proper service organization. Unfortunately, however, the specific features of the Canadian medical system are such as to overproduce costly curative services frequently at the expense of less costly services with more value to the patient.

This is due, above all, to the structure of the Canadian medical system which at every level is characterized by the competitive pursuit of private profit. In this regard, the organization of physicians has already been considered. Since they operate as individuals selling health care as a commodity on a fee-for-service basis, their economic interests lie with the provision of more, relatively costly curative services — and with the broadest purvue of their trade.[19] It's not suprising that virtually every study of medical practice shows that substantial proportions of physicians' services — from drug prescriptions to major surgical procedures — were without medical justification, in the process exposing patients to the risks associated with powerful surgical and chemical interventions.[20] It also appears that few medical procedures are supported by adequate evidence of their efficacy.[21]

Having said this, it is extremely important to stress that physicians themselves are but a part of the problem, and indeed are often unwitting victims of forces beyond their own control. They are not the only ones whose economic interests lie with the development of more costly medical services. The suppliers of medical equipment and drugs must also be considered. These profit-seeking corporations benefit directly from the development of high-powered capital-intensive medical care and the discovery of cures for new diseases which they promote by aggressive marketing as well as direct and sponsored research. Extensive time-consuming testing of medical procedures involving new products, let alone circumspect claims from the results obtained, are hardly in their interests. The individual physician — given the paradigm of modern medicine with its technological bias, given the prestige and income associated with being at the forefront of medical practice, and given patients who have heard about particular new drugs or procedures and threaten to go elsewhere for them — typically is in no position to judge or resist.

The same factors which foster the overproduction of curative services limit the quality of care that is provided. Here, only a few points can briefly be noted. The sale of medical care on a fee-for-service basis transforms care into a cost of doing business, both in physicians offices and in hospitals, exacerbating the de-humanizing tendency inherent in scientific medicine. Physicians have a real economic incentive to transform their office into medical assembly lines, and to acquiesce to (if not actively to promote) limits on the amount of patient contact time allowed nursing and other support staff in order to free hospital resources for hardware, and the personnel to operate it. The result is care which is less thorough, less reassuring, less prompt and more dangerous due to the greater fatigue and frustration levels of hospital staff than is desirable.

The fragmentation inherent in a system characterized by individualism and competition defies proper service delivery. On the one hand, the numerous cracks in the system repeatedly undermine the continuity of care. On the other, such organization ensures, however rational the behaviour of its constituent elements, the rationality of the whole will suffer. Emergency services are a case in point. It has long been clear that effective treatment of acute emergencies (accidents, heart attacks) entails the *prompt receipt* of basic medical attention by the victim. Consequently, the key to prompt delivery of emergency care lies with the development of a well-organized, accessible and skilled ambulance service. This is hardly what exists in most of Canada. The focus instead has been on the development of sophisticated emergency departments in hospitals, choc o'bloc with "state of the art" technology of dubious value. Ambulance services to get people to the hospital have been almost an afterthought, so much so that not infrequently, these are contracted out to small businessmen. These services are typically fragmented rather than operationally integrated. The accessibility of existing services, moreover, is compromised by the absence of a simple emergency call system (i.e., a 999 telephone number) in many major Canadian cities. Finally, for several reasons, not least the legal monopoly over medical practice enjoyed by physicians, ambulance attendants have been provided with limited training and equipment.

From Health Insurance To The Canada Health Act

Health Insurance, then, promised much more than it could deliver. Moreover, the design of provincial health insurance programmes was such that the benefits, however limited, could not be cheap. In 1956, prior to the enactment of hospital insurance, personal health care expenses accounted for 3.4 percent of GNP. By 1972, when medical insurance was in place across the country the figure was 6.4 percent, rising further to roughly 8 percent of GNP in the 1980s.[22] Several factors underlay this increase in health care expenditures, including the efforts of hospital workers to raise their wages above the poverty line, but the most important was physician behaviour.

Health insurance was little more than a blank cheque made out to physicians: the state guaranteed to foot the bill for any physician provided services (at rates formally set by physicians themselves) and for any associated hospital costs. Major increases in medical fee schedules in the 1960s (to win physicians' support for health insurance) led directly to major increases in physician incomes. In addition, physician incomes were further inflated not by an increase in numbers of patients but by a reorganization of their practices which "generated more income from a given number of initial patient contacts."[23] This shift to more intensive medical practice entailing more tests, surgery, etc. increased the demand for hospital facilities, causing the whole health system to expand.

The growth in health care costs came as no surprise. In 1956, the federal Director of Health Insurance Studies had warned that "if we have no control over the doctor under a pre-paid hospitalization plan, we have no control over unnecessary use of hospital beds."[24] However, in responding to rising costs, it was not physicians' control over hospital and medical services which the state challenged, but the limited benefits workers obtained from health insurance. As events would have it, this challenge was not long in coming.

The pursuit of social justice through welfare state reforms in capitalist societies has always been conditioned upon successful capital accumulation to provide a margin for the implied redistribution. Health Insurance, however, arrived just as advanced capitalist countries like Canada were passing from the postwar boom into a sustained period of economic crisis and stagnation, reminding (sometimes forgetful) governments that their primary concern is with the health of capital. Confronted by intense international competition, capital is restructuring/rationalizing its operations on a national and global scale, a central objective being to increase the productivity and/or decrease the cost of labour. In this context, the welfare state has posed a serious obstacle to capital's interests. As a source of employment, the welfare state kept the reserve army of labour, so useful in exerting downward pressure on wages, lower than it otherwise would have been. No less significantly welfare state programmes constituted a social wage, limiting the dependence of workers on their employer and the willingness of workers to acquiesce to capital's demands.

The counterattack on health insurance really began with the publication of *A New Perspective on the Health of Canadians* by the Federal government, in 1974. Echoing with the criticisms of the limits of modern medicine and the need to address the socio-economic causes of disease raised by the women's movement and leftwing critics of the welfare state, the document had a radical veneer to it. This, however, was deceptive, for at its heart was a fundamentally conservative message: "patient, heal thyself." The focus of the document (subsequently reinforced by federal programmes like Participaction) was on the importance of "lifestyle" — on the link between the incidence of disease and individual decisions to adopt "behaviour and living habits which adversely affect health."[25] In seeking to establish that the sick were to a significant degree victims of their own malfeasance, the document tried to mobilize support for limiting public expenditures on health services, and intentionally or otherwise, opened the door to the introduction of user fees.

A number of substantive measures accompanied this ideological initiative. New restrictions were placed on the ability of foreign physicians to enter Canada. More importantly, the federal government undertook to stem the flow of federal funds into the health care system. In 1977, the open-ended shared cost programmes which allowed federal involvement in areas of provincial jurisdiction like health care, were replaced by the Established Programmes Financing and Fiscal Arrangements Act (EPF), which imposed ceilings on federal contributions to the financing of medicare and hospitalization.

Whatever the actual short run impact of EPF[26] on the level of federal expenditures, it provided a welcome justification for provincial governments, already engaged in a struggle to enhance their attractiveness to capital, to intensify their own efforts to reduce health expenditures. A number of provinces, notably B.C., Alberta and Nova Scotia imposed direct charges on some or all users of health services, in the name of discouraging abuse and/or providing an incentive for people to adopt a healthier lifestyle. Provinces exercised their "power of the purse" over hospitals to force reductions in the number of hospital beds per capita.[27] Hospitals were also urged, sometimes backed by budgetary incentives, to reduce staffing levels through contracting of work and adopting approaches to the organization of work based in "Scientific Management."[28] Pay levels for the remaining staff were subject to strict control. Formal wage controls, indeed, were in place under the 1975-78 federal Anti-Inflation Programme(AIP). Restraint continued informally until 1982, when most provinces again imposed formal controls in the wake of federal legislation (C-124) suppressing collective bargaining rights for all workers under federal jurisdiction.[29]

The fee schedules according to which physicians were reimbursed for their services did not escape restraint either. Physicians claimed that being independent suppliers of services to the health system, their fees — like drug equipment prices — were their own business and not subject to negotiation with governments. Nonetheless, there have been regular provincial negotiations since medicare came into existence. Physicians' fees were subject to the 1975-78 AIP limits. Afterwards, provinces continued to insist on restraint, not least of all because of the difficulty of doing otherwise, in view of the hard line being taken against hospital workers. Given physicians' determination to assert their freedom to set their own fees, governments began to lower the percentage of the official fee schedule (originally 90 percent) that physicians received from public insurance. It was in this context that physicians began to resort to extra or balance billing, charging patients the difference between the fee schedule and what they actually received from the provincial plan, to obtain incomes commensurate with their own exalted sense of self-worth, while provincial governments (who more often than not shared the physicians' view) turned a blind eye.

Rationalizations of direct charges to patients as necessary to deter abuse of the system, or as appropriate, given the contribution of individual lifestyle decisions to disease rates, are ingenious to say the least, involving a resort to the crudest sort of "blame the victim" ideology. Yet how can people distinguish health from disease when physicians (together with the drug industry) have made virtually every physical and emotional sensation a symptom of something, while keeping virtually all medical knowledge as their own exclusive preserve? As for individual culpability in the incidence of disease, far more weight must be given to socio-economic conditions over which individuals have no control; working conditions, ecological conditions, family structures and income levels. "Exercise more" is rather pointless advice for a single parent, a manual worker or indeed, most urban wage and salary earners for whom work and getting there alone consume some ten hours daily.

The re-emergence of direct charges to patients has eroded significantly the benefit workers achieved from health insurance. The most thorough study of the effect of user fees was based on examination of the impact of a government imposed user fee initiated in the late 1960s by the Saskatchewan Liberals under Ross Thatcher. Overall, health services utilization fell 7 percent, virtually all of which was due to a utilization rate decline of 18 percent among the lowest income groups.[30] Studies of extra-billing by physicians reveal similar effects. The patients of physicians who have opted-out of medicare are found to have incomes some 20 percent higher than those of non opted-out physicians. Furthermore, opted-out physicians report significantly greater proportions of patients who have delayed seeking treatment than their opted-in counterparts.[31]

Clearly, this exercise in cutting back the welfare state led to the stabilization of health care costs and at a level far below that in the U.S., much to the dismay of right-wing ideologues for whom the profligacy of government relative to the private sector is an article of faith. That the quality of care, as defined by McKeown, has suffered cannot be seriously disputed, with chronic and aged patients, in particular, frequently experiencing appalling levels of neglect. At the same time, by the late 1970s, direct financial charges to patients once again had become a common experience. With the gains achieved by health insurance so visably threatened, the labour movement could not but respond.

In 1979, the CLC initiated the formation of a broad coalition to counter this threat. As framed by the CLC, the coalition's response was unfortunately highly defensive in nature, essentially calling for the restoration of the status quo ante. Any improvements sought were limited in nature; the funding of more chronic beds, home care services and community health centres, was secondary to the central objective of "saving medicare." There was virtually no attempt by the left, inside or outside of the CLC's coalition, to advance a serious critique of the health care system which workers were being asked to finance. Those few voices trying to do so — the nursing associations which raised the need for putting physicians on salary stand out — were marginalized. Whatever the reasons for this reticence on the part of most of those socialists and feminists who had been developing such a critique over the past decade, it certainly suited the CLC who viewed the coalition primarily as a means of generating electoral support for the NDP.

The popular hostility to any weakening of health insurance so readily tapped by the CLC and the NDP undoubtedly helped prompt the newly elected Conservative government, in 1979, to once again ask Emmett Hall to undertake an inquiry, giving him a broad mandate to review health care policy generally. Hall, who was certainly not about to pick up where the

CLC and NDP had left off, declined the opportunity, choosing instead essentially to confine his attention to the erosion of the principles underlying the original legislation. Condemning extra-billing as "a head tax on the sick" his principle recommendation was to call for it to be prohibited.

Despite having his report ready within a year, the Conservatives were not around to deal with this report of Hall's either, and it fell to the born-again Trudeau Liberal government to respond. They were in no hurry as the economic pressures which led them to undermine the very reforms they had authored, were, if anything, more intense. But finally, in a last ditch effort to stave off looming electoral defeat and reminiscent of the party's sudden embrace of hospital insurance in 1956, the Canada Health Act was introduced. This act attempts to eliminate user fees and extra billing by taxing the provinces in an amount roughly equal to the costs born by individuals in purchasing the services covered under the 1958 and 1966 legislation.

Any assessment of the Canada Health Act at this point could be premature, but it does appear that it will largely eliminate the various user fees which appeared since public health insurance was enacted. This is not to be confused with the restoration of the status quo ante. There can be no doubt that the health services now dispensed are less prompt and less humane than a decade ago, or that the working conditions, if not the wages, of hospital workers have sharply deteriorated. As well, all the other shortcomings of the status quo remain. The structure of power within the health care sector remains intact at the expense of effective care. Private profit will still govern the production of medical services and the incidence of disease will not change as long as prevention remains subordinate to cure.

* * * * *

The limits of health insurance cannot be overcome by banning extra-billing, user-charges, or even insurance premiums. Naively or otherwise, many proponents of health insurance, and of the welfare state, believed that meaningful lasting reforms could be realized in the sphere of consumption while leaving capitalist relations of production intact: that what working people lost in the sphere of production (and in the case of women, in the sphere of reproduction — control over what is produced, how, and when); control of themselves — could be recaptured in the sphere of consumption. Shedding this illusion can at least help us to see what remains to be done.

NOTES

1. E.M. Hall, *Canada's National-Provincial Health Program for the 1980s,* 1980, Table 5, 18.

2. See for example, H. Grubel, "The Costs of Social Insurance," in G. Larmer (ed.), *Probing Leviathan,* Vancouver, 1982.

3. B. Gilbert, *The Evolution of National Insurance in Great Britain: The Origins of the Welfare State,* London, 1966, 452.

4. See *Report of the Advisory Committee on Health Insurance,* March 1943, 57, also known as the *Heagerty Report.*

5. W.L. Mackenzie King, *Industry and Humanity,* Toronto, 1973, 222.

6. For a more detailed examination of the development of health insurance in Canada see D. Swartz, "The Politics of Reform: Conflict and Accommodation in Canadian Health Policy" in L. Panitch ed., *The Canadian State: Political Economy and Politial Power,* Toronto, 1977, 311-344.

7. L. Panitch, "The Role and Nature of the Canadian State" in L. Panitch ed., *The Canadian State,* 20.

8. Memo to the Deputy Minister of Health, 21 February 1952, P. Martin Papers, vol. 28.

9. Quoted in T. Allan and S. Gordon, *The Scalpel, The Sword,* Toronto, 1971, 97.

10. Swartz "The Politics of Reform...", 329.

11. See Allan and Gordon, *The Scalpel...,* 93.

12. N. Roos, et al., "The Impact of the Physician Surplus on the Distribution of Physicians Across Canada," *Canadian Public Policy II,* 2 1976, 189.

13. See for example, J. Siemiatycki, "The Distribution of Disease," *Canadian Dimension,* June, 1974, 15-25.

14. R. Beck, "Economic Class and Access to Physician Services Under Public Medical Care," *International Journal of Health Services, III,* 1973, 341-355. See also P. Manga, "The Income Distribution Effects of Medical Insurance in Ontario," *Ontario Economic Council,* Occasional Paper 6, Toronto 1978.

15. T. McKeown, "A Historical Appraisal of the Medical Task," in T. McKeown and G. McLaughlin, eds., *Medical History and Medical Care,* N.Y., 1971, 29.

16. A summary of this evidence is found in M. Renaud, "On the Structural Constraints to State Intervention in Health," *International Journal of Health Services,* 5:4, 1975, 559-72.

17. T. McKeown, *The Role of Medicine,* Oxford, 1979. Lest anyone attribute the centering of Canadian health care policy on such a limited model to ignorance, it is important to note that the observations of McKeown and others are neither novel or recent. During World War II, when the Liberal government believed it might be necessary to carry out its long-standing promise of health insurance to gain working class acquiescence to the continued rule of capital, the Federal Health Department was asked to develop a plan. In addition to an insurance fund to cover medical costs, the proposal developed called for an extensive public health programme. Testifying before a parliamentary committee in 1943 regarding this plan, Dr. Heagerty observed with respect to Britain that while their health insurance plan of 1911 had been a political success, it had done nothing to improve the health of British workers, something which rested on yet to be enacted public education and preventive measures.

18. Ibid, chap. 10.

19. See P. Armstrong, "Female Complaints: Women, Health and the State," unpublished manuscript, Vanier College, Montreal, 1986.

20. An overview of some of these studies is found in Swartz, "The Politics of Reform..." Naylor, "Medical Aggression", *The Canadian Forum*, April 1981, 5-9.

21. A. Cochrane, *Effectiveness and Efficiency: Random Reflections on Health Services*, London 1972. See also Naylor, "Medical Aggression;" H. Waitskin, "A Marxist Interpretation of the Growth and Development of Coronary Care Technology," *American Journal of Public Health*, 69:12, 1979.

22. The figures for 1956 and 1972 are from D. Swartz, "The Politics of Reform...," Table 2, 331. For the 1980s, see *The Globe and Mail*, 17 September, 1986 (one of an excellent series of articles comparing the U.S. and Canadian health care systems, by Anne Silversides, September 15-17, 1986). See also D. Angus, "Health Care Costs: A Review of Past Experience and Potential Impact of the Aging Phenomenon," in D. Coburn, et al. *Health and Canadian Society: Sociological Perspectives*, 2nd edition, Toronto, 1987, 57-72.

23. R. Evans, "Beyond the Medical Market place," S. Andrepoulos ed., *National Health Insurance: Can We Learn from Canada?*, Toronto, 1975, 162.

24. Memo to the Deputy Minister of Health, 21 February 1952, Martin Papers, Public Archives of Canada, vol. 28.

25. M. Lalonde, *A New Perspective on the Health of Canadians*, Ottawa, 1974, 34.

26. For a discussion of this impact, see G. Weller and P. Manga, "The Development of Health Policy in Canada" in M. Atkinson and M. Chandler, eds., *The Politics of Canadian Public Policy*, Toronto, 1983, 223-46.

27. E. Hall, *Canada's National*, Table 19, 52.

28. P. Armstrong, "Female Complaints...."

29. See L. Panitch and D. Swartz, *From Consent to Coercion: The Assault on Trade Union Freedoms*, Toronto, 1985.

30. R. Beck, "The Effects of Co-payment on the Poor," *Journal of Human Resources*, 9, 1973, 129-142.

31. A. Wolfson and C. Tuohy, *Opting Out of Medicare*, Ontario Economic Council, Toronto, 1980, 25-26, 70-71.

Contributors

JIM ALBERT teaches in the School of Social Work, Carleton University. He has written in the area of social policies for children and is currently working on the impact of organizations on front-line social workers. He is also engaged in a study of the participation of people in managing their own health and social services in Nicaragua.

BRUCE CURTIS teaches in the Department of Sociology and Anthropology, Wilfrid Laurier University. He has written extensively on the history and politics of education, including *Pedagogy, Punishment and Popular Resistance: Building the Educational State in Canada West, 1836-1871* (in draft). At present he is co-director, with P. Corrigan, of "The Canadian State Formation Project."

GLENN DROVER is the Director, School of Social Work, University of British Columbia. He is the editor, with A. Moscovitch, of *Inequality: Essays on the Political Economy of Social Welfare* and is author of *Welfare and Worker Participation* with P. Kerans, to be published in 1987. He has been recently engaged in a major study of child care policies.

DENNIS GUEST teaches in the School of Social Work, University of British Columbia. He has written on the history of Canadian income maintenance programmes, including *The Emergence of Social Security in Canada*. He is currently working on a history of social welfare in British Columbia.

ALLAN IRVING teaches in the Faculty of Social Work, University of Toronto. He has written on Canadian social welfare history including articles on Harry Cassidy and Leonard Marsh. He is currently writing a biography of Harry Cassidy and working on a history of social welfare research in Canada.

BRIGITTE KITCHEN teaches in the Department of Social Work, York University. She has written extensively on income maintenance policies for families and children, including family allowances and child tax credits. Currently she is working on a manuscript on the *Economics of the Family*.

WENDY MITCHINSON teaches in the Department of History, University of Waterloo. She has written extensively on Canadian women's history. Her most recent work is the co-editing with J.D. McGinnis *Essays in Canadian Medical History* (forthcoming). She is currently pursuing research on the medical treatment of women in Canada, 1850-1900.

ALLAN MOSCOVITCH teaches in the School of Social Work, Carleton University. He is editor (with G. Drover) of *Inequality: Essays on the Political Economy of Social Welfare,* and author of *The Welfare State in Canada: A Selected Bibliography, 1840-1978.* His current research is an examination of Marshall's conception of social rights and its relevance for the study of the Canadian Welfare State.

JEFFREY PATTERSON is senior programme director and director of research at the Social Planning Council of Metropolitan Toronto. He has written many articles on housing and other social policy issues. Currently he is writing a summary report on spending cutbacks in Canada and launching a research project on the integration of social and economic development policies.

LEONARD RUTMAN is a partner in Price-Waterhouse and the author of *Evaluation Research Methods, Planning Useful Evaluations, Understanding Program Evaluation* and *In the Children's Aid* (with A. Jones). He is currently engaged in programme evaluation and government programme consulting.

R. L. SCHNELL teaches in the Department of Educational Policy and Administrative Studies, University of Calgary. He is the author of a number of publications on the history of child welfare and the involvement of women in social reform including *Studies in Childhood History, Discarding the Asylum* (with P. Rooke), and *No Bleeding Heart: Charlotte Whitton, A Feminist on the Right, 1896-1975* (with P. Rooke, forthcoming). His current work is on the history of the participation of women in the Social Question Section of the League of Nations.

JAMES STRUTHERS teaches in the Canadian Studies Programme, Trent University. He is the author of *No Fault of their Own* and has published articles on the history of social work and social welfare. He is currently doing research on the history of the welfare state in Ontario.

DONALD SWARTZ teaches in the School of Public Administration, Carleton University. He has published on Canadian health policy and on worker participation and is the author of *From Consent to Coercion: The Assault on Trade Union Freedoms* (with L. Panitch). At present he is engaged in a study of the rank and file movement in Canadian unions.

JOHN H. TAYLOR teaches in the Department of History, Carleton University. He has written on social and urban history and is the author of *Ottawa: An Illustrated History*. Currently he is involved in a study of Canadian cities during the Depression of the 1930's.

NEIL TUDIVER teaches in the School of Social Work, University of Manitoba. He has published in the area of management trends in the social services. He is currently doing research on the relation between military policy and social policy and on provincial fiscal and social policy.

B. L. VIGOD teaches in the Department of History, University of New Brunswick. He has written extensively on Quebec history and is the author of *Quebec before Duplessis: The Political Career of Louis-Alexandre Taschereau*. He is currently working on a history of the career of Sir Lomer Gouin.

Garamond Books:

Books on the leading edge of research and debate in Canadian social science and the humanities, written and priced to be accessible to students and the general reader.

• Stephen Brickey and Elizabeth Comack (eds): *The Social Basis of Law*
• Robert Brym (ed): *The Structure of the Canadian Capitalist Class*
• James Dickinson and Bob Russell (eds): *Family, Economy and State*
• Murray Knuttila: *State Theories*
• Peter Li and R. Singh-Bolaria (eds): *Racial Oppression in Canada*
• David Livingstone (ed): *Critical Pedagogy & Cultural Power*
• Allan Moscovitch and James Albert (eds): *The Benevolent State: The Growth of the Welfare State*
• Jorge Niosi: *Canadian Multinationals*
• Jon Young (ed): *Breaking the Mosaic: Ethnic Identities in Canadian Schooling*

The Network Basic Series

• Pat Armstrong and Hugh Armstrong: *Theorizing Women's Work*
• Pat Armstrong et al: *Feminist Marxism or Marxist Feminism: A Debate*
• Howard Buchbinder et al: *Who's On Top: The Politics of Heterosexuality*
• Howard Buchbinder and Janice Newson: *The University, Corporations and Academic Work*
• Varda Burstyn and Dorothy Smith: *Women, Class, Family and the State*; Intro by Roxana Ng
• David Livingstone: *Social Crisis and Schooling*
• Graham Lowe and Herb Northcott: *Under Pressure; a Study of Job Stress*
• Meg Luxton and Harriet Rosenburg: *Through the Kitchen Window: the Politics of Home and Family*
• Roxana Ng: *The Politics of Community Services*
• Leo Panitch and Don Swartz: *From Consent to Coercion: The Assault on the Labour Movement*
• Henry Veltmeyer: *The Canadian Class Structure*
• Henry Veltmeyer: *Canadian Corporate Power*
• Robert White: *Law, Capitalism and the Right to Work*

Garamond Press, 67A Portland St., Toronto, Ont., M5V 2M9
(416) 597-0246